THE SENIOR GOLFER'S ANSWER BOOK

THE SENIOR GOLFER'S ANSWER BOOK

Happier, Healthier Golf for the Middle-Aged Player and Beyond

by
Syd Harriet, Ph.D., Psy.D.

and

Sol Grazi, M.D.

BRASSEY'S
Washington & London

Editorial Offices: Order Department
4380 MacArthur Boulevard, N.W.   P.O. Box 960
Washington. DC 20007   Herndon, VA 20172

Brassey's books are available at special discounts for bulk purchases for sales promotions, premiums, fund-raising, or educational use.

Please note: The medical advice in this book is not intended to replace what your doctor tells you. All health-related problems require professional intervention, and you should see your doctor before any of our recommendations are used. Any application of the recommendations is at your discretion, and neither the authors nor the publisher assumes any responsibility or liability therefor.

Library of Congress Cataloging-in-Publication Data
Harriet, Syd.
    The senior golfer's answer book : happier, healthier golf for the middle-aged player and beyond / by Syd Harriet & Sol Grazi.
        p.   cm.
    Includes bibliographical references and index.
    ISBN 1-57488-141-8
        1. Golfers—Health and hygiene.   2. Middle aged persons—Health and hygiene.   3. Golf injuries.   4. Golf for the aged—Health aspects.   I. Grazi, Sol.   II. Title.
    RC1220.G64H37   1999
    613'.088'79635—dc21
                                                            98-42352
                                                            CIP

First Edition

10 9 8 7 6 5 4 3 2 1
Printed in Canada

CONTENTS

PREFACE

The popularity of golf has reached dizzying heights. Interest in overall emotional and physical well-being has also increased. The purpose of *The Senior Golfer's Answer Book* is to provide advice that can help your senior years—on and off the course—to be healthier and happier. We make a number of recommendations about prudent physical and psychological strategies for approaching the game of golf. Our goal is to show you that getting older doesn't have to result in illness or the inability to play golf.

Daily exercise and golfing can play major roles in maintaining your health. Not only does physical exercise help with such medical problems as hypertension, but it can be an important step in preventing illness and injuries.

Being healthy and fit also will improve the way you perceive yourself and will provide you with more energy. It's also helpful in playing pain-free and worry-free golf for years. The benefits are endless.

Before you embark on any of the suggestions in the book, we strongly advise that you get a physical examination to determine what level of training is best for you. Once you get the green light, the secret is to get into the habit of exercising on a regular basis. Your goal should be to increase the amount of exercise in very small increments so that you can reach the ideal twenty to thirty minutes that's necessary to benefit from an aerobic workout. Remember, you don't have to exercise long hours to get the benefits.

Exercise is beneficial if it accelerates the heart rate to a prescribed level and if you keep the activity going for at least 20 minutes. We recommend that you set an exercise intensity level, for example 60–80 percent of your maximum heart rate, depending on your age, sex, and medical condition. (See "Aerobic Exercise" in chapter 3.) To get the full benefits from exercising, you must do it at least three times a week. We recommend such activities as walking, swimming, bike riding, rope jumping, rowing, and aerobic dancing. We also suggest that you exercise whenever you can. For example, use the stairs rather than an elevator or park your car some distance from the supermarket and walk the rest of the way.

As you use this book, you will discover that you can take steps to guard against injuries. That's why we spend some time on injuries related to exercising and golfing. We offer preventive measures to keep you from running into misfortune. For example, being in good shape physically can help you from developing lower back pain.

Also, you need to know that chronic medical conditions can lead to difficulties in exercising and playing golf. For example, if you are taking medicine for your allergies, it can affect your ability to play well. Diabetes mellitus can have an impact on your game if your insulin levels change during a game.

And not to be overlooked is the profound impact your mental attitude can have upon your ability to play. We show you how to control your emotions so that you can improve your play and enjoyment of this wonderful game. We also provide answers to questions about mental quirks that take place on the course—wait until you read about where your anger really comes from.

Finally, we urge you to carry a cellular phone in your bag. Of course, we recognize how phones can distract you and your partners during play. If you are several holes away from the nearest phone, however, the time you save calling on your cellular could make the difference between life and death during an emergency. Just leave it off during the round.

We put together *The Senior Golfer's Answer Book* to help you maintain your health and extend the joy of your days of golfing. That's why we present easy-to-understand information about physical and mental mishaps, illness, and exercise and offer nutritional recommendations. We also provide information to help you have a better understanding of surgery or other treatment plans that might be recommended by your doctor.

We organized the material in this book according to subject. Sol is the author of chapter 1, "Golf Injuries," and chapter 2, "Health Problems of Senior Golfers." Syd is the author of chapter 4, "Mind over Aging Matter"; Appendixes A, "Aging, Memory, and Personality Change"; and Appendix B, "Grief: Time Heals All, But Is There a Quicker Way?" Both of us contributed to chapter 3, "Exercise"; chapter 5, "Nutrition"; and chapter 6, "Miscellaneous Tips for Healthy Golfing." Each chapter is structured around a series of questions, diagnoses, treatment plans, and tips and/or advice. To make the information easier to find in each chapter, we arrange it in alphabetical order by the condition, injury, or specific problem that you might encounter on and off the course. We also include information about getting the most out of a golf lesson (Appendix C), a directory of golf psychologists (Appendix D), a resource guide for contacting organizations for seniors, a glossary, a bibliography, and an index.

The appendixes offer in-depth information not covered in the main text of the book. The glossary provides brief definitions of medical and psychological terms that might be unfamiliar to you.

Use the index to find information that you need immediately. Most topics are listed by their common names.

We believe that the answers are concise and easy to read, but we cannot overemphasize the importance of your doctor's role in your emotional and physical well-being. Thus, our book is only a beginning. Although it provides simple diagnoses and possible treatment plans to help you understand injuries, illnesses, and emotional problems, only your physician can take into account other factors that must be considered in a particular problem. Diagnosis and treatment are unique for each individual.

Your active role in your well-being is the key to making the best of your golfing days. Check out a chapter now, and see how it will help you to understand any problem that you have and how you can make the most of your golfing experiences.

Sydney Harriet, Ph.D., Psy.D.
Sol Grazi, M.D.

ACKNOWLEDGMENTS

Syd: I can only say thanks once more to Rosa for her patience and willingness to be there during the not-so-good times. Deep gratitude is hard to articulate and yet that is probably the closest I can come to express how I feel toward my lifelong golf teachers—Geneva Kretsinger, Dr. E. A. Kretsinger, Hans Wiedenhofer, and Carl Romanovich; they taught me all that I know about this great game. I also want to thank Frank Hokr, who showed me through example how to stay young and see the joke of it all. To my sister Edith, I express many caplets of appreciation for showing me how to embrace serendipity. Finally (I know they are still playing golf at the best course in the universe) in loving memory, I thank my golfing buddies—Frank Artado, Bob Blanchard, and Oscar Gamache—for having taught me that camaraderie, loyalty, and friendship are the true immortal treasures that golf provides.

Sol: I am deeply indebted to my wife Martha, who kept her patience during the many hours of research and writing. I also indebted to my daughter Lila, who helped in the copy and taught me how to get around the Internet, and to my other children, Becky, Letty, and Jacob, who gave me the space to work and the encouragement to continue. Thanks go out to Dr. Dale Carnegie, DPM, and golfer who brought his expertise to the manuscript and unending encouragement. Finally, I am especially grateful to Margie Harbrecht,

M.D. Her personal and professional support were invaluable. Wordsworth had no better sister.

Sol and Syd: Our deepest appreciation goes to Terry Belanger whose superb copyediting made this book so much easier to read. We are also most indebted to Jeff Ehmke, who patiently withstood the pressure for meeting deadlines and sacrificed his holidays to comb the manuscript for omissions and mistakes. Thanks too to Maureen Keane, a wonderful author/nutritionist and fantastic colleague who gave her precious time to make sure we were nutritionally on track. Much appreciation to Ed Luethke, PGA golf professional, for generously sharing his teaching expertise. We offer a hearty handshake to Bob Kozar, publisher of *Golf Today,* a great editor and an in vivo golf god. Appreciation goes to Dr. Tom Kubistant, who unselfishly helped compile one of the most definitive bibliographies on golf (we owe you, Tom). Finally, this book would never have happened without Don McKeon, our editor at Brassey's, who offered unending encouragement throughout this project despite the many bogeys we experienced along the way. Don, we are indebted to you.

INTRODUCTION: WHY A BOOK ABOUT HEALTH FOR MIDDLE-AGED GOLFERS?

If you want to be healthier and more independent as the years go by, find ways to have time for exercise, get over your worries about medical conditions while playing golf, and learn how to understand the psychology of the game, you've chosen the right book.

On the brink of the new millennium, aging for golfers is a completely different phenomenon from what it was just thirty years ago. We have senior tours and senior retirement communities. The notion that being a senior means living an active and quality lifestyle is quite common. There are marathon runners in their seventies, and professional golfers still compete during their sixties. In fact, sixty years ago, the age of fifty was considered old. Today, a fifty-year-old, relatively speaking, is considered a youngster who is just approaching middle age.

Life changes are gradual, and usually they occur without our awareness. Perhaps we're inclined, like a character in Kurt Vonnegut's *Slaughterhouse Five,* to exclaim: "How did I get to be so old?" The realization that we have grown older can elude us for years and then end up staring us in the face one morning when we look in a mirror. We notice the grayness of the hair and the crinkling lines near the eyes, and the epiphany has a numbing effect. How did we change since we last took a long, hard look at ourselves? More so, we ask, why didn't we realize it until now? There are no simple answers, only the time-honored profound ones. We look at snapshots of years past and see the transformation. Surely, the mirror must be lying to us. Unconvinced, we go on with our lives only to discover that the radio is playing "our" music on the "oldies" station. Our children leave home. We become grandparents as our own parents and friends die—more inevitable events hinting at the passage of time. Sooner or later, we put our defenses aside and accept that our biological clocks are, at best, beginning to run down.

Yet time is nothing more than an idea, subjective at best. We feel either younger or older than we are. Some of us look sixty when we are forty-five, while many folks in their seventies don't look their age. We are living longer, remaining healthier, and even retiring earlier. Just look at photographs of those who were your age at the turn of the century and compare them to yourself. They will probably look older—perhaps much more so—than you appear to yourself and to others.

It has been suggested that our maximum life span is about 110 years. Occasionally, we hear of people who live longer than that. The reasons we are programmed to live about 100 years or so are unknown. This maximum life span may have existed for thousands of years. Only our life expectancy has changed: By the year 2000, it's expected to average 80 years among both men and women (on average, the latter already live beyond the age of 80).

Yet we spend the first half of our adult life going through the traditional stages of development and past the hallmarks of time: school, marriage, rising through the ranks. At about forty, this progression of new events slows to a snail's pace. Most of us reach a point where things begin to stabilize. The dreams of youth are realized or abandoned. The wish to be thirty different things has, by choice or by fate, trickled down to no more than a few. We work in every profession—alas, few are professional athletes. Those who are find only a handful of their contemporaries doing what they do. Life hands us choices to make, and the consequences of the choices land us—for better or worse—where we are at age forty or forty-five. The idea that the rest of life may be downhill with no further growth can be distressing. If we think that the only thing left is deterioration, we can become devastated, to say the least.

Nonetheless, many of us reverse our careers in midstream. We quit our nine-to-five jobs and run off like Gauguin to become artists. Some of us, like Jay Sigel, abandon sales positions and join the senior golf tour. Others leave husbands and wives and take up with younger women and men. Yet the fact remains: The predicament facing all of us is that we have so much to do during our senior years. It reminds us how mortal we are. It's not just knowing in an intellectual sense that all living things must die, but that we must die, too.

The question that resonates during spare moments is: How then do we use our precious time? It's a difficult call because we don't know how much time remains. To behave at this stage as though we are not going to die, however, is foolish. Wills and other legal documents become essential. Contingency plans are needed.

Although retirement might be sometime off, arrangements for it require advance planning. It's important to review the benefits, as well as the risks, of retiring too early and to determine our financial needs once the steady flow of a salary ends. The choices we make at this time are crucial. As Teddy Roosevelt said after he left the Oval Office and ran off to spend a year in a remote jungle, "It's my last chance to be a boy."

So we try to spend our time and money wisely. If playing a golf course demanding $100 green fees and advanced skills makes us feel uncomfortable, it may not be the right thing to do, especially if it takes money out of our savings that could affect someone else. But if we decide to play the course, we should not toil over what each shot and each hole are costing us. The choice has been made; it's now best to forget the playing fee and enjoy ourselves.

During many of our daily activities, we often ruminate about the future and lose sight of the wonder of the moment. This often happens when we play golf. Perhaps we rarely enjoy the experience of just playing. Instead, we think of a bad shot that we made or the swing that we plan to use next. Seldom do we smell the white mums frilling in the warm sun or gaze toward the electric orange spectacle left by a setting sun. Yet the moment is there, and it's now; it isn't in the future. By middle age, we have mastered or left behind our child-rearing duties as parents. Our careers are on cruise control. No additional effort at this age is required to establish ourselves and make our marks. We can do things because we want to and because they are there to do. No longer do we have to be obligated or execute tasks merely to survive. This is when we live: in the present, right this minute.

This is what *The Senior Golfer's Answer Book* is about. All you can do about your game of golf or your life is to take it as it comes, adjust to change, and learn the art of being fully aware that every plan has potential uncertainties and hidden disasters. Illness and injury, missed shots, and disappointments await on and off the course. Plans fail. Expected failures become wild successes. How arbitrary and capricious life and golf can be!

The purpose of *The Senior Golfer's Answer Book* is to help you with these vicissitudes of living. The one choice you have is how you react to them—how you can grab opportunity, embrace misfortune, or take steps to prevent illness and injury. Experience has taught us how to deal with certain aspects of the unknown, but there are always more waiting to be heaped upon us. What worked before might not work now. That is the challenge: when to make adjustments and when not to, or when to surrender to what we cannot change.

To that end, we offer hundreds of answers to questions about your physical and emotional well-being on and off the course. We have compiled treatment plans and recommendations to help you recognize the wonder of the moment and to become more aware of what you can do to maintain a healthy lifestyle. Finding how to seize the moment can free you to appreciate and experience the "now." Learning about proper exercise, good nutrition, and appropriate responses to illness or injury can give you control over your physical well-being.

The realization that you are growing older and have not developed an exercise and diet program can be frightening. You might feel that if you don't start soon, you will never get out of the sedentary habits that are contrary to good health. *The Senior Golfer's Answer Book* can help you to develop strategies to move beyond your sedentary funk. Our ultimate goal is to assist you in realizing that the transition to a healthy golfing lifestyle is not as difficult as you might think.

We would also like to talk to you and answer your questions. Please feel free to ask us anything—even what you think is a dumb question. Your so-called dumb question could be one that hundreds of other golfers have, and it will help us when we revise this book to make it even more user friendly. You can reach Sol at grazis @essexVCHSC.edu and Syd at SH062@csufresno.edu. Your first one hundred questions are free. Any more than that, you have to pay for the golf round and lunch. Fair enough?

GOLF INJURIES **1**

Golfers often don't think of golf as a sport that causes a lot of injuries, even among players who are physically unprepared. Actually, it taxes the imagination to consider what could possibly bring about an injury. In truth, golf injuries are rare, and they are more common among professionals than amateurs. No doubt this has to do with the nearly constant level of activity undertaken by the top pros. They not only play eighteen to thirty-six holes a day, but they might also hit several hundred balls on the practice range. Such intensive play will definitely increase the likelihood of injury.

Amateurs are in a different position. Typically, they don't work as hard as pros, but they also aren't in the same physical shape as professionals. In a survey presented in the *British Journal of Sports Medicine,* 57 percent of the amateur respondents reported injuries. The most common injuries involved the wrist, back, elbow, and knee. The most significant injuries were musculoskeletal, especially in the ribs and trunk. As expected—and the reason that I emphasize reading chapter 3 on exercise—poor physical preparation was the predominant cause of injury. This being the case, perhaps the most appropriate caregivers for golf injuries are physical therapists and golf pros who teach proper techniques. Many injuries are obviously the result of poor golfing skills.

A good start in taking control of your physical well-being as a golfer is to acquire information. That's what this chapter is all about. It will help you to avoid a number of injuries that can result from not knowing what aging does to your body. Your physician probably doesn't have the time to coach you into becoming knowledgeable about golf injuries. So let me step in with a little preventive and reparative advice. Before discussing injuries, however, a word or two about ice and heat.

There has been much discussion regarding the use of ice or heat in an acute or chronic injury. The conventional mode is to use ice during the acute phase (the first twenty-four hours) and then use heat. The rationale is good. Ice helps to reduce swelling, and it inhibits torn blood vessels from bleeding by causing them to contract. Heat promotes the dilation of blood vessels, thus allowing more blood and healing nutrients to get to the injured area. Both ice and heat help to reduce pain, although the effect of ice seems to last longer.

I am a card-carrying member of the "ice school." Ice releases muscular spasm, but heat does not. People who have drowned in the San Francisco Bay did so not because of fatigue and exhaustion but because their muscles could not contract in the cold; hence they became weaker as they got colder. This suggests that ice prevents or decreases muscle contraction. In addition, it is felt that if an injured muscle continues to spasm, it does not heal as quickly. The repair of the muscle goes on for weeks, but the most active changes occur during the first week. Ice constricts the blood vessels, thus causing the fluid in the injured tissue, with its toxic by-products, to return to the blood vessels and get out of the area. Once the ice is removed, the blood vessels expand as a reflex to the extreme cold that they have experienced. This process brings fresh blood and nutrients to the injured area. Because the area already has been cleared of a lot of waste, the new materials do not have to compete in the injured space, and they get to the work of healing more quickly.

Although heat is immediately soothing to the patient, the spasms return more quickly with the use of heat. Ice is initially discomforting, but its effects are more lasting. I recommend progressive cooling. Place a cloth, preferably wet, between the injured area and the source of ice to prevent freezing the skin. When the cloth is removed some minutes later, the skin is already partially anesthetized. This makes the direct cold more tolerable. I usually recommend ice for 15 minutes on and 20–30 minutes off. Some doctors apply heat directly after removing the ice, but I do not because it can increase the potential for the muscle to spasm again. By allowing the body to warm slowly with its own heat, muscle spasms are less likely to occur.

Because you will read the questions in this chapter individually, it is important to remember that not all of the answers will remind you of the possible problems associated with certain medications. This is particularly true of nonsteroidal anti-inflammatory drugs (NSAIDs), aspirin, acetaminophen, and steroids.

All NSAIDs have the potential to cause gastric pains and bleeding. Aspirin presents the same risk. In fact, aspirin is the most common cause of gastric bleeding diagnosed in emergency rooms. It is *very* important that you do not take these drugs together and that you do not take them if you have a problem with stomach pains or bleeding. When you see any of these medications recommended in the following sections and you have one or both of these problems, do not take them until you first check with your doctor. Gastric problems sometimes can be avoided by using enteric-coated aspirin, but rely on your doctor's recommendation.

These medications can also predispose and aggravate general bleeding problems because of their platelet-inhibiting function. They are good for people with heart problems but not so good for someone who has a bleeding problem or who is taking Coumadin (warfarin). Again, be warned.

Even though acetaminophen is considered to be relatively safe, it also have some risks. The most important risk is potential damage to the liver. At first, this was considered a problem in people who overused it, but we are now seeing that acetaminophen in combination with alcohol can cause severe liver damage. This doesn't happen to everyone who takes acetaminophen or we would have known about it long ago, but the association is there.

You will notice that steroid injections are frequently mentioned in this chapter. This is not because I often prescribe them, but rather for completeness of the treatment sections. In actuality, I do few steroid injections; I prefer more conservative treatments. Very rarely do I inject an acutely injured part and then only for a person who requires an untimely return to activity, such as a professional athlete. The conditions for that person are very specific, and the athlete is stronger, has a greater potential to heal quickly, and has less chance of sustaining greater damage as a result of the treatment. In most instances, I inject steroids for chronic conditions that are not amenable to more conservative treatments.

Ultimately, I am a subscriber to the maxim that the safest treatment is that which is least invasive. I would recommend that you stop playing golf for awhile, spend time reading up on the game, rent a few golf instructional videos, and get some tips. Before you know it, you'll be back where you left off. If you don't believe that the rest will be good for your body, see what Syd has to say about the other benefits of not playing in chapter 4.

■ ABDOMINAL WALL SPRAIN

Question: "I was doing some warm-up exercises before teeing off and felt this pain soon after every time I breathed in. When I swung at the ball, I felt this sharp pain in my stomach. What happened?"

Answer: You probably injured the muscles or tendons of your abdominal wall. In other words, you probably pulled a muscle in your stomach. If the pain went away as you played, you would have had what we call a 1st degree sprain. The sprain would be diagnosed as a bit more severe—2nd degree—when there are torn muscle fibers. If you couldn't continue playing because of the pain, it is likely that you ruptured the muscle-tendon-bone attachment—3rd degree. Risk for this kind of injury increases with stretching exercises, decreased circulation caused by cardiovascular illnesses, obesity, poor nutrition, previous abdominal sprain, and/or poor muscle conditioning.

Treatment: The chance that this was a sprain is greatest if the pain was not in the area where a tendon connects with a bone. Eliciting the pain with pressure and movement is going to tell you more than an X-ray. Ice to the area reduces swelling and pain. Heat can help with the pain and will bring blood and its healing constituents to the area. Aspirin, acetaminophen, or ibuprofen and topical liniments and ointments will help to reduce pain. Physical therapy is often helpful if you have moderate to severe muscle sprain. If this is the first time you have felt the pain, slower and more deliberate movements might prevent recurrence. Movement, as long as it does not strain the injured area, actually enhances the healing. If continued activity causes persistent or increasing pain, a leave of absence from playing and exercising should help to prevent any complications. When a sprain occurs while you're in the middle of the course, I recommend that you stop playing and put ice on the sprained area. Whirlpool treatments can help as a way to heat the area.

Tip: Remember to contact your doctor if the pain persists longer than 10 days. If your doctor determines that you have moderately to severely torn ligaments, you might need to refrain from activity for several months. If the problem is resistant to conservative treatment, a trigger point injection with a corticosteroid can help the area to heal. Once everything gets back to normal, I recommend that you begin doing crunches or participate in a supervised weightlifting program to build up the strength of your stomach muscles.

■ ARM INJURY

Question: "I took a hard swing at my ball and hit the ground before I hit my ball. On the next shot, I felt pain shoot through my arm. What should I do?"

Answer: The injury could have been to the biceps muscle or tendon, or it could have been to the biceps tendon sheath in the upper arm and shoulder. The biceps muscle is a large muscle in front of the upper arm. Symptoms include pain while moving or stretching the biceps, muscle spasms, swelling over the injured area, loss of strength, a cracking feeling and sound when you press the area with your fingers, muscle or tendon calcification, and/or inflammation of the sheath covering the tendon. If you can't move your arm and the pain is severe, you need to stop playing and get medical attention.

Treatment: I'm assuming you have stopped playing. At that point, the best thing to do is to wear a protective device for support and to prevent further injury. Obviously, you won't have one with you while you play, so a brace or splint might be indicated if the pain persists after you stop playing. In the interim, apply ice to the injured area. Cold prevents swelling and bleeding and slows down inflammation. Don't put the ice on your skin, however; wrap the area in a towel or a pack and keep a bandage on it. Be careful not to wrap your arm so tightly that you constrict blood flow.

Depending on how severely you injured your arm, I would rest it until it's safe to continue. When you do, play less golf than you normally do (nine holes, not eighteen).

Also, periodically elevate your injured arm above your heart to reduce swelling. Finally, aspirin, ibuprofen, acetaminophen, or other mild pain medication can help to reduce the pain.

Tip: If you have persisting chest pain, pain down your arm, heaviness in your chest, persistently uneven heartbeat, breathlessness, wheezing, difficulty in catching your breath, light-headedness, nausea, extreme fatigue, numbness, or any pain that cannot be related to a cause, stop playing and head for the clubhouse. If the symptoms don't subside or if they recur when you exert yourself, don't take any chances. It could be a heart attack. Call your doctor's office or, probably better, have somebody call for an ambulance, i.e., 911.

ARM STRAIN (TRICEPS) ■

Question: "I get this dull pain whenever I extend my forearm. I don't feel it so much when I'm playing, but after a round I do. Can you tell me what's wrong?"

Answer: You probably have injured the triceps muscle or tendon, which is at the back of your upper arm. In layman's terms, you might have a pulled muscle. Arm strain symptoms include what you described: pain with stretching, moving, or forceful extension of the forearm at the elbow joint. Sometimes, swelling around the injury and muscle spasms occur.

Treatment: If this is the first time you've felt pain in your triceps, you should allow sufficient time for healing before playing or practicing golf again. When the injury also involves a torn ligament, it can take as long as a fractured bone to heal. Average healing times are 2–10 days for mild strains and up to 6 weeks for more serious ones. Several times a day, use ice massage for fifteen minutes on the affected area. If you feel improvement after a few days, you might want to apply heat by using hot soaks or taking hot showers and letting the water stream onto the affected area. Aspirin, acetaminophen, or ibuprofen; topical ointments and liniments; and/or pain medication can help to reduce minor discomfort. If the strain is severe, your doctor might order a sling.

Tip: You can prevent arm strain by using one of our exercise programs in order to build up strength and flexibility. I also recommend careful warm-up before you practice or play. If the strain continues after 10 days, or if the pain or swelling worsen even after treatment, call your doctor.

■ BACK PAIN (DISK)

Question: "Tell your readers the worst pain anyone could ever feel is what I'm experiencing right now. My doctor diagnosed my low back problem as a herniated disk, or slipped disk. I have no idea how it happened. I did pick up something a little heavy one morning and bang, my hell began. A sharp pain started in my buttock and went down the back of my leg to the great toe. Will I ever be able to golf again?"

Answer: Yes, you will, but you'll need to go through a bit of time away from the game for a full recovery. Let me say that I empathize with you. My patients, friends, and relatives with this problem have made similar testimonials about the unbearable pain. A herniated disk is the result of weakening and rupture of the disk material that, in turn, puts pressure on the nearby spinal nerves. The pain can be sudden when it results from an injury, or it can be due to stress that is caused by constant lifting or being overweight. In some rare cases, it may be the result of a preexisting condition called spondylolisthesis, in which there is a sudden or gradual break in the supportive ligaments surrounding the spinal disk. Disks of the neck or lower spine are usually the most common areas. Symptoms include severe pain in the low back or in the back of a leg, buttock, or foot. Pain usually occurs on one side and gets worse if you move, cough, sneeze, and especially if you try to lift your golf bag or strain yourself while performing some heavy chore.

The pain down the back of the leg is a hallmark of sciatica or sciatic nerve compression. Despite the pain, you are not in immediate danger. If you experience weakness in the affected leg or foot, you should immediately see a doctor. Seeking medical help is even more important when urinary or fecal incontinence occurs after such an injury.

Treatment: After the initial pain, apply ice packs to the area during the first 72 hours and continue to do so if the ice provides relief. Also try heat lamps, hot showers, hot baths, or a heating pad. For minor pain, try aspirin or ibuprofen. If the pain is severe, your doctor might prescribe muscle relaxants and pain relievers. In some instances, NSAIDs help to reduce inflammation around the ruptured area. You might need laxatives or stool softeners if constipation becomes a problem.

There are different schools of thought on how to treat sciatica before deciding on surgery. I prefer that the patient move around as soon as possible. If bed rest is necessary, stay in bed for as short a time as possible because the more you rest, the weaker your muscles will become. They then become part of the problem, and full recovery takes longer.

If conservative treatment does not work, you might need X-rays and/or a computed tomography (CT) scan or magnetic resonance imaging (MRI) to confirm a protruding ruptured disk. Many disks can protrude without contributing to sciatica. The disk must actually impinge on the nerve if surgery is to be effective. Another way to determine if the nerve is actually affected is by a nerve conduction study. This is not a comfortable procedure, but it is a darn sight less onerous than a surgery you don't need. If the disk is impinging on the nerve, surgery can help to relieve nerve pressure.

In many cases, however, bed rest, usually for as long as two weeks, has been effective in helping patients recover, although it is best to use bedrest sparingly. If, during recovery, the pain increases, you experience loss of bladder or bowel control, and/or you have new symptoms, call your doctor immediately.

Tip: Here's something I urge you to consider. If there is a family history of low back pain or disk disorders, make an extra effort to follow these preventive measures. You need to practice proper posture when lifting. To lift properly, always bend your knees and not your back. By bending your knees, you reduce the stress on your back. You also need to exercise regularly by doing crunches that will help tone up your stomach and back muscles. If you happen to have a spastic attack on the course, stop golfing. If you can't move, have a member of your foursome call for help.

■ BACK PAIN (GENERAL)

Question: "I have back problems, and I'm on the verge of quitting the game. Is there anything I can do to keep on playing?"

Answer: The back is made up of the spine (the bones in the back), the spinal cord and nerves, disks, and the soft tissues. Assuming that your doctor has examined you and determined that you have no major illnesses causing your back pain (i.e., disease of the kidney, heart, or gallbladder), the most likely source of your problem might be one of the anatomic structures listed above.

The back is probably the most important part of the body to condition, and it is often the least considered. There are essentially two parts to its well-being: (1) the back itself and (2) the "front" of the back, or the abdomen. A strong back requires a strong abdomen. Why do women get back pains during pregnancy? When the baby grows, it pulls on the back. The normally straight back is pulled farther and farther forward. This puts pressure on the sacroiliac joint, which starts to stretch and hurt under the strain. It also stresses the back muscles, which have to work harder to keep the back more upright. The result is a weaker, more tired back, and, more often, a continuous nagging pain. Excessive weight (fat) is equivalent to having a baby in the abdomen. The pressure on the back is the same in each case.

Treatment: The basic approach to relieving back pain from strain or minor injury is immediate bed rest with an ice pack and aspirin or

NSAID, such as ibuprofen, ketoprofen, or naproxen, to reduce pain and inflammation. Once the inflammation subsides, applying heat can soothe and restore muscles and connective tissue.

If the back pain is immobilizing, your doctor might prescribe an over-the-counter or prescription painkiller and possibly even a muscle relaxant. Be warned, some muscle relaxants, such as methocarbamol or cyclobenzaprine, can cause nausea, disorientation, and drowsiness, so these medications shouldn't be taken for more than a few days.

Long-term bed rest is no longer a way of treating most cases of back pain. In fact, the lack of activity can actually contribute to recurring back problems. In most cases, your doctor will instruct you to start normal, nonstrenuous activity within 24 to 72 hours, after which controlled physical exercise should begin.

Tip: Swing modification may be just what you need. To do that, you have to throw to the wind those classic teachings you get from golf professionals or read about in golf magazines. Keep in mind that such instructional programs target the player without back pain. For example, a large shoulder turn and a small hip turn are good for distance but suicide for your back. I recommend that you do just the opposite. Make a smaller shoulder turn and a larger hip turn. By doing that, you avoid the resistance in the back muscles that can cause an injury or make one worse. Obviously you lose distance, but you increase your playing days with less pain.

To swing in this new manner, you'll want to modify your swing in the following way. In his excellent book, *The Golf Doctor*, Dr. Bill Mallon recommends that you get up on your toes, especially the left toe on the backswing. Letting the left heel come off the ground is the approach Jack Nicklaus used for decades, and he seemed to play very well. Your finish is just the opposite where you complete your swing by coming up onto the right toe early into the follow-through. This frees up your hip turn. The bottom line is that you end up decreasing the stress that's placed on your lower back. The problem I have seen with some of my golfing patients who have tried this approach is the tendency to move off the ball, which can cause quite a number of mis-hits. Another approach would be to see your golf pro and be fitted for lighter and whippier clubs. Again, you would make a larger hip turn, and allow the lighter club and flexible shaft to make up for the smaller shoulder turn.

Exercises to strengthen the back and abdomen can greatly lessen back problems. The most important exercise are crunches (see chapter 3). No matter what shape your abdomen is in, doing crunches will make it stronger. When you do them, as the exercise buffs say, "Let it burn." But just let it burn a little. Don't try for an all-out conflagration.

Finally, if all else fails, you might want to ask your pro for help in developing a shorter swing. The longer your swing, the more stress you put on your back. The paradox here is that you might not only learn how to reduce the risk of back pain, but you'll probably end up hitting the ball a greater distance because the likelihood of your making better contact with the ball will increase.

■ BACK PAIN (LOWER)

Question: "When I practice putting for a while, I notice my lower back hurts the next morning. What can I do to prevent this?"

Answer: Welcome to the club. Many of the injuries to players on the PGA and Senior tours involve the back. Jack Nicklaus, Greg Norman, Payne Stewart, Fred Couples, and Fuzzy Zoeller are just a few who have suffered from lower back problems.

Most lower back pain is the result of back muscle and ligament strain. Sometimes, however, the cause can be spinal compression, fractures, spinal stenosis, or tumors. Tenderness, severe pain, and swelling are some of the symptoms that result from violent overstretching of the lower part of the spine. If there is tearing of some ligament fibers in that area, there is usually little loss of function; however, a significant rupture of a portion of the ligament or complete separation of the ligament from the bone might require surgery.

Treatment: If you have a mild strain, use ice several times a day. Place ice chips or cubes in a plastic bag and wrap it in a moist towel. Put the bag on the injured area for 15–20 minutes. After several days, apply heat instead of ice. You can use a heat lamp, hot soaks, hot showers, a heating pad, or heat liniment or ointment. If you can get a gentle massage, by all means do so. It will not only provide comfort, but decrease swelling. To relieve the pain, take acetaminophen or ibuprofen.

Tip: Although you are just practicing your putting, doing a few warm-up exercises is a good habit. Warming up can help prevent the morning-after pain that you describe. Another approach is to putt for five minutes and then walk for a few minutes.

Syd suffers from lower back pain when he practices putting. His remedy is to putt for five minutes, take a break, and walk to the clubhouse a couple of times before going back to his practice session. This procedure not only helps his back but gives him a chance to reflect on his putting. Another approach is to adopt one of the new long pendulum-type putters. If that doesn't work, consider a conventional putter with a longer shaft. In fact, longer shafts on all your clubs will keep you from bending and reduce the strain on your lower back.

A number of the senior players on the tour have switched to longer putters because of back problems and not necessarily because they want to putt better. Bending over for any reason for any period of time can cause a ton of pain for anyone with back problems. By using one of the longer putters, you bend less and that, in turn, puts less stress on your back. Regular putters are anywhere from 34 to 36 inches long; the long putters are fifty inches long or more. If you decide to start using one, I recommend that you take a lesson with your pro to learn the best way to hold the club. (Note: longer shafts may make the clubs harder to control.)

Jogging, cycling, and racquet sports can also worsen your back pain. If you suddenly develop lower back pain after a swing, don't press your luck. Stop playing, and let the back rest. The golf course will be there tomorrow. I have known golfers who continued to play despite the pain and eventually were unable to play for weeks.

■ BACK SPRAIN

Question: "I have this on-and-off pain in my back. Sometimes it occurs right above my right buttock, sometimes below my right arm and above my right waist, and sometimes on the left side of my waist. I have learned to live with these aches but was wondering if I had something that needed medical attention."

Answer: You're describing pain that shoots into the buttocks or your hip that results from violent overstretching of one or more ligaments in the sacroiliac region of the spine, right above your buttock, the dorsal spine region (the area you describe as below your right arm and above your right waist), and the lumbar spine region (that area near the left side of your waist). When a ligament in those areas is overstretched, it becomes tense and gives way at the weakest points. The sprain is usually diagnosed as mild if there is some tearing of ligament fibers and muscle spasms but no loss of function. It's considered severe if there is a complete rupture of the ligament and total loss of function, which usually requires surgery. It sounds as though your sprains are mild.

Your back sprain in the regions you described could have been caused by sudden improper movements during your swing where you twisted too suddenly on either your backswing or downswing, or you took a swing off balance or lost your balance. Sometimes being overweight can cause these areas in the back to sprain, especially if you have not been conditioning the muscles in the lower back, stomach, buttock, hip, and dorsal spine. Other symptoms can include tenderness, swelling, bruising, muscle spasms, and sometimes a feeling of popping or tearing in one or all of the areas you describe. Usually, your doctor will X-ray your hip, pelvis, and/or lumbar spine to rule out fractures. If your doctor determines that your condition is chronic, it could be due to repeated injury to the area over time, which has resulted in arthritis.

Treatment: As soon as you can, use an ice pack several times a day for up to fifteen minutes. Wrap the pack in a moist towel, and place it over the injured site. After several days, replace the ice treatment with heat, such as a heat lamp, hot soaks, hot showers, or a heating pad. If you can, take whirlpool treatments. If the pain doesn't subside with aspirin, acetaminophen, or ibuprofen use, your doctor might prescribe muscle relaxants or stronger pain relievers. A mild sprain will take 2–10 days to heal. If you have a severe sprain, it can take up to 6–10 weeks for complete recovery. It could be that your pain keeps recurring because you haven't given the area(s) enough time to heal.

Tip: Because we aren't getting any younger, we need to participate in strengthening, flexibility, and conditioning programs to reduce the chances of this common injury. For your back pain, consider some of the programs that we recommend (see Section on Exercise in chapter 3). Also, before you play or practice, use one of the several warm-up exercises described in chapter 3. I know many golfers who use a back brace, which helps to reduce the tearing of ligaments during abrupt swings that are often caused by bad lies, especially those in the rough.

BLISTERS ■

Question: "Every time I get through playing or practicing, I find my hands have blisters on them. Do I have thin skin? And what can I do to reduce blisters?"

Answer: I suspect that you either play a lot of golf or you practice for long stretches. A blister is caused by friction and rubbing, which might be the result of a loose grip where the club is moving in your hand somewhere during the swing.

Treatment: Most blisters caused by friction or minor burns do not require a doctor's care. You may be able to soothe ordinary friction blisters with vitamin E ointment or an aloe-based cream. Never puncture the blister unless it is large, painful, or likely to be further irritated. If you do try to puncture it, use a sterilized needle or razor blade; put the point or edge in a flame until it is very hot, or rinse it in alcohol. Wash the area thoroughly, make a small hole, and gently squeeze out the clear fluid. Then apply hydrogen peroxide to the area to protect against infection. If the fluid released is yellow or white, the blister is infected and needs medical attention. Do not remove the skin over a broken blister because the new skin needs this protective cover.

Although many blisters heal on their own, a few require medical care. Blistering caused by toxic agents or disease must be treated not only to relieve discomfort but also to address the underlying cause.

Tip: It's hard to be aware of how your hands are moving off the club while you swing, so you might want to have your pro check to see if you are loosening your grip during your swing. You want to keep your grip pressure the same while you take the club back and when you swing at the ball. If your pro determines that you are not loosening your grip, you might consider the amount of time that you spend in practicing. Long practice sessions can dry and crack your skin. Before I start a long practice session, I usually lubricate my hands with the ointment used for hemorrhoids. If you don't want the greasy feeling while you practice, apply a little bit as soon as you finish.

Please be warned that I am not recommending that you

tighten your grip. You want to hold the club firmly but not to the point where you tighten the muscles in your hands and arms.

If you get blisters on your glove hand, make sure that your glove is the right size. Perhaps you have noticed that different gloves in your size do not have the same fit. When I buy gloves, I usually try on two or three in my size to find one with a snug fit. I recommend that you do this, too. Finally, it certainly won't hurt to check your grips to see if they are clean. As they get oily, they naturally slip in your hands. Also, if you begin to see some wear, it's time to change the grips.

BROKEN BONES ■

Question: "I'm a woman golfer and am concerned about all the news I hear about fragile bones. I'm getting on in years and am wondering what I can do to keep my bone structure healthy and strong."

Answer: What you are describing is osteoporosis, which is a health threat for 25 million Americans, 80 percent of them women. Symptoms are often not present until bones are so thin that they can fracture from bumping into something, slipping, or even being hugged. As people get older, their bones become thinner. They lose calcium, which is the filler in the bone matrix that keeps it strong. The thinning is more evident in women after menopause because it is a direct effect of a decrease in estrogen. Bed rest, disuse, and immobilization cause a remarkable lessening in bone density in both women and men. Those with osteoporosis experience increased fractures and often debilitating bone pain. Older people tend to shrink. This is due to fractures of the spine. The weight of the body can cause multiple fractures of the vertebrae, which occur in 40 percent of women who have osteoporosis, and the whole back becomes shorter. Weak bones are a poor foundation for joints. As the bones deteriorate, the joints become distorted. This speeds the destruction of the joints along with the bones.

So far, there are no definitive tests for radiologic detection of osteoporosis; however, a test called single photon densitometry is used to measure bone in the forearm. Two tests are used to determine risk for spine and hip fractures—dual photon densitometry and quantitated computerized tomography—but they are quite costly. Also, there is no universal agreement that any of these tests can accurately determine a person's level of osteoporosis.

Treatment: Many current studies demonstrate how estrogen replacement therapy (ERT) and calcium help to improve bones by preventing osteoporosis and even building up their density after osteoporosis has set in. ERT works best when it is started during the first few years of menopause, but it can still offer benefits if started later, even beyond age seventy. Consult your doctor about possible side effects and safety concerns that might apply to you.

Another drug approved by the Food and Drug Administration (FDA) is calcitonin—a hormone that blocks bone loss and promotes bone growth.

Exercises, such as walking, strength training, and participating in sports, can also help. Research demonstrates that estrogen alone does little for increasing bone density, but adding exercise could increase bone density by 8.6 percent, a fourfold increase. Men don't need estrogen to get this benefit. In fact, they do not get osteoporosis to the extent that women do. Calcium supplements with vitamin D also might be prescribed. Calcium intake helps to prevent further bone loss.

Tip: Fractures from osteoporosis are most common in the spine, hip, lower leg, and wrist. I recommend a carefully supervised weight-bearing exercise program. The most popular is walking on the golf course. Strength training with weights is quite effective in retarding the progression of bone thinning. For women receiving ERT, I suggest engaging in exercise and combining it with a calcium supplement of at least 1,200–1,400 mg per day. I also recommend including plenty of low-fat milk and yogurt products in the diet. Adding tofu, canned salmon and sardines, and leafy greens, all of which are rich in calcium, can also help to reduce bone loss. If a fracture occurs, a physical therapy program to strengthen specific muscle groups near the site can be most beneficial.

Be warned that if you're considering a regimen of ERT, it can result in an increased risk of uterine cancer, if you don't get progesterone with it. On the other hand, ERT can halt bone loss and reduce the incidence of broken bones; eliminate hot flashes; restore flexibility, secretions, and lubrications in vaginal tissues; and possibly reduce the risk of heart disease. Recent studies suggest that a woman can get benefit from lower dosages of estrogen than were previously recommended.

With all the above pros and cons, I suggest that you work closely with your doctor so that the decision you make will be the correct one for you.

CARPAL TUNNEL SYNDROME ■

Question: "I was an avid golfer who played three times a week for thirty years until I started having problems with my wrists. I was told I had carpal tunnel syndrome. Two surgeries later and after damage to my middle finger, I have no feeling, and I no longer play. What happened? I was told the surgery was supposed to get rid of the pain. Instead, it ended my golfing career. I haven't played in five years and I sure miss the game."

Answer: Carpal tunnel syndrome (CTS) results when the median nerve is compressed at the wrist by a thickened ligament that wraps over the nerve. When that happens, a sharp pain, similar to the pain that results when you hit your funny bone, occurs in the area of the wrist. Numbness and a tingling sensation in the fingers are also common symptoms. CTS is often caused by repetitive overuse of the wrists and hands. Syd developed it after he began an aggressive practice program of hitting a thousand balls a day, and I recently had difficulty swinging a club because of an injured wrist. Keep in mind, however, that pain and numbness in the hand can be caused by other things as well, such as pressure on the nerves of the arm that originate in the neck. Consult your doctor before doing anything.

Treatment: Please consider surgery *only* after all else fails. I recommend an initial treatment of aspirin. In addition, I offer my patients wrist splints to inhibit wrist movement and decrease inflammation. As you recover, exercise to strengthen the wrist and hand is important. Squeezing a rubber ball is an ideal wrist-strengthening tool. If you're looking for an alternative treatment approach, note that some patients have been helped by using vitamin B_6. Cortisone injections also are used to decrease inflammation; however, because of the risk of tendon rupture, I don't usually administer more than one injection.

Finally, if you do decide to have surgery, there are two approaches to discuss with your doctor. The first is a small incision on the palmar side of the wrist, which releases the ligament overlying and compressing the nerve. The second procedure is arthroscopic surgery, in which several small incisions are made. There's more risk of complications with the second approach, and it's best to get the full details from your doctor before you decide to go this route. Both approaches can be performed on an outpatient basis, and recovery usually takes several weeks.

Surgery is not a substitute for arm and wrist conditioning, which can also make the difference between a successful surgery or an unsuccessful one.

Tip: With Syd's carpal tunnel problem, he decided not to resort to any of the above treatments. He merely stopped hitting golf balls for several months, and now he rarely hits more than a small bucket at a time. His carpal tunnel has not bothered him since. The body is incredibly wise. It knows exactly what to do to take care of itself.

COLD HANDS AND FEET ■

Question: "Although the sun is out and the temperatures are mild, I recently have been noticing that my hands and feet get cold while I play a round. My hands will get deathly pale, then very purple. Often I have to put a glove on my bare hand as I walk to my ball. Is there something wrong?"

Answer: What you are describing is a phenomenon called Raynaud's disease. When the small blood vessels of the fingers and toes and sometimes the tip of the nose go into spasm, blood flow is reduced or halted to the area. As a result, your fingers or the bottom of your feet first turn white from receiving too little blood, then blue from blood that's poorly oxygenated. Finally, the redness returns as the blood flow comes back.

Exposure to cold can set off an attack and so can touching something cold, such as your club or a can of soda. Most people don't have an underlying medical problem when diagnosed. Other conditions, however, are associated with secondary forms of Raynaud's symptoms. They include connective tissue autoimmune diseases, such as lupus erythematosus; rheumatoid arthritis; and scleroderma. All of these can produce inflammation of the blood vessel walls, which can lead to reduced blood flow to your hands and fingers. Raynaud's disease often occurs in people who have spent a lifetime operating equipment or tools that vibrate.

Tip: You require no treatment if you have a mild form of Raynaud's disease. With a more severe case, you might be able to prevent the cold-related symptoms you described by protecting your hands with special golf gloves that are now available in your local pro shop. Get a glove for each hand. Avoiding cold surfaces helps to reduce the likelihood of an attack. When other disorders cause a secondary form of Raynaud's, medical intervention, which includes the use of vasodilator drugs to open the small blood vessels in your hands and feet, is your best bet.

Syd has Raynaud's phenomenon and carries a hand warmer while he plays. There are numerous models. One model can be heated in the microwave, but it stays warm for only ½–1 hour at best. When exposed to air, other models keep warm for 7–8 hours. You can find these devices in sporting goods stores. There are numerous brands, and it's best to experiment to find the one that best suits your style of play.

Another technique that has helped some of my patients is swinging your arms around in sweeping circles as if you're trying to shoo away flies. This motion rushes blood to your extremities.

Having this problem is another reason not to smoke. Smoking aggravates Raynaud's phenomenon.

■ CUTS

Question: "I cut my leg on the course while looking for a ball in the rough. It was bleeding a lot. What should I have done?"

Answer: The obvious answer is to stop the bleeding, but this might be more difficult than it would seem. Most cuts require only direct pressure. However, if the cut is deep and the bleeding profuse, especially if it is pulsing (this means that you cut an artery), a tourniquet is necessary. For a cut on the arm, place the tourniquet around the upper arm; for a cut on the leg, place the tourniquet on the thigh. A tourniquet can be made from any cord, such as the one connecting your club covers. A belt is often the most available device. Use a stick to twist the tourniquet tightly enough so that the bleeding diminishes or stops. If a stick is not available, a putter, although unwieldy, will work. Then get off the course, and go to an emergency room immediately. On the way, loosen the tourniquet every 15 minutes to give the limb some blood.

For less significant cuts, keep some Band-Aids in your bag. They can protect minor cuts or blisters and allow you to continue playing.

If the cut appears to require stitching, this should be done within 8 hours.

Tip: Always keep a small supply of Band-Aids and butterfly bandages in your bag for small injuries. A day will come when they will be indispensable.

ELBOW PAIN (See also Arms, Hands, and Wrists) ■

Question: "My elbows hurt when I play golf and especially after the round. Is there such a thing as tennis elbow for golfers?"

Answer: Yes. In fact, golfers' complaints about elbow pain number close to complaints about their backs. Pain from elbow sprain results from overstretching one or more ligaments in the elbow joint. The pain in your elbow is probably the result of hitting the ground with your club before you hit the ball. That causes the elbow to bend sideways or backward, which puts stress on a ligament and temporarily forces the elbow out of its normal location.

Tendinitis is another cause of elbow pain. Elbow tendinitis is caused by the force of your grip at impact that sends shock through your forearm muscles to your tendons. The little bone (lateral epicondyle) on the exterior part of your elbow is harnessed to most of the forearm muscles by a small tendon on each muscle. When the tendon becomes inflamed, you get that painful and tender feeling in your elbow. The little bone (medial epicondyle) on the inside of your elbow, the one nearest your rib cage, is also the cause of pain and soreness that you might experience when you grip the club hard. This transmits a lot of force to your tendons, which can cause shock and inflammation.

Answer: If the sprain is causing constant pain, see your doctor immediately. Treatment consists of the application of a cast, tape, elastic bandage, or sling. A Velcro band that wraps around the forearm can also reduce the strain on the affected tendon. If you have severe pain while you're playing, place ice chips or cubes in a plastic bag, wrap the bag in a moist towel, and place the bag over the painful area.

The best preventive treatment is to build up your forearm muscles. Strong forearm muscles can absorb the shock of impact more effectively and prevent it from moving down your forearm and impacting your tendons. Also, it's prudent to warm up before practicing or playing. Taping the elbow before playing is also helpful.

Tip: The easiest way to build up forearm muscle strength is by squeezing a tennis ball continuously wherever the opportunity arises. You can do it at the office or while you're walking. I do it often while I'm in meetings. When things get out of hand, I squeeze a rubber ball, which also helps me to vent some of my frustration.

I also recommend hand weights and practicing wrist curls (see chapter 3).

There is one contraindication, as we say in the profession, which refers to a treatment or activity which would be inadvisable. Don't do any of these exercises if you experience pain in your elbow. If that is the case, give the inflammation in the tendons a chance to heal through rest.

Finally, I recommend a visit to your pro to seek advice about how to alter your golf swing by slightly bending the classic straight left arm or by developing a stronger grip where your left hand is turned more to the right. You also might want your pro to see how tightly you are holding the club. Also, consider Jack Nicklaus's classic recommendation of gripping your club as though you were holding a small bird in your hands. Your pro can also take a look at your golf equipment to determine if a change in the kind of shafts you swing might help to reduce shock to your elbows.

See your doctor if the pain persists. The doctor can fit you with a brace, just below the elbow, that is helpful in absorbing some of the shock. Other options include cortisone injections and, if all else fails, surgery.

FACIAL CONTUSION ■

Question: "Somebody hit a ball that went into my fairway and struck me on the cheek. I was knocked to the ground and had this large round or egg-shaped bump on my cheek. Later I was OK, but I want to know what I should do if this happens again. (Please don't tell me to duck because I did that and still got hit.)"

Answer: When you were hit by the ball, the skin was bruised and the underlying tissue of the face were bruised. A direct blow to the cheek, as you experienced, can cause bleeding from ruptured small capillaries, and the blood can be absorbed by muscles, tendons, and soft tissues. Symptoms include local swelling, pain and tenderness, feeling of firmness when you put pressure on your cheek, and discoloration under the skin that goes from redness to a black-and-blue bruise.

Treatment: You need to see a doctor right away unless the blow was very light. Your doctor will order X-rays of the facial area to rule out the possibility of a fracture. If there are no broken bones, treatment will consist of using an ice pack three or four times a day. Wrap ice in a plastic bag and wrap the bag in a moist towel. Place it on the injured area for 20 minutes every 6–7 hours. After several days, you can use a heat lamp, hot soaks, hot showers, a heating pad, or heat liniment. Gently massaging the area can provide comfort and decrease swelling. If you have pain, you can use acetaminophen or ibuprofen, or your doctor might give you a prescription for pain medicine.

Tip: Please note: if the swelling doesn't go down in a day or two and if the skin shows signs of infection—drainage, increasing pain, fever, headache, muscle aches, or dizziness—call your doctor's office for another appointment so that the doctor can examine the contusion again. An infection in this area can have serious implications.

■ FINGER PAIN (TRIGGER FINGER)

Question: "I have found lately that when I bend a finger, it locks into place. When I try to move it back to its original position, I can, but it hurts when I do so."

Answer: Orthopedists call your problem "trigger finger." It's a variation on tendinitis in your hand, and any of the fingers can be affected. The condition is usually caused by a thickening of one of the tendons in your palm. When little nodules form, they sometimes get caught in a gap in the tissue around your tendons. This keeps you from flexing your finger.

Treatment: If you can put up with the inconvenience, trigger finger won't harm you in any way and no treatment is needed. When you play, however, it might distract you. If this is the case, you might want to consult an orthopedic surgeon about a regimen of steroid or cortisone injections. If they don't help, surgery can be performed on an outpatient basis.

Tip: The only problem affecting your game will occur when you try to let go of your club. You might have to force your fingers off the club. As for changes in your equipment or swing, they really won't help.

FINGER SPRAIN ■

Question: "I don't know how it happened, but after hitting a large bucket of balls, my index finger began to swell. Right now my finger is really tender. What happened?"

Answer: Your finger pain could be the result of mis-hitting the ball or hitting the ground before the ball. The club turning while you swing could be another likely cause. The sprain is caused by violent overstretching of one or more ligaments that hold the finger joints in place. You could have torn or ruptured a portion of the ligament. If the latter occurred, surgery might be required. As you described, symptoms are swelling and tenderness. A sprain can also cause severe pain and a popping or tearing feeling inside the finger when it occurs.

Treatment: The first step is to rule out fracture. Often, however, treatment includes a splint or tape whether the injury is a fracture or a sprain. If pain persists, your doctor might order stress X-rays to determine the degree of the ligament's looseness or the presence of a fracture. If the ligament is badly torn, surgery might be the treatment of choice.

If the sprain occurs while you're playing, apply ice and discontinue playing. Once you get home, use an ice pack three or four times a day. If the pain is severe, you can use aspirin, acetaminophen, or ibuprofen and topical liniment or ointment. Sometimes, I inject a corticosteroid (triamcinolone) to reduce inflammation.

Tip: Remember that if you don't allow for proper healing time, you could injure the area again. I'd recommend a leave of absence from playing for 2–6 weeks if the sprain is mild, 2 months if it is moderate, and 3 months if it is severe. Sometimes swelling around finger sprains requires 3–6 months to heal. Call your doctor if pain and swelling are present for more than 2 weeks.

■ FOOT AND ANKLE INJURY

Question: "I was walking in the rough when a hole 'grabbed' my foot and turned it. My ankle has swollen, and I can hardly walk without feeling pain. Should I seek medical attention?"

Answer: Ankle sprains often occur on golf courses that are hilly or that have tall grass where holes are not visible. You probably tore the lateral ligaments in your ankle. As you continue to play, you are irritating those torn ligaments when you swing at the ball and turn off your ankles.

Treatment: If the sprain is mild, ice and an ankle support might enable you to continue playing at least some golf. If the pain persists, however, it's time to take a rest from playing and practicing. This will help to reduce the swelling that you describe. If you do start playing after resting for awhile, it's a good idea to ice down your ankles after a round even if you ride in a cart. Again, it's the stress on your ankle ligaments during your swing that can cause swelling.

If you must play despite the swelling and pain, you might want to tape your ankle, but this could impact the free flow of your turning away from the ball and maintaining your balance. However, I once taped my ankle to play in a tennis tournament, and I did pretty well.

Tip: A golf equipment store can provide devices for ankle sprains or back problems. You might want to buy an ankle brace to keep your ankle protected.

Sometimes playing in a good pair of walking shoes rather than your spike shoes will take some of the strain off the ankle.

If resting and using ice to reduce the sprain isn't working, steroids might help to reduce the swelling faster. Steroid medication has side effects, however, and it might not be an appropriate treatment if you have other other chronic medical conditions, such as kidney disease. As a subscriber to the maxim that the safest treatment is the one that is least invasive, I suggest that you just stop playing for awhile and spend the time reading up on the game. If you don't like to read, rent a few golf instructional videos and get some tips while you're giving your game and swing a rest.

FOOT PAIN (BONE SPURS AND PLANTAR FASCIITIS) ■

Question: "My pro suggested that I use my feet more during my downswing. He recommended that I push off my right foot to start the downswing. I've been doing that now for two weeks and I get this on-and-off pain in my ankle. I also noticed this little irregular bump sticking out of my foot. What's the problem?"

Answer: You might have a bone spur or calcium deposits, probably resulting from the repeated pressure that you have been putting on your foot. This is an abnormal buildup of bone at the lower part of the heel or other foot bones as a result of repeated pressure on the area. Either you are forcing a lot of pressure on your foot before your downswing or you are playing a ton of golf. It could also be the result of weakened muscles or conditioning, which can promote improper movement that creates extra stress on the ankle and foot bones. In addition to changes in the contour of bones, symptoms include a loss of the ability to push off your foot rapidly and a low level of pain in your foot.

A more common scenario involves pain on the sole of the foot as well as the heel. This is the result of an injury to the connective tissue on the sole, which is known as plantar fasciitis. You are likely to notice this injury by a sharp pain in your foot when you first put pressure on your feet as you get out of bed. After the pain subsides, you are pain free for a few hours before a nagging ache plagues you for the rest of the day. You can identify this injury as plantar fasciitis if the bottom of your foot is sore to the touch from most of the heel to the ball.

Treatment: A short-term treatment approach for both conditions is to apply ice regularly. Stretching the plantar fascia will keep it from reinjury. The best way to do this is to roll your foot back and forth on a cylinder. Some people use a juice can full of ice, which serves both purposes. It is best to do this both before and after a round of golf. Ointments and heat liniments are also helpful. If your golf facility offers whirlpool treatments, try them. Gentle foot massage not only will be comforting, but it can help to decrease swelling.

Tip: Even before the pain begins to subside, begin daily progressive rehabilitation exercises as soon as your doctor gives you the green light. I also recommend using ice massage before and after you play or practice. Fill a large Styrofoam soda cup with water and freeze it, then tear a hole in the top so the ice sticks out. Use this to massage the foot area that is painful.

I suggest that you stay away from drug therapy. If you must get some relief, take aspirin or ibuprofen.

At times, the injury can be severe enough that the best thing to do is rest the injured foot for 2–4 weeks. You might want to consult with your doctor to determine if a splint or crutches will help. Also, while sitting, elevate the foot. Whether or not rest is required, warming up always will be necessary because the healing fascia will contract, thus making it more prone to injury.

■ FOOT PAIN (BURSITIS)

Question: "I noticed lately that I've been experiencing tenderness in my left big toe. It usually happens the morning after I play golf and walk during my round. Can you tell me what my problem is?"

Answer: If your doctor rules out such things as gout and fractures, you might be suffering from inflammation of a bursa in your foot. A bursa is a cushion overlying a joint or tendon. Injury to the bursa can cause mild irritation. Bursas can occur about the Achilles tendon; the heel bone; and, in your case, next to the base of the big toe. Redness, pain, tenderness, swelling, foot and toe restriction, and even fever are common symptoms. Bursitis can result from injury to a joint, acute or chronic infection, arthritis, or gout.

Treatment: The treatment of choice is to use ice massage (placing or rubbing ice on the affected area) and, after a few days, to apply heat to the painful area. If the inflammation is severe, I tell my patients to use crutches so as to prevent excessive weight on the tender area. If there is swelling, I suggest keeping the foot elevated, which also helps to prevent fluid buildup. Prop your foot on pillows when you are in a lying or sitting position. Depending on the severity of the bursitis, NSAIDs might be prescribed. For mild pain, you can use acetaminophen or ibuprofen. For severe and persistent pain, I inject triamcinolone (an anti-inflammatory steroid medicine) into the bursa. Check with your doctor about this treatment.

Tip: Obviously, you should not play golf until the symptoms clear up. To prevent a recurrence, wear shoes that fit. When Syd developed this problem, he realized that it was caused by a pair of golf shoes that were a half size too small. I also recommend warming up by using some of the techniques described in chapter 3. Finally, wear warm socks in cold weather and wear extra protection, such as wraps or toe supports, over the affected area.

GROIN STRAIN ■

Question: "I took a hard swing at my ball in the rough. When I walked away, my groin area hurt. What happened?"

Answer: You probably injured the muscles or tendons in your groin area, which is where the abdomen meets the thigh. It's made up of muscles, tendons, and the attached bones that act to stabilize the pelvis and allow us to move. A mild strain in that area refers to pulling a muscle. A moderate strain indicates some tearing of fibers in a muscle or tendon. A severe strain is a rupture of the muscle-tendon-bone attachment. The most common tissue strained in this area is the inguinal ligament. Chronic strains usually result from overuse. Acute strains are caused by direct injury or direct stress. The symptoms include groin pain, especially when you move or stretch your leg at the hip joint. Some golfers experience muscle spasms in the stomach or thigh, groin swelling, and occasional loss of strength if the strain is severe. An overweight golfer is more prone to inguinal strain than a golfer of average weight because the abdomen is already putting stress on the ligament.

Treatment: Treatment usually consists of resting to allow for sufficient healing before resuming your game. Average resting times range from 2–10 days for a mild strain to 6–10 weeks for a severe strain. If you continue to play, you could eventually develop a chronic injury that might resist healing. Treatment at the time of injury includes rest, ice, and compression. If the area begins to feel better, replace the ice with heat. Your doctor might order elasticized bandages to support the injured area.

Tip: Research has shown that participating in a strengthening, flexibility, and conditioning program helps to reduce the risk of groin strain. If such a program is not possible for you, make sure that you warm up correctly before you practice or play (see chapter 3).

■ HAND PAIN AND TINGLING

Question: "I get a lot of hand pain and tingling after I play golf or hit practice balls. My doctor assured me I didn't have arthritis or carpal tunnel syndrome. Can you tell me what might be wrong?"

Answer: Paresthesia (pain and tingling) in the hands is often caused by pressure on the spinal nerves in the neck that is due to bone spurs (from arthritis) or herniated disks. The symptoms you describe are usually the result of the swelling and inflammation of the tissues caused by this nerve-pinching pressure. Your problem can be diagnosed with MRI and/or a nerve conduction study to determine if the cause is related to herniated disks in your neck and/or bone spurs pressing on a nerve.

Treatment: Surgery is often the treatment of choice, but other possibilities are medication and physical therapy. Research suggests that nonsurgical therapy has little impact on the actual causes of nerve pressure, although it can considerably reduce symptoms. Continuing pain and tingling in your hands, along with weakness of hand muscles, might eventually lead to nerve damage. If this occurs, surgery is required.

Tip: Before you go under the knife, make sure that your doctor has ruled out joint inflammation caused by arthritis, gout, bursitis, tendinitis, carpal tunnel syndrome, sprained ligaments, muscles, tendons, or fractured bones in the hand, bone infections (osteomyelitis), and (in some rare cases) rheumatic fever.

HAND SPRAIN ■

Question: "I hit a large bucket of balls yesterday and woke up this morning with my left hand feeling tender. While I was hitting balls, I noticed a sharp pain and a tearing sensation inside my hand. Did I break something?"

Answer: You might have severely overstretched the ligaments in your hand, either by hitting the ground before you hit the ball or by violently snapping your hand during your swing. A hand sprain involves several ligaments that cause more complications than a single-ligament sprain. When you overstretch a hand ligament, it will become tense and give way at some point. If the ligament is torn, we call that a mild strain. If there is a rupture of a portion of a ligament, you probably developed some swelling in the hand. A complete rupture of the ligament results in a total inability to use your hand. Surgery might be needed. Symptoms include severe pain during your swing; a popping or tearing inside the hand; tenderness; swelling; and, in some instances, bruising.

Treatment: Because ligaments have a poor blood supply, it can take 2–6 weeks for the hand to heal if the sprain is mild and 8–10 weeks if it is severe. When you don't allow your hand enough time to heal, prolonged disability can result. Should you continue to sprain the hand, you could develop arthritic hand joints.

Immediate treatment at the time of the sprain includes resting the hand and using ice. Your doctor might apply a cast, tape, or an elastic bandage. After 72 hours, I suggest that you apply heat instead of ice if the hand begins to feel better. You can take aspirin, acetaminophen, or ibuprofen for minor discomfort, or your doctor might prescribe stronger pain relievers or a long-acting local anesthetic to reduce the pain. If there is a lot of inflammation, corticosteroid injections of triamcinolone can help.

Tip: Build up your hand strength by squeezing a rubber ball (see chapter 3). You might want to tape weakened joints before you practice or play. If the sprain occurs while you are practicing or playing, stop right away to avoid further injury and/or long term complications. If you continue to feel pain in your hand or if the swelling or bruising worsens despite the treatments noted above, call your doctor right away. And, please, don't resume golfing until you get the green light from your doctor, even though your hand feels fine. A lot of golfers reinjure the ligaments by resuming their golfing routines too soon.

■ HAND TENDINITIS

Question: "I feel this pain in my hand whenever I swing my club. I don't recall having hit the ground or done anything out of the usual. I do hit a lot of practice balls before a round and afterward notice some redness in my hand. Can you explain what might be happening?"

Answer: You could have inflammation of a tendon (tendinitis) on the lining of a tendon sheath (tenosynovitis) in your hand. This lining secretes a fluid that lubricates the tendon. When inflammation of the lining occurs, the tendon has difficulty moving smoothly in its covering. Symptoms for hand tendinitis include constant pain or pain when you move your hand, hand and wrist motion restriction, cracking sounds, and redness and tenderness at the site of the injured tendon. Hitting too many practice golf balls or swinging too hard at the ball can cause hand tendinitis.

Treatment: I have my patients wrap their hands and wrists with an elasticized bandage until the pain goes away. Also, I advise applying ice packs or heat—a heat lamp, hot soaks, hot showers, a heating pad, or heat liniment or ointment—to the affected areas. If the pain persists, you can use nonprescription drugs, such as aspirin. Should your doctor prescribe pain medication, don't take it longer than 4–7 days. In some rare cases, I inject the tendon covering with a combination of a long-acting local anesthetic and a steroid, such as triamcinolone.

Tip: I recommend that you participate in an adequate warm-up before you start whacking a bucket of balls. If necessary, wear protective gear and get a golf lesson to learn the proper moves and techniques for swinging at the ball. It's possible that your hand tendinitis is the result of flaws in your swing. Finally, turn to chapter 3 for tips on strengthening your wrists and hands.

HEATSTROKE AND HEAT EXHAUSTION ■

Question: "I was playing in hot weather and walking when I started getting dizzy and felt like I was going to faint. I'm in excellent health, and I couldn't figure it out. I rested for a bit and then I felt better. But a few minutes later, it happened again. Was I suffering from heat exhaustion?"

Answer: Good diagnosis; however, do not confuse heat exhaustion with heatstroke. Both are very common complaints of athletes. Heat exhaustion is diagnosed if your skin is cool and clammy, you are perspiring profusely, your pupils are dilated, your pulse is rapid, you become nauseated, you experience cramps in your legs and stomach, and you feel dizzy and faint.

Heatstroke results when your body temperature goes above 102°F. Your skin becomes hot, dry, and flushed, and your pupils become constricted. Your pulse rate is too high, and you have a sense of confusion. Seizures and unconsciousness can result if you don't follow the advice given below.

Treatment: Don't take any of the above symptoms lightly. For heat exhaustion, head immediately to a shaded area. Once there, lie down or sit down and elevate your feet. Put cool, wet towels on your forehead and body. When you're able to swallow and breathe easily and are feeling somewhat better, you can drink a little water; however, avoid *all* alcoholic and caffeinated beverages.

For heatstroke, you need to get into a cooler location as soon as possible. If you're in the middle of the course, get to a drinking fountain and soak wet cloths to put on your forehead and body. Try fanning yourself, and do not eat or drink anything until the symptoms subside.

Tip: I also recommend packing salt tablets in your bag, especially on hot days. When you are aware of the symptoms described above and follow the treatment recommendations, you will reduce the chance of more serious complications. If you don't feel any better after a bit, however, it's prudent to call for emergency medical assistance.

HERNIA ■

Question: "When I stood in one place for a while, for example, while waiting to tee off, I got this dull pain in my groin. I noticed that I also had this little soft lump down there that hurt, but it felt better when I pressed on it. My buddies told me I had a hernia and told me I could wear this corset rather than go under the knife. What's your recommendation?"

Answer: A hernia is a protrusion at an internal organ through a weak or abnormal opening in the muscle surrounding it. Common types of hernias that affect golfers and other athletes include inguinal hernias, which are more common in men, and incisional hernias, which occur frequently in women. Symptoms, as you describe, include scrotal swelling, with or without pain, and a lump or protrusion that usually goes away with gentle pressure when you lie down. This weakness in connective tissue and the muscle wall could have been present when you were born, or could have occurred later. In golfers and other athletes, hernias usually result from straining or being overweight.

Treatment: Hernias can be treated by using a supportive garment or truss, but only if it causes very little discomfort and you can live with it. Surgery is the best way of repairing a hernia. It almost eliminates the possibility of strangulating the hernia, which can lead to blood supply loss and can cause severe illness, severe pain, and shock. My argument is: Why take the chance?

Tip: Syd had his hernia surgically repaired and reports that he played golf three weeks later. He now avoids heavy lifting or straining. To prevent getting another hernia, you should also avoid straining during a bowel movement and stay away from weight-lifting equipment until you get the hernia surgically repaired. If you must lift something, make sure to bend your knees, keep the object close to your body, and lift it by using your leg muscles. Never bend from the waist to lift anything.

■ HIP PAIN (BURSITIS)

Question: "The outside of my hip usually hurts while I swing at the ball and especially after I get through playing. Don't ask me what it feels like the next morning! Any suggestions for what I can do other than give up golf?"

Answer: When the pain is on the outside of your hip, it's usually caused by bursitis, specifically in the trochanteric bursa. The trochanteric bursa is a fluid-filled sac near the bone on the outside of your hip. Its purpose is to cushion the hip. Your hip has a number of large muscles and tendons that this sac protects from irritation. Because your hips are instrumental during the golf swing, they can cause overcompression of this sac by the tendons, which results in bursitis.

Treatment: Modifying your swing by turning your hip more will, paradoxically, take stress off the hips by increasing your lower back rotation. By doing this, you reduce the chances of sliding those tendons and the sac at the hip.

If this maneuver doesn't work, I suggest rest to reduce the inflammation. Icing the area that hurts usually speeds up the recovery time. Aspirin, ibuprofen, or an anti-inflammatory prescription can also help to reduce inflammation, but take any of these medications with care if you have ulcers or a history of stomach problems.

Tip: If you are not getting results from the treatments suggested above, you might want to see your doctor for a shot of cortisone. You might not get results, however, because the trochanteric bursa is deep and hard to reach with a needle. Even many orthopedists require the use of a fluoroscope. This instrument is more commonly found in a hospital than a doctor's office.

INSECT BITES AND STINGS ■

Question: "What should I do when I get bitten or stung by an insect?"

Answer: The only insects you need to be concerned with on the golf course are hornets, wasps, ants, yellow jackets, fire ants, and bees. These fellows don't normally cause a problem if they bite or sting you unless you are allergic to them. Then the reaction can be fatal.

When you get stung or bitten, your immune system might respond to the chemicals in the venom right away or the venom might have a delayed reaction. Under normal circumstances, a bee sting is just irritating. It causes pain and a local inflammatory reaction: heat, swelling, and redness. If you are allergic to the venom, however, you could go into anaphylactic shock, an allergic reaction in which the allergen-antibody combination causes a cascade of events that sets the whole body into a tailspin. Your blood pressure drops precipitously; your bronchial tubes close up; you swell up in your face, mouth and throat; and you get a rash. Other serious symptoms include nausea and vomiting. Death can also result from a severe allergic reaction.

Treatment: To treat an insect sting or bite that generates a mild reaction, first examine the site of the sting. If the stinger is left behind, remove it immediately. Then apply ice to reduce swelling. If you can get back to the clubhouse, apply baking soda and water to help relieve the pain. If the area itches, apply calamine lotion. Ibuprofen will help to reduce inflammation. For pain, take aspirin or acetaminophen. For strong reactions, try diphenhydramine or another nonprescription antihistamine. If you are highly sensitive and have had a severe reaction to a sting in the past, immediate medical attention is necessary. Your doctor or outpatient emergency room will usually treat you with a shot of epinephrine (adrenaline).

Tip: I recommend that people who have strong reactions to insect stings carry a bee-sting kit with them. The kit consists of a tourniquet, one or two preset doses of epinephrine, and an antihistamine. Please remember, however, that administering your own medication is not enough. You still need to see your doctor right away!

Studies have demonstrated that allergy shots can help to prevent severe reactions to bee stings. You might want to consider them if you play a lot of golf.

The best advice is to prevent insect stings and bites. Avoid wearing bright colors and bold-patterned golf shirts that insects could mistake for flowers. Also, do not wear fragrances and scented cosmetics.

■ KNEE PAIN (BURSITIS)

Question: "I get a pain and swelling on my knee. Mainly, it is just a bother. Initially, it came up with pain, but now it's just swollen and a nuisance. Since it doesn't hurt much, should I worry?"

Answer: If this swelling feels mushy and is confined to your knee-cap, you might have a prepatellar bursitis. It results from trauma to the protective cushion of the patella, which has filled with fluid and blood. This condition is also called "housemaid's knee" because of the trauma endured when one cleans the floor on hands and knees. Although the condition can be painless, it is also associated with redness and pain. In fact, resolution of the pain with a lidocaine injection into the area is considered by some doctors to confirm the diagnosis.

Treatment: Prepatellar bursitis is not dangerous, but if it is not treated over a period of time, it can be quite persistent. The best thing to do is to get medical attention as soon as possible. Your doctor will drain it, inject it with a steroid and possibly a local anesthetic, and wrap it with an Ace bandage. You should then stay off your feet for at least a day and maintain a low profile for a week. Keep the affected area compressed and iced.

Tip: Prepatellar bursitis is not uncommon. The worst aspect of the condition is a possible recurrence. You can reduce this possibility by getting it treated immediately. The same can be said about a bursitis of the elbow.

KNEE PAIN (RUNNER'S KNEE) ■

Question: "A few years ago, Lee Trevino claimed that his golf game improved by running two miles prior to a round. I started doing that, and it actually helped. However, the other day I started feeling this aching pain around my kneecap after my two-mile run. When I got on the course, the pain became worse, especially when I had to walk up a hill. What happened?"

Answer: You might have developed runner's knee. It's more likely to happen if you are a woman. That aching pain you describe is caused by the kneecap not being able to track properly, perhaps because of some abnormality in your legs (e.g., a thigh bone that is turned inward slightly or flat feet). Lack of strength or flexibility in the muscles around your kneecap also can be a cause. Too much stress to the knee as a result of running, especially on pavement, can create an imbalance in the leg muscles, thus causing the knee-cap to be pulled sideways. In addition to the pain you describe, symptoms can include soreness and a sensation of the knee giving way.

If you feel as though your knee is slipping, you might have an anterior cruciate ligament (ACL) that's not functioning. The ACL is the ligament that crosses over the front of the knee and prevents the tibia from falling forward. If it ceases to work correctly, you can have a very painful situation. Ruptures, sudden stops, and turns will cause the knee to come out.

On the other hand, if you feel that something is getting caught in your knee and it locks, you might have a meniscus tear. The meniscus is the cartilage in the knee that cushions the force to the knee.

Treatment: In rare cases, shoe inserts or a knee brace can help to correct the problem if it is caused by flat feet or the thigh bone turning inward. Often, treatment is not necessary other than starting one of the strength and flexibility training programs provided in chapter 3. If you're experiencing a lot of pain, rest becomes crucial. You'll only make the condition worse if you try to work through the condition. Stay away from kneeling or climbing steps unless absolutely necessary. Apply an ice bag for 10 minutes several times daily. After a few days, apply heat; use a heat lamp, hot soaks, hot showers, a heating pad, or heat liniment. If the pain doesn't go away, aspirin, ibuprofen, and/or another type of NSAID might help.

Tip: When you start feeling better, begin an exercise program to strengthen and condition the upper leg and hip muscles. Avoid deep squatting and other activities that compress the knee. Also, you might want to lift your left toe slightly during your backswing and lift your right toe as you complete your downswing.

If your symptoms don't go away after you rest for several days, call your doctor. You might be a candidate for arthroscopic surgery. It is a very effective procedure for repair of most knee problems. Depending on the problem, the recovery time is within 2 weeks for a meniscus to as long as 9–12 weeks for an ACL reconstruction. Before you go under the knife, however, talk to your doctor about the pros and cons. Loss of ACL function can not only cause cartilage tears in your knees, but it can eventually be the site for degenerative arthritis. If you are a candidate for the operation, though, the procedure is effective in preventing future cartilage tears and helpful in reducing the eventual risk of arthritis in the knee. The downside is that it could take up to a year after surgery for your knee to heal.

The FDA has recently licensed a new drug (Carticel) that uses a patient's own cartilage cells to repair cartilage. So far, results have been encouraging, especially in patients with injuries. Check with your doctor to get the full details.

LEG SPRAIN, LOWER ■

Question: "I was walking up a hill at my course when I felt this tearing inside of my lower leg. I had to stop playing. What happened?"

Answer: You might have sprained a ligament in your leg by putting too much stress on it. Leg ligaments can be violently overstretched when you climb a steep hill. When leg ligaments are overstretched, they become tense and give way at their weakest point, either where they attach to bone or within the ligament itself. Leg sprains occur quite frequently in runners, walkers, and athletes who often accidentally land on the side of their feet. Symptoms are severe pain at the time of the injury, the popping and tearing feeling inside your leg that you described, tenderness, swelling, and bruising.

Treatment: If the sprain is mild, I instruct the patient to use an ice pack several times a day and to wrap the injured leg with an elasticized bandage between ice treatments. If the area feels better after several days, I instruct the patient to use a heat lamp, hot soaks, hot showers, a heating pad, or heat liniment or ointment instead of ice. If pain persists, I prescribe aspirin, acetaminophen, or ibuprofen and continued use of the topical ointment or liniment.

If the sprain is severe, I will apply a cast from the toes to the knee to protect the affected area. A stronger pain reliever is sometimes needed.

Tip: It's important that you build up your leg strength. Refer to the leg-strengthening exercises in chapter 3. Always warm up before a round of golf and, if necessary, tape your ankles before you practice or play. If the pain persists for more than 2 weeks after applying the above treatments, call your doctor.

■ LIGHTNING STRIKE

Question: "Every afternoon in my state, we have quite a number of lightening storms in the summer. Can you review the steps to take when lightning strikes?"

Answer: The most dangerous weather event you can encounter on the golf course is lightning. Almost a third of those struck by lightning die immediately. This is due to the electrical shock that stops the heart. We have known for several decades what a proper amount of electrical current can do to "reset" a heart with an abnormal rhythm. A disordered heart can be set right, but if too much current is given or if it comes at the wrong time during the electric cycle of the heart, then the muscle can stop working.

Actually, lightning does the same thing but with significantly more energy. For comparison's sake, the cardiovascular output is about 300 watt-seconds (it's not important to know much about this measurement). Lightning has the power of about 20 billion watt-seconds, and its bolt has a diameter of about 20 feet. It can affect objects 100 feet away.

If lightning ever strikes someone in your group, be aware that the electricity comes and goes quickly. In other words, the afflicted individual will not pass an electrical shock to others. Cardiopulmonary resuscitation (CPR) must be started immediately (see the section, Heart Attack First Aid, in chapter 2). The heart will sometimes restart by itself if the injured person has enough oxygen and blood circulation is good. At the very least, prompt action might allow enough time for medical help to arrive. If you don't know CPR, learn it. Courses in CPR can be found in cities and towns everywhere. Avail yourself of this lifesaving knowledge. It is vital in many situations, not just lightning strikes.

People who survive lightning strikes might suffer from other injuries, such as severe and persistent myalgia (muscle pain). This is probably the result of the significant contraction that such a large jolt of electricity will cause to a muscle. Convulsions are also common, sometimes with recurring amnesia and memory deficits. Electroconvulsive therapy (ECT), or "shock therapy" as it is frequently called, does to the brain what cardiovascular shock does to the heart. Other possible effects from lightning include damage to the kidneys, probably as a result of the massive debris that they must filter from the muscle damage. Cataracts also can result from lightning. Finally, burns from the lightning as it travels over the skin can cause the same branching configuration on the body that it does in the sky.

Tip: The smartest decision you can make when you hear thunder is to find shelter, but do not get under an isolated tree or metal-topped pavilion; either of these could attract lightning. Scatter from one another if there is no shelter because bodies close to each other can be affected by the same strike.

MUSCLE CRAMPS ■

Question: "I was standing over a putt when my legs started to cramp. I had to fall to the ground and rub my legs for a minute or so until I felt better. I was wondering what causes muscle cramps and what I can do to prevent them in the future?"

Answer: Painful involuntary muscle cramps are caused by contractions resulting from disorders of the nervous system or by chemistry changes in muscle cells. Such contractions and chemical changes are often the result of vigorous physical activity, potassium or calcium deficiencies, nerve disorders (e.g., pressure on nerve roots near the spinal cord), nerve fiber abnormalities, enzyme deficiencies, diabetes, alcoholism, chronic kidney disease, hardening of the arteries, and/or a reaction to medication.

Treatment: In most cases, muscle cramps go away by themselves. In some situations, they can be controlled by treating the underlying medical problem. Increasing fluids can also reduce the frequency of muscle cramps. Warm soaks, ice, and/or gentle massage can help to relieve pain and soreness in muscles, as will stretching and rubbing the cramped muscles. You are probably aware that you can combat a cramp by contracting the muscles opposite those that are cramping. So, if you get a cramp in the calf of your leg, you can force the front of the foot up toward the knee.

Tip: I recommend a diet of fluids, especially water, before and during play. If you have frequent cramps, eat a lot of foods high in potassium, such as dried apricots, whole-grain cereals, dried lentils, dried peaches, bananas, peanuts, and citrus fruits. Also make sure that you have sufficient calcium in your diet. (If you are taking potassium supplements, be sure to get your doctor's OK in case you are taking drugs that can raise your potassium levels.)

■ NECK PAIN

Question: "I woke up this morning with a sore neck. It happens every time I play golf. What can I do about it?"

Answer: One explanation for your sore neck after playing might be that you try extra hard to keep your head still while you play. This causes too much overstretching of one or more ligaments in the neck. By trying to keep your head perfectly still during the entire swing, you generate extreme twists and turns on your back, which lead to the soreness you describe. Other symptoms include muscle spasms, stiffness, tenderness, swelling, and sometimes bruising.

Emotional stress also contributes to tight muscles, especially those in the neck. They become tired, and tired muscles become sore.

The issue of muscle pain is actually a function of muscle tension and muscle strength. Strong muscles can take a lot more stress than weak muscles.

Treatment: To reduce pain, use an ice pack for about 15 minutes several times a day. Sometimes heat is more helpful than ice. Find which works best for you. Use a heat lamp, hot soaks, hot showers, a heating pad, or heat liniment or ointment. If you can, get a whirlpool treatment. If the pain is persistent and discomforting, take aspirin, acetaminophen, or ibuprofen.

Stress reduction will reduce muscle tension. Exercise increases muscle strength. A combination of the two is the best way to reduce pain and prevent injuries. Stretching will also reduce tension.

Tip: Give yourself permission to move your head a little while your shoulders rotate away from the ball. If you sense that you're losing sight of the ball, accept that. Blind golfers can hit golf balls, too. If you watch Jack Nicklaus, you will notice a slight turning of his chin to the right of the ball just before he swings the club back. Thus, Jack reduces the chance of causing strain to his neck. Don't get me wrong—Jack is also doing this to keep his head behind the ball.

Consider doing neck stretches before play or when you encounter a bottleneck on a hole. Try standing with your hands on your hips and your legs spread out, much like you set up to the ball with a driver. Slowly turn your neck to the left, stretch it, and hold it in the stretched position for 5–10 seconds. Then, turn your neck to the right and do the same thing. For a more complete exercise program, consider the recommendations in chapter 3 for neck exercises to strengthen and condition the muscles and ligaments in the region of the neck.

■ NOSE INJURY

Question: "I got hit with a golf club, which caused a bloody nose. It was very difficult to stop the bleeding. What should I have done?"

Answer: The most significant nose emergency you will find on the course is trauma. It can be mild and cause only a bloody nose, or it can break a bone and disrupt the nasal passages and the ability to breathe properly. Most often, you can notice the latter by a change in the shape or a deviation of the nose. This is best seen immediately after injury and before the nose swells significantly.

Treatment: The first thing you should do is stop the bleeding. Most nose injuries such as yours result in bleeding from the front of the nose, which is easy to stop. Wet a tissue, napkin, or piece of cloth and put it in the nose. Apply pressure on the outside of the nose, and lie back (for instance, against a tree) for a few minutes. Continue to keep the paper or cloth in the nose for at least 15 minutes as you get on with your game.

If your nose appears crooked, get an X-ray to see if it is broken. If so, it should be reduced (put back into place).

Tip: The best way to deal with a nose injury is to prevent it from happening. Watch out for flying balls—and clubs!

■ POISON IVY

Question: "Ever since I was a kid, I was warned about poison ivy and other poisonous plants. The other day I hit my ball into the rough and came out with rashes on my arms and hands. Did I get poison ivy? Any tips to recognize it and treat it?"

Answer: Skin eruptions come within hours to days after contact. Redness and blistering occur at the site of contact. The burning and itching can be intense, but avoid scratching the rash because that is the best way to spread the poison and cause a secondary infection.

Poison ivy grows just about everywhere east of the Rockies, even toward the border with Mexico. It is most likely to be found on flood plains, in forests, and on banks and shores. Although usually a small plant, it can grow into a vine or shrub if nothing is growing around it. The leaves are glossy and in clusters of three. The flowers are greenish white to cream-colored, and the berries are tan to yellow.

Poison sumac is a tall shrub, growing as high as 15 feet. The leaves are bunched seven to eleven on a stem. The berries are yellow or cream. You might have seen this variety when you were younger; poison sumac is found in wet places (bogs, swamps, and wetlands) east of the Mississippi. The nonpoisonous variety has red fruit and is almost never found in wet locations.

Poison oak is found more often on the West Coast, although at camp we were dedicated to discovering an eastern species. With leaves and berries similar to poison ivy, it has leaves like an oak that grow in groups of three.

All of these plants carry the same substance, an irritant called urushiol. Even indirect contact with urushiol, such as inhaling the smoke from a burning plant, can cause significant irritation to the nose, throat, and lungs. If this happens, get to a doctor quickly.

Treatment: If you break out from poison ivy or any of its cousins, do not scratch it. You will only spread the rash and the itch. To minimize the adverse reaction on your skin, remove all contaminated clothes and wash them thoroughly. Calamine lotion soothes itching skin. You can also use a cool potato or an oatmeal-mash compress. If necessary, you can use Benadryl, but be careful. It dries the membranes and causes drowsiness, and it can also slow down your golf game. Mild steroid creams, such as hydrocortisone (½–1 percent) can speed the healing of the blistery rash.

Tip: Be aware of what these poisonous plants look like if you are golfing in a region where they exist. The best treatment is prevention.

■ **RIB STRAIN**

Question: "After I hit a driver, I felt this pain in my chest on subsequent shots. While I walked, my chest hurt. When I touched the area near my heart, it was tender. What happened?"

Answer: You might have injured the muscles or tendons that attach to the ribs. Muscles, tendons, and their attached ribs make up a unit that stabilizes the chest, breastbone, and upper spine. The function of this unit is to allow free movement of your upper body. If there is a weakness in it, a strain results. Symptoms include pain while moving, breathing, coughing, or swinging a golf club; muscle spasms, tenderness, or swelling; and a crackling feeling and sound if you press the area with your fingers. If you swing incorrectly or too hard at the ball on a regular basis, you can wear down and overuse this muscle-tendon-rib unit and cause a strain.

Treatment: Most rib strains are more painful than disabling. If this is the first time that you have felt strain in your ribs, just laying off practice and play for a bit will prevent any further complications. If the strain is mild, stay away from playing for 2–10 days. If it's a moderate strain, you might have to rest from 10 days to 6 weeks. I recommend rest and ice, including ice massage several times a day, to my patients. After 24 hours, I have them apply heat instead of ice if the area is feeling better. For discomfort from the strain, I recommend aspirin, acetaminophen, or ibuprofen and a topical ointment or liniment. If the pain is severe, I prescribe stronger prescription pain medicine. There is little justification for an elasticized bandage or rib belt. Such devices do not materially help healing or symptoms, and they can reduce a person's ability to breathe well.

Tip: The best way to prevent rib strain in the future is to participate in one of the strengthening and conditioning exercises recommended in chapter 3. Also, always warm up before you practice or play. If you get rib strain often during play, I recommend going to a golf pro to determine how your swing might be contributing to the problem.

SHINSPLINTS ■

Question: "For no reason that I can think of, I began getting this pain that ran down the front of my lower left leg. I had to stop playing as a result. Please explain to me what might have caused this."

Answer: Shinsplints will cause the pain you describe. It will also cause pain along the back and inner side of the lower leg and ankle. Usually, shinsplints is the result of excessive exercise or playing a lot of golf, especially if you are walking. The pain is the result of inflammation caused by a shearing of the covering of the bone. This is most common in actively growing young children, but it is not unheard of in adults. When there is an imbalance of the calf muscles, inflammation will result, which often happens when you're walking a hilly course with rough terrain.

Treatment: Complete recovery can take between 2 weeks and 2 months. The best advice is to stop playing golf and stop exercising with your legs until the pain subsides. You can also put ice on the affected area for several days, followed by heat—a heat lamp, hot soaks, hot showers, a heating pad, or heat liniment or ointment. If the pain is discomforting, you can take aspirin or ibuprofen or have your doctor prescribe anti-inflammatory medication. Wrapping the affected area with an elastic bandage is also helpful in promoting healing.

Tip: In the future, avoid walking on hard, uneven surfaces, and warm up adequately before you play or practice. Also, make sure that you wear golf shoes that offer good arch support while you play. Finally, be aware that the symptoms you describe could be the result of a stress fracture or increased pressure caused by constricted tissue covering the muscles or nerves. If the pain doesn't subside, call your doctor. You might need X-rays of the lower knee and ankle just to play it safe.

■ SHOULDER PAIN (IMPINGEMENT)

Question: "I feel like my shoulder joints are loose when I swing at the ball. Sometimes, I hear this clicking sound and occasionally a popping noise when I swing at the ball. Then I get this sharp pain that radiates down my arm on the downswing. What's going on?"

Answer: You could be experiencing an impingement syndrome. The front of the shoulder has a ligament that attaches the clavicle (collar bone) to the scapula (shoulder blade), thus forming the anterior limits of the very flexible shoulder joint. Sometimes a wild movement can catch the bursa that protects this joint, called the acromioclavicular (AC) joint, which creates a lot of pressure and injury to both the bursa and the joint. Sharp pain occurs with a downward motion of the arm when it is above the shoulder and with rotation of the arm across the chest.

Treatment: Depending on the severity of the injury, the treatment varies from rest to trigger-point injections of a corticosteroid or, rarely, surgery. Ultimately, exercise and a rehabilitation program are indicated for shoulders to reach their full strength.

Tip: The first order of treatment is to rest the shoulder, sometimes with a sling. This rest must be balanced with passive motion so the shoulder does not freeze. Anti-inflammatories can help, as can ice. The mainstay is tincture of time to allow the injured tissues to heal.

This can take up to 4–5 months. Corticosteroid injections sometimes hasten the healing, but an AC injection is a challenge because the medication must get into the bursa in order to be fully effective. In a severe second-degree or third-degree tear, surgery might be necessary to return the shoulder to full function.

If you injure this ligament often, I urge you to see your pro to work together on ways to shorten your swing.

The best way to prevent shoulder problems, as is the case with most other golf injuries, is to warm up carefully by using some of the exercise suggestions in chapter 3.

SHOULDER PAIN (ROTATOR CUFF) ■

Question: "I play golf quite regularly and am told I take a hefty swing at my ball. A few months back, I developed shoulder pain and it really hurts anytime I overswing. I saw my doctor, and he told me I might need surgery on my rotator cuff. What happened?"

Answer: A rotator cuff injury is the most likely cause of shoulder pain in golfers, but especially those in their thirties and forties. If you have pain in the back of your shoulder with muscular activity or if it hurts to raise your arm above shoulder level, you should suspect a rotator cuff injury. Shoulders have intricate fluid-bearing joints, with twenty-six muscles working to build complex movement. There are four chief muscles and tendons in each rotator cuff that help to keep the upper arm bone firmly secured to the shoulder blade and collarbone. Making a sharp move or putting too much physical stress on the soft tissues that hold the shoulder together can cause this injury.

Treatment: The good news is that most rotator cuff injuries don't require surgery. Rest, ice, compression, elevation, and resting your shoulder are often the best treatments. Applying ice helps to reduce inflammation. If your shoulder hurts while you sleep, elevation will help. Anti-inflammatory medication, such as aspirin or other over-the-counter medications (Advil, Nuprin, Motrin, or Aleve), is also beneficial. Beware, however, of possible side effects, such as stomach upset or even ulcers, with excessive use. If you have kidney disease, consult your doctor before using any of them.

Finally, if your physician recommends surgery, an orthopedist might recommend an acromioplasty. This procedure removes a portion of the bone overlying the rotator cuff. If your rotator cuff is completely torn, it might need repair and your recovery rate will take longer. Both surgical procedures can be done on an outpatient basis.

Tip: Smooth, relaxed swings (try not to kill the ball) help to promote a healthier rotator cuff. In fact, any stressful motion can increase your risk for injury. Also, before a round, I suggest that you spend a little time in exercising the muscles around the rotator cuff in order to strengthen them. To do that, stand vertically and hold light weights, such as soft drink cans, in both hands with thumbs pointing down to the floor. Bring your arms up and forward slowly in a "V" pattern to your shoulder height and slowly return on the same path. Another exercise to strengthen your inner rotator is to pin the working arm against your ribs and pull slowly against resistance until your hand reaches your stomach, then slowly let your hand move back to its original position. To strengthen the external rotator, do the same motion but move your arm away from your stomach.

■ SHOULDER PAIN (TENDINITIS)

Question: "Two hours after hitting a bucket of practice balls, I noticed that my shoulder was sore. Did I do something wrong while I practiced?"

Answer: You might have strained your shoulder while swinging at the ball. This could have happened if you did not warm up properly and/or if you swung at the ball very hard. Shoulder tendinitis occurs when the lining of the tendon sheath in the shoulder becomes inflamed. This lining secretes a fluid that lubricates the tendon, but when the lining or the sheath becomes inflamed, the tendon has difficulty sliding smoothly in its covering. If this happens, pain results either with or without shoulder movement. The shoulder also feels weak, especially when you try to lift your arms.

Treatment: As in all connective tissue injuries. I recommend ice before heat. I often give my patients a shot of cortisone in the ligament and tell them to rest the inflamed area. In some severe cases, I prescribe a sling to rest the shoulder and nonprescription pain relievers to reduce the pain.

Tip: Rest is crucial. If you start hitting balls too soon, you could reinjure the shoulder. So that you will avoid shoulder tendinitis, I strongly recommend that you participate in the strengthening, flexibility, and conditioning programs described in chapter 3. Also, it's crucial to warm up adequately before practicing or playing. Finally, have your pro take a look at your swing to see if you are moving improperly or misusing swing techniques. It's amazing how many of my golfing patients unknowingly make subtle changes in their swing that result in injuries.

SPINAL STRESS FRACTURE ■

Question: "My pro told me if I twist my back more during my backswing, I'll be able to get more distance off the tee. Instead, I ended up with this severe pain in the neck. What happened?"

Answer: Sometimes, a hairline fracture of the spine can occur in the neck or back when it's repeatedly stressed. A stress fracture, also called a fatigue fracture, might not appear on X-rays. It can involve any segment of the spinal column in the neck or back; any joint that connects segments of the spinal column; or any soft tissues, such as muscles, nerves, tendons, ligaments, bone covering, blood vessels, and connective tissue, that surround the fracture site. In addition to the pain you describe in your neck, pain can also occur in the back. Swelling, tenderness to the touch, and warmth are other symptoms of a stress fracture.

Treatment: Although healing time varies, depending on your age, sex, previous health, and general conditioning, the average time is about 3 months. Healing is considered complete when there is no pain at the fracture site and when X-rays show complete bone union. Ice massage is part of the continuing care program. This is followed by heat treatments once the area begins to feel better. I prescribe aspirin for mild pain and prescription pain relievers for more consistent and severe pain.

Tip: You need to participate in one of the strengthening, flexibility, and conditioning programs recommended in chapter 3. Building up your muscle mass will help to protect bones and underlying tissues from future hairline fractures. While you are recovering, I also recommend exercising all the muscle groups not affected by the injury.

■ THIGH PAIN (HAMSTRING)

Question: "I was walking to the next tee when I felt this severe pain just above the back of my knee. I did have to climb a hill and did stretch a bit to get to the tee, but I've done that before without difficulty. What happened?"

Answer: You could have strained a hamstring muscle or tendon or injured their bony attachments. The hamstring tendons are located behind the knee on either side and feel like a tightly wound rope. Their function is to stabilize the knee and hip as you move. The strain injury usually occurs at the weakest part of the hamstring muscles, which run from the pelvis and femur to the back and side of the knee. Symptoms include pain when moving or stretching your leg, muscle spasms in the injured area, swelling, weakened leg muscles, crackling feeling and sound when you press the area with your fingers, and inflammation of the sheath covering the hamstring tendon. Hamstring strains can range from mild, where a muscle is slightly pulled, to severe, where the muscle-tendon-bone attachment is ruptured. The latter injury, which often occurs in professional football players, requires surgical repair. Diagnostic procedures, such as X-rays of the pelvis and knee to rule out fractures or an MRI, are not usually necessary unless you are a professional football player who needs to know if the extent of the injury will prevent you from playing in next week's game.

Treatment: If this is a first-time hamstring injury, the most effective treatment approach includes rest, ice, and stretching. The best stretching maneuver is to put your foot on a chair or table, then bend forward and try to put your head on your knee. You will feel your hamstring stretching during this action. If the ligament or tendon is torn, healing can require as long a period of time as that for a fractured bone. If a muscle ruptures or the muscle-tendon-bone attachment loosens, surgery might be necessary.

Mild strains usually heal in 2–10 days, severe strains require 6–10 weeks of healing time before you can resume golfing. Treatment includes ice packs 3–4 times a day and heat after several days if the area begins to improve. If there is minor discomfort, you can use nonprescription medicines, such as aspirin, acetaminophen or ibuprofen, and/or topical liniments and ointments. For severe pain, stronger medicine, such as codeine, might be needed.

Tip: To avoid future hamstring strains, I recommend that you use one of the strengthening, flexibility, and conditioning exercises described in chapter 3. Also, make sure that you warm up adequately before your next round or practice session. Finally, begin daily rehabilitation exercises immediately after getting the OK from your doctor.

■ THIGH STRAIN

Question: "I took a golf lesson, and my pro told me to turn my right knee in and toward my left leg on the backswing. I played using that technique, only to feel this pain in my thigh during the round. What happened?"

Answer: Beware of golf lessons in which your pro tells you to try a swing modification engaging muscles and tendons that have not been conditioned or used for awhile. You probably injured the muscle or tendons of the thigh and strained the weakest part of a unit of muscles, tendons, and their attached bones that stabilize the hip and knee and allow you to move. Symptoms are pain when moving or stretching your hip or knee, muscles spasms, swelling at the location of the injury, crackling feeling and sound when you press the injured area with your fingers, and inflammation of the sheath covering the tendon in the thigh. The possible cause, as mentioned above, could be overusing muscle-tendon units in the thigh that have not been used before.

Treatment: If this is your first experience with this type of strain, sufficient healing time before you play golf again should prevent any further complications. If a ligament or tendon has torn, it could take 6–10 weeks to heal. Apply rest, ice, Ace bandage or elastic support compression, and elevation to the area that is strained, and use ice massage several times a day for 15 minutes at a time. After several days, use heat—a heat lamp, hot soaks, hot showers, a heating pad, or heat liniment or ointment—instead of ice if the area begins to feel better. If you have minor discomfort, take aspirin, acetaminophen, or ibuprofen. Often, topical ointments are especially helpful. If the strain is moderate or severe I will protect the area with a cast or splint, I might ask the patient to use crutches for several days or longer.

Tip: Remember, your risk of injury increases when you use muscles and tendons without first warming up, especially those that have not been used before. Also remember that when you change your swing, you will engage tendons and muscles not previously used. It is important to participate in one of the strengthening, flexibility, and conditioning programs described in chapter 3.

THUMB SPRAIN ■

Question: "I was hitting practice balls when I noticed this popping sound in my thumb, which was followed with bruising and a lot of pain. Is it possible to break a thumb by swinging a golf club?"

Answer: You probably sprained your thumb, which occurs with violent overstretching of ligaments in the joint of the thumb. When you overstretch these ligaments (usually when you change your grip or have had a previous thumb injury), the joint becomes tense and gives way at its weakest point. With a mild sprain, there is rarely loss of function. If the sprain is severe, you could have a complete rupture of the ligament or complete separation of the ligament from the bone, at which point surgery might be required. Symptoms include pain, the sensation you describe as a popping sound, tenderness, swelling, and bruising that appears right after the injury. X-rays of the thumb, wrist, and hand are often done to rule out fractures if you show no improvement after one week of resting the thumb.

Treatment: Just resting the thumb and using the following treatments can reduce prolonged disability. Rest is the best way to avoid further problems. If the sprain is mild, you usually can resume golfing in several weeks. Use an ice pack several times a day on the thumb. After a few days, a heat lamp, hot soaks, hot showers, a heating pad, or heat liniment or ointment can be used. If you have minor discomfort from the pain, you might want to take aspirin, acetaminophen, or ibuprofen. Occasionally, I inject cortisone into the area to reduce inflammation. In rare cases, a cast, tape, or pre-formed brace for the thumb might be needed.

Tip: I recommend taping the vulnerable area before practice or competition to prevent reinjury. Your doctor will show you how to do this so that the tape doesn't interfere with your grip.

■ WRIST SPRAIN

Question: "I hit my ball into the knee-deep rough. When I swung at the ball, I hit a rock that I didn't know was there. As a result, I felt this pain in my wrist, which started swelling after the round. Will I need surgery?"

Answer: Probably not, but it is likely that you sprained your wrist. Surgery is needed only for a complete rupture of a ligament or for a complete separation of a ligament from the bone with total loss of function. Your sprain is probably mild, with partial tearing of some ligament fibers.

Wrist sprain is caused by sudden or violent overstretching of one or more ligaments in your wrist joint. When you hit the rock, the ligaments in your wrist were stretched and one or more gave way at the weakest point where they attach to bone. Symptoms, as you describe, are pain, a popping or tearing inside the wrist, tenderness, swelling, and bruising.

Treatment: If the pain is quite severe, X-rays might be ordered by your doctor to rule out the possibility of a fracture. Otherwise, the gold standard of treatment includes rest, ice, compression, immobilization with a wrist splint, and elevation. If you don't need a cast, apply ice to the wrist several times a day and wrap it with an elastic bandage between treatments. After several days, replace the ice with heat—a heat lamp, hot soaks, hot showers, a heating pad, or liniment or ointment. If the pain is too discomforting, take aspirin, acetaminophen, or ibuprofen. Your doctor might prescribe stronger pain relievers or a shot of cortisone and lidocaine.

Tip: A mild sprain can require 2–6 weeks for healing, which means staying away from practice and play. If you play before the wrist heals, you can prolong the healing time. Also, I recommend working on a conditioning program (see chapter 3) while you're away from the course.

2 HEALTH PROBLEMS OF SENIOR GOLFERS

All of us are genetically programmed, and our genes are a significant influence on the status of our health as we age. Personal risk factors (i.e., bad habits) and our environment (as well as a lot of luck) also have much to do with why we get sick. Obviously, we can't trade in our genes for new ones, but we can make changes in our environment and habits. For example, not wearing seat belts, drinking alcohol excessively, smoking, and abusing drugs can result in poor health and/or a shorter life expectancy.

This chapter can help you to recognize the importance of taking responsibility for your own well-being. Syd and I hope that through early detection of symptoms and preventive medicine, you can avoid poor health and prolong your golfing career.

Thumb through the chapter to find symptoms similar to any that you are experiencing. If you believe that you might have a disorder described here, your best chance of improving your health is to take an active role and follow the recommendations for possible treatment approaches.

This chapter can help you to take control of your physical health. The treatment plans and recommendations are based on the latest data-driven research related to treatments of the most common aging disorders.

AGE (GENERAL) ■

Question: "I feel like I'm losing it. I'm not the golfer I was when I was twenty. Anything I can do about it?"

Answer: Because aging is the result of both genetic and environmental factors, my answer is both yes and no. Gerontologists continue to discover genes that program certain biochemical reactions in our bodies, and they have also learned that these genes turn on and off during various stages of cell life. For example, when Leonard Hayflick, a researcher, spread a few skin cells in a dish, the cells divided and filled the dish. He then placed a few of these cells in another dish. They divided again and filled the second dish. This doubling continued about thirty-five times, but then the rate of division began to slow. By the fiftieth division, the cells stopped dividing altogether. Hayflick's experiment suggests evidence for the hypothesis of a "genetic clock," or a limit beyond which survival would not continue.

Your environment also can impact the length and quality of your life. Ultraviolet light, smoking, air pollution, contaminated water, and your diet can contribute to aging, too. Fortunately, most environmental factors are within human control.

Treatment: Although you have no control over your genes, you can increase your life expectancy. Avoid smoking, refrain from consuming fatty foods, control blood pressure and blood cholesterol, and properly manage such diseases as diabetes. In addition, increasing your commitment to an exercise program and engaging in physical activities can help to slow down the aging process.

Tip: One specific approach has been proved to slow the aging process. Maximal life span potential has been stretched up to 40 percent in mice and rats whose caloric intake was reduced by one third to one half. Although there is no evidence of this holding true for humans, it won't hurt to watch your calories. Some researchers suggest daily consumption of about 1 gram of protein and no more than ½ gram of fat for each kilogram (2.2 pounds) of your current body weight. If you weigh 165 pounds, for example, that would break down to a daily intake of about 75 grams of protein and slightly less than 40 grams of fat. Don't start any diet, however, without first talking it over with your family doctor.

■ AGE-RELATED CHANGES

Question: "I noticed that there are changes going on with me physically. I developed a potbelly, and I eat the same amount. I'm also getting less distance off the tee. Any information on what's happening to me physically?"

Answer: Everyone begins to lose maximal muscle capacity as they age. If you are not on an exercise program, you will have a steady decline in muscle strength after age fifty. Although you will still be able to do regular chores, you will find golf or other sports more difficult because of a loss of muscle function.

Treatment: By engaging in an exercise program, staying physically active, and continuing to play golf, you can slow, but not stop, this age-related loss in your muscles. Even if you maintain the body weight that you had when you were thirty years old, the amount of muscle decreases and the amount of fat increases. Muscle loss usually begins during the middle forties, and, if not counteracted by exercise, it will continue at a rate of about 1.5 percent a year. Fat requires less energy to maintain than muscle, so you need fewer calories to keep the same weight.

Tip: The more muscle mass that you have, the more calories that you'll burn, which helps to keep your weight down. In other words, the changes you describe have more to do with an inactive lifestyle than they do with aging. Perhaps you eat the same amount of food as you did when you were thirty, but you burn fewer calories. These calories are stored as fat, and, probably in your situation, this results in your potbelly.

Get involved with an exercise program recommended in chapter 3, such as crunches and weight lifting, and consider the suggestions about diet and nutrition in chapter 5. By the way, Syd's potbelly almost disappeared after he engaged in a routine of two hundred crunches a day.

ALCOHOLISM ■

Question: "I love my beer. There's nothing more enjoyable for me than to drink and play. The best part is when I get to the clubhouse and have a few there, too. Is my drinking affecting my performance on the course?"

Answer: Consider that alcohol can cause numerous problems when you combine it with golf. Its effect on the brain is obvious. A small amount can actually improve your swing by inducing relaxation, but a large amount will impair your eye-and-hand coordination, which is crucial for delicate shot play. Alcohol also acts as a diuretic, which causes blood vessels to dilate in the skin. This, in turn, causes heat loss during cold weather. Vodka and Russian winters have conspired to cause many lost fingers and toes as the result of frostbite.

Another serious problem that a person can have with alcohol is not recognizing that he or she is drinking too much. Several criteria and self-tests have been developed to determine whether a person is an alcohol abuser, but a simple test confirms possible alcohol abuse if "yes" is the answer to each of the following questions:

■ Have you ever felt that you should cut down on your drinking?

■ Have people annoyed you by criticizing your drinking?

■ Have you ever felt guilty about your drinking?

■ Have you ever had a drink (eye opener) first thing in the morning to steady your nerves or to get rid of a hangover?

A more comprehensive screening can be done with the Michigan Alcoholism Screening Test (MAST). If you do fit the criteria for alcohol abuse, you could be the last person to know because denial is a large part of the syndrome. Often, people think of an alcoholic as a sloppy drunk, but many alcoholics get by at work and at home without their condition becoming obvious to the casual observer.

Treatment: Alcohol is one of the few drugs that, when abused, can cause serious problems, even death, when its consumption stops abruptly. A hangover is a mild form of withdrawal; delirium tremens is the most severe form. The latter is characterized by hallucinations, disorientation, sweats, and trembling, all of which can be excruciating. If you experience these symptoms, go to a hospital or detoxification center immediately so that you can be monitored during the acute phases. If you are too far away or the symptoms are coming on too fast, a small amount of alcohol will temporarily allay the symptoms. Then get help immediately. The symptoms will recur!

Long-term treatment must start with admitting that you have a problem—a serious one. The only true treatment for alcoholism is abstention. Because of its emotional and physical attraction, staying away from alcohol cannot be accomplished alone. Some alcoholics might claim that they stayed sober without outside support, but if they actually did do it alone, they were playing a long shot. Many counselors and support groups, particularly Alcoholics Anonymous, are available to help you.

A few studies suggest that alcoholism might have a genetic component. Even if this is true, the only treatment is to avoid alcohol.

Tip: Unfortunately, many alcoholics are golfers. Alcohol seems to be the drug of choice in golfing circles. When used to excess, alcohol contributes to nutritional deficiencies, not to mention a bad game, bad relationships, and a bad life. If you think more about the next drink than about the next stroke, consider that you could be an alcoholic and get help. (See the section, "Alcohol Abuse," in chapter 4.)

You probably would need less in the way of any drugs if you simply remember some of the basic parts of life that also make golf fun: exercise, proper nutrition, relaxation, and good relationships with people. They can get you on a "high" that chemicals and drugs can't touch.

ALLERGIES ■

Question: "I feel fine until I get out on the course, where my game falls apart. I find myself sneezing and coughing a lot. Can you give me some tips on how to keep my allergies in check and still go out and play golf?"

Answer: The difference between an allergic reaction and a nonallergic reaction is essentially this: With a nonallergic reaction, the immune system senses an invader in the form of a toxic substance, virus, or bacterium and attacks it. It tries to make the body as inhospitable as possible and brings cells and other substances to the invader. The defenders try to swallow or digest the invader. Sometimes, a fever ensues during the process because some bacteria and viruses do not like climate changes. Also, drainage might increase from the location of the invader as it is washed out of the body. In other words, the immune system uses all of its power to expel or kill the invader. In an allergic reaction, the offending agent is similar to agents that the body already harbors but different enough for the immune system to identify it as foreign. It then attacks the invader. This might be the reason that a viral infection has a limited time frame, whereas an allergy can remain in the body for a long period. There are only so many viruses to fight, but there is a lot of them in the body. The immune system can fight at great length without running out of ammunition.

The symptoms of allergic reactions and viral infections are the same: itchy, watery eyes; stuffy, runny nose; scratchy throat; dry cough; occasional sneezes; skin rashes; chills; and other sundry, uncomfortable manifestations. If you have a fever or your body aches, however, the cause is more likely a virus or a bacterium, such as streptococcus. Except for bacteria, which might be better fought with antibiotics, the invaders are treated the same: symptomatically.

Treatment: The best treatment is to avoid the substances that trigger allergic reactions. The basic medication for allergies is antihistamines, which counteracts the histamine chemicals that cause allergic reactions. Prescription corticosteroid drugs might be used for severe symptoms. In emergency situations, when anaphylactic shock (e.g., a severe reaction to wasp venom or penicillin) occurs, injections of epinephrine are used to dilate bronchial passages.

Skin allergies are treated with a variety of corticosteroids, usually hydrocortisone. Hives often need no medication, but severe cases might require a prescription antihistamine, cimetidine, terbutaline, or an oral corticosteroid.

Hay fever is generally treated with over-the-counter antihistamines, but your doctor may prescribe other drugs, such as cromolyn, if your symptoms are severe.

Food allergies are best treated by avoiding those foods that cause a reaction. Skin rashes associated with drug allergies are generally treated with antihistamines.

Tip: The most severe and dangerous allergic reaction is anaphylaxis, or anaphylactic shock, which begins within minutes after exposure and advances quickly. Although any allergen can trigger anaphylactic shock, the most common are insect stings; certain foods, such as shellfish and nuts; and injections of certain drugs. Emergency treatment includes an injection of epinephrine to open up the airways and blood vessels; in severe cases, cardiopulmonary resuscitation (CPR) is sometimes necessary.

ALZHEIMER'S DISEASE ■

Question: "A good friend of mine panicked when we approached the first tee and yelled that his golf clubs were missing. They were on the rack next to the clubhouse. He also forgets and tells me the same story every ten minutes. What really surprised me was that when we took a break to get a drink after nine holes, he thought we had played eighteen. Can you tell me what my friend is going through and if there is anything that can be done?"

Answer: The most common worry that I hear from my aging patients is that they believe they are losing their minds. As aging golfers, we are part of the fastest-growing segment of the population. The National Institute of Aging estimates that the number of Alzheimer's patients will be around fourteen million by 2050.

Alzheimer's disease occurs when there is a degeneration of the nerve cells in brain tissue that are used for memory. Affected nerve cells lose their ability to secrete the neurotransmitter acetylcholine, a chemical that sends messages between nerve cells in the brain. Researchers are trying to find an effective treatment to halt the breakdown of acetylcholine and hopefully reduce memory loss. The reason that the brain cells die is unknown. Some theories suggest the cause to be genetic; the result of viruses; and/or, especially, environmental toxins.

It's also important to understand that although Alzheimer's disease is the most common form of senile dementia, dozens of other disorders that cause memory problems can be reversed with treatment after a thorough assessment. Some examples are multi-infarct dementia, which results from many small strokes; brain disease, which often causes physiological changes that lead to impaired thinking; and depression, which has a proven track record for effective intervention. Other disorders that can mimic the symptoms of Alzheimer's disease are chronic alcoholism, liver failure, vitamin B_{12} deficiency, diabetes, kidney failure, malnutrition, and hypothyroidism (a disorder in which the thyroid gland produces inadequate thyroid hormones that results in physical and mental decline).

Treatment: At the present time, there is no cure for Alzheimer's disease, and no standardized test is available to make a diagnosis. That doesn't mean all hope is lost. Hundreds of millions of dollars are being spent on this disease, and researchers are getting closer to finding a way to curb its dreadful effects. The drug of choice currently being used to help reduce some of the symptoms of Alzheimer's disease is called donepezil (trade name, Aricept). Assuming that your friend has Alzheimer's disease, you might want to recommend that he or she talk to their doctor about this drug.

■ ARTHRITIS (GENERAL)

Question: "Every morning when I get up, my hands and legs feel stiff. I also feel pain in my joints, especially when the weather is damp. My doctor tells me that I have a little arthritis and that after age fifty all of us get it. Anything I can do to get rid of it?"

Answer: Arthritis is caused by joint inflammation. There are many kinds of arthritis, but the one that you describe is probably degenerative arthritis. It occurs as a result of wearing out a joint that might have been involved in an injury when you were younger.

If joints everywhere in your body ache, the disorder is called rheumatoid arthritis. Arthritis is classified as an autoimmune disease, one in which the body's immune system attacks joints and organs.

Treatment: This is a tough call. Treatment depends on how much the pain and stiffness keep you from an active lifestyle. I often have my patients engage in a physical therapy program to maintain motion in the affected joints. Heat, ice, and drugs can alleviate symptoms. If the pain is severe, joint replacement offers an effective intervention.

The drugs are mainly anti-inflammatories or Tylenol. Despite the greater marketing of both prescription and over-the-counter nonsteroidal anti-inflammatory drugs (NSAIDs), aspirin is still the cheapest, most effective anti-inflammatory medication. Because recent studies suggest that the joints in rheumatoid arthritis do not diminish their rate of deterioration with the use of NSAIDs, pain control has become the goal. This has prompted many physicians to recommend Tylenol, especially in light of the side effects of NSAIDs (e.g., stomach irritation and bleeding problems).

Heat is also a mainstay for arthritis pain. It reduces swelling and increases flexibility. It is especially effective when the joint has been immobile for a while, as when you're sleeping. The morning ritual of a hot bath for the person who has hip, back, and knee arthritis makes for a more mobile day.

Finally, easy motion, with just a tad of increased stress on the joint, keeps it flexible, as well as the muscles and ligaments that support it. Ultimately, a weak and degenerated joint is as good as the structures surrounding and supporting it.

Tip: Obviously, arthritis makes playing golf extremely difficult, but I want to emphasize this point: Even though you hurt while you play, don't give up the game! By moving your joints during play, you are combating muscle deterioration and working out the stiffness in your joints. The pain is there, I know, and it hurts to play, but a gentle warm-up before playing helps to reduce the degree of pain while you play.

I also recommend that you wear warm clothing to heat up stiff joints. It's also crucial that you get to the course early and spend some time warming up (see "Warm-Up" in chapter 3). Also, you may want to skip playing on a damp, wet, or very cool day.

As you probably know, you can have your pro put oversized

grips on your clubs. This helps you to close your hands on the clubs.

If you can't get relief, you may want to consider surgery. Knee, hip, and shoulder joints are the most common sites for replacement.

■ ARTHRITIS (HIP)

Question: "I have arthritis in my hip, which my doctor says was caused by aging. I can play limited golf, but I'm in a lot of pain, especially when it's damp out. What can I do to help relieve my pain?"

Answer: If you have a headache, it usually goes away. Unfortunately, that is not the case with arthritis. You will have good periods followed by bad periods—back and forth. Inflammation of the joints is the cause of pain in arthritis. Despite the recent hoopla in books promising cures, there are none nor is there one on the horizon. Nonetheless, numerous chronic pain and inflammation medications can offer temporary relief for hip arthritis.

Treatment: Whatever you can do to take the stress off a painful hip is a form of treatment. If you don't mind using a cane to get around when you're off the course, it can help. I knew a golfer who used his 3-iron much like a cane as he walked a bit on the course.

Another treatment is to have your pro help you design a shortened swing to reduce hip turn. I like the early Jack Nicklaus swing. He lifted his left toe at the top of his backswing and lifted his right toe after the downswing.

The gold standard treatment for any kind of arthritis is the regular use of analgesics, aspirin, acetaminophen, ibuprofen, or naproxen, but any of these can cause complications. Nonsteroidal anti-inflammatory drugs (NSAIDs), such as aspirin, ibuprofen, and naproxen, frequently cause indigestion, heartburn, stomach pain, nausea, and loss of appetite. They can also cause ulcers, as well as bleeding or perforated ulcers that sometimes become life threatening.

Tip: If you do respond well to any of the drugs mentioned above, I recommend taking a leave of absence from them occasionally so as to minimize their potential danger and give your stomach a chance to heal itself. If the pain and inflammation become intolerable, take acetaminophen during your off days. Also, keep in mind that heavy use of acetaminophen and NSAIDs increases the risk of liver disease. Also, see the previous section, "Arthritis (General)."

If the hip is degenerated enough to warrant replacement and you decide to have surgery, keep in mind that replacement hips last about 10–20 years, at which point they begin to loosen and start causing pain again. Most golfers have little difficulty after the surgery.

ASTHMA ■

Question: "I usually get an asthma attack when I play golf. I know I'm allergic to trees and pollen from flowers. Do I need to give up exercising or playing golf because I have asthma? If not, what can I do to prevent an asthma attack when I play?"

Answer: Asthma is a chronic respiratory disease that causes a tightening of the chest and difficulty in breathing. Asthma sufferers have trouble with breathing out. During an asthmatic episode, muscle spasms and swelling bronchial tissues narrow the airways, which then become clogged with mucus. Because stale air gets trapped in the lungs, it is necessary to use the top part of the lungs to gasp for air. Brief incidents of asthma generally cause only breathlessness and wheezing. In severe cases, however, the airways become so narrow and clogged that breathing becomes extremely difficult.

Symptoms usually occur as reactions to various environmental factors such as pollen, animal dander, tobacco, and smoke. Some patients experience only mild reactions. For others, the episodes are frequent and serious and often require emergency medical treatment.

Asthma has no single cause. It can result from a variety of factors working alone or in combination. Allergies are the primary offenders—50 percent to 90 percent of patients have allergies. When an allergy-causing substance, such as pollen, grass, dust, or mold, is inhaled, it can trigger the release of histamine and other body chemicals, which results in an allergic reaction.

Lung infections can also induce asthma. Bronchiolitis, a viral respiratory infection, is a common cause of asthma in children. Bronchitis develops as a result of an upper respiratory infection. Other causes of asthma include vigorous exercise, air pollution, cold weather, and emotional stress.

Treatment: Many effective new treatments for asthma are available. The ones most commonly used are bronchodilators, such as Proventil, and inhaled steroids, such as Vanceril or Asmacort. Less often used are oral theophyllines and, for acute episodes, oral steroids, such as prednisone. The best approach is to take a puff or two of Proventil before playing so as to reduce or eliminate any potential for wheezing on the course. If you also have long-term, moderately severe, or chronic asthma problems, ongoing use of the inhaled steroid can effectively reduce or eliminate wheezing. The only reason for using prednisone is if you recently had a trauma (this could even be a severe cold in some people) that couldn't be controlled by the inhalers. Nowadays, the only people who use theophyllines are those who have become accustomed to them or those who use inhalers but need an extra push. Antibiotics should not be considered unless there is evidence of a bacterial infection. They should never be used "just in case."

Warning: Bronchodilators are potent drugs. If they are overused, they can cause dangerous side effects, such as high blood pressure.

Tip: A number of Olympic athletes have asthma. Most folks with asthma can play golf without too much concern. Some environmental conditions, however, such as extremely cold or hot weather, can cause an asthma attack. The best approach to exercising in these conditions is to breathe through your nose. On a very smoggy day, I suggest that you limit the amount of your golfing or other exercise you do.

ATHLETE'S FOOT ■

Question: "The other day I got through playing golf and had this terrible itch on my toes. I guess I had athlete's foot. What is it and what can I do to prevent it?"

Answer: Athlete's foot is a common fungal infection. It is contracted in warm moist places, where the fungi flourish. The skin becomes rough, thick, cracked, and red. It can break down in moist areas, such as between the toes. The skin is mildly inflamed from the infestation and can feel itchy and hot. Because the fungi are in the skin, athlete's foot is difficult to eradicate, but it will not react as much, or at all, if the feet remain cool and dry.

Treatment: You can effectively treat athlete's foot with a number of prescription and over-the-counter (OTC) medications. Nizoral, Diflucan, and Mycelex (prescription) and Tinactin, Desenex, and Cruex (OTC) are just a few. You might want to try a few of these to find the one that works best for you.

Tip: To prevent athlete's foot, I recommend that you keep your feet clean and dry. Powder is helpful for feet that sweat a lot. Cotton socks absorb sweat and discourage infection more than do nylon or rayon socks. When a fungal infection appears, treat it quickly to prevent it from spreading.

■ CATARACTS

Question: "Lately, I have been having trouble following the flight of my ball. I see this haziness and this blurry sensation. Also, I sometimes see double when I look at the pin. Do I need new glasses?"

Answer: As the eyes age, the lenses can start to cloud up, which sometimes produces opaque vision. What you describe as hazy vision might be caused by a cataract.

Cataracts long have been one of the inevitable consequences of growing older. With modern medicine, however, it's now possible to reduce the risk of cataracts. Although cataracts are often hereditary, many are caused by eye trauma, diabetes, or even by certain drugs. Also, working near high levels of X-ray and microwave radiation might make one susceptible to cataracts. One study showed a relationship between cigarette smoking and cataract formation. Other studies have shown a link to excessive exposure to ultraviolet sunlight.

Treatment: The best bet to reduce the chance of getting cataracts is by protecting your eyes from sunlight at all times. (Note that more golfers now wear hats and sunglasses as they play.)

Unfortunately, surgery is the treatment of choice. During the operation, the eye surgeon removes the clouded lens. It is replaced with eyeglasses, a contact lens, or an intraocular lens implant. The implant procedure is frequently used with great success. Lens removal and implant are usually done during same surgery. The procedure is now quite simple and restores almost perfect vision.

Tip: I strongly urge you to wear sunglasses whenever you go outside. It is important, however, to get a pair that offers protection from ultraviolet radiation. If you buy sunglasses from the drugstore, check the tag for the category of the lenses. I recommend buying glasses that block out 95 percent of UVB radiation, 60 percent of ultraviolet radiation (UVA), and 90 percent of visible light. If you wear prescription glasses, have your doctor fit you for a pair that offers the maximum amount of protection because you'll be playing golf in them.

CHRONIC OBSTRUCTIVE PULMONARY DISEASE ■

Question: "I was told recently that I have developed chronic obstructive pulmonary disease. Can you tell me a little about it and what I should do so it doesn't affect my golfing too much?"

Answer: The main cause of chronic obstructive pulmonary disease (COPD) is smoking. Cigarette smoke eventually destroys normal lung tissue and causes inflammation of the lungs. Symptoms include shortness of breath, especially during activity, and quite a bit of coughing. Respiratory infections are common during the cold months. In some instances, hyperemia, a very dangerous disorder, can cause organ malfunction and even death.

Treatment: One treatment approach to consider while you play golf, interestingly enough, is exercise. According to your ability to tolerate it, exercise is one of the mainstays of COPD treatment. Walking is by far the best thing you can do. It increases the size and strength of the lung muscles and improves the body's metabolism to accept more oxygen from the lungs. If you can't walk the whole course, take a cart but walk intermittently.

Other treatments that can help you while you play golf include bronchodilators. A good proportion of people with COPD have some wheezing, and many of them have found Atrovent to be helpful. Fluids are especially important because people with COPD have more difficulty breathing when they are mildly dehydrated. This is especially true of those who tend toward wheezing.

Some golfers who have COPD play golf with a supplemental oxygen supply to maintain normal blood levels of oxygen, although this is more a requirement for those with advanced cases of COPD.

Tip: Before you play golf or exercise again, ask your doctor for a medical evaluation. I have a lot of my COPD patients take classes in a supervised pulmonary rehabilitation program. You can call your local hospital for more information, or check with your doctor's secretary. Some patients respond well to a regular aerobic exercise program. I also recommend a balanced strengthening program for your arm, chest, and back muscles, which will help you to breathe with less discomfort.

Finally, as one would expect, high altitudes are detrimental because there is less oxygen in the air and your lungs must work harder. Please consider the altitude of the location that you plan to visit on your next vacation.

■ CONSTIPATION

Question: "This is an embarrassing question. Often I play golf while constipated. I wish I didn't have that feeling so often. Is there something I can do to help relieve the symptoms before I play?"

Answer: Constipation is characterized by hard stools, a decreased urge to defecate, occasional abdominal bloating and pain, and temporary or persistent difficulty in moving your bowels. Temporary constipation occurs when your regular diet or routine is interrupted. You describe chronic constipation, however, which can be the result of a poor diet, dehydration, stress, and/or certain medications. Although it can be associated with many diseases that affect the nerves, muscles, and vessels of the intestine, most often it is a result of anxiety and inappropriate expectations about bowel regularity.

Anxiety has a strong effect on the gut. It can slow it down, speed it up, or cause reverse peristalsis. The latter is a process in which the intestinal muscles contract in a disordered way, which prevents food from properly moving forward. Certain medications, such as opiates, can cause reverse peristalsis. The most common form of anxiety-caused constipation is irritable bowel syndrome (see "Irritable Bowel Syndrome" in this chapter), in which constipation is often followed by diarrhea.

Almost everyone becomes constipated at one time or another as a result of mild temporary anxiety accompanied by a poor diet. Eating too few low-fiber foods, too many fried foods, and drinking insufficient amounts of fluids are the dietary correlates.

Though not particularly life threatening, constipation can be uncomfortable. Dry, hard stools can irritate and tear the mucous membrane of the anus, which results in so-called anal fissures. Also, the effort to expel hard stools can cause hemorrhoids.

Treatment: The most important immediate treatment for constipation is alteration of your diet. Increase fluid intake to at least 2 quarts per day. While playing golf or doing heavy exercise, fluid intake should be even higher. This fluid requirement should not be fulfilled by drinking coffee or alcohol, both of which actually promote the loss of fluids by increasing the need to urinate.

Diet changes should revolve around an increase in fiber intake. The fiber absorbs water to make a larger, more moist stool, which is to move better able along the intestine. Fiber foods include grains, especially whole grains; fruits; and vegetables. Alfalfa sprouts, iceberg lettuce, and fruit juice have little fiber, whereas a baked potato, spinach, and dried fruits have a lot. Meat has effectively no fiber. Meat alternatives, especially beans, are excellent sources of fiber.

Learning to control anxiety goes a long way toward relieving constipation (see the sections in chapter 4 titled "Anticipatory Anxiety" and "Anxiety during Competition").

It is worth noting that a sudden onset of constipation that does not resolve itself in a timely fashion can be a symptom of colon cancer. This is rarely the case, compared with the overwhelming numbers of people who have constipation from other causes, but this type of constipation probably should be reviewed by your physician.

Mild laxatives might help to relieve temporary irregularity, but they should be used with caution. If you use them regularly, you could irritate the intestinal lining and weaken the bowel's muscle tone.

Tip: Keep in mind that regularity varies from person to person. Some people have daily bowel movements or two or three a day. Other people have no more than three bowel movements a week. With a mild case of constipation, nature usually takes over and regularity returns.

Again, I strongly recommend increasing the amount of fiber you consume. Eat more grains, fruits, and vegetables, but do so gradually to avoid excess gas and indigestion. I also recommend exercise, which stimulates the bowels.

If you still have problems after several weeks, see your doctor.

■ CONGESTIVE HEART FAILURE

Question: "I was diagnosed as having congestive heart failure. Does that mean I must restrict the amount of golf I play?"

Answer: The term *failure* can be frightening, but it's misleading. It means that your heart is working but it isn't able to pump enough blood to your body's tissues and organs to meet their needs. The term *congestive* refers to the buildup of fluid. Blood returning to your heart builds up because less blood leaves your heart. As this happens, fluid from your blood collects in vital organs, such as lungs and liver. Fluid can also build up in surrounding tissues and cause swelling.

Congestive heart failure is usually the end result of many cardiovascular problems. Causes include coronary artery disease, diseased heart muscle, hypertension, abnormal heart rhythms, heart valve problems, congenital heart disease, alcohol abuse, and/or toxic substances.

There are no symptoms at first. Eventually, you might experience shortness of breath after exertion. Fatigue or weakness; swelling in your feet, ankles, and abdomen; swollen or distended neck veins; rapid weight gain; and enlargement of the heart are other symptoms of fluid buildup.

Treatment: The problem is frequently difficult to eliminate, so the goals of treatment are to prevent further damage to the heart and to assist its pumping capacity through drug therapy. Angiotensin-converting enzyme (ACE) inhibitors are the mainstay treatment. Drug names include Vasotec, Prinivil, Zestril, and Capoten. ACE inhibitors allow blood to flow from the heart more easily by decreasing production of the hormone angiotensin II that constricts the arteries and raises blood pressure. At the same time, they also decrease production of the hormone aldosterone that causes your body to retain sodium and water.

Tip: I recommend ACE inhibitors with a warning that they cause an irritating cough in about 20 percent to 25 percent of the people who use them. If you have asthma and find that it worsens while you're on an ACE inhibitor, I recommend diuretics, often known as water pills. The problem with a diuretic is that it will make you urinate more frequently. The diuretics that I usually prescribe are Bumex and Lasix.

The only asthma-related problem you should worry about while playing golf is the fatigue that results from too much exertion. I usually advise my patients to rent a cart during play and park it a distance from where they hit their balls. That way they get some exercise from walking. If a partner rides with you, have him or her drive the cart while you walk a few holes.

CORONARY ARTERY DISEASE ■

Question: "My doctor just told me I have coronary artery disease. What is it, and what can I do about it so that it doesn't interfere with my golfing?"

Answer: Not getting enough blood to the muscles of the heart is the primary result of coronary artery disease. It's caused by atherosclerosis (blocked arteries), which prevents the blood from traveling through the arteries. Cholesterol buildup and blood clots are the main causes of blockage. When a patient complains to me about pain in the chest while exercising (angina), I immediately suspect coronary artery disease.

Treatment: If diet and medication don't improve your condition, either coronary artery bypass surgery or angioplasty, a procedure that opens blocked blood vessels, is the treatment of choice.

Tip: I recommend a complete examination by your doctor if you have persistent pain in the chest while you walk or exercise. Your doctor will order an exercise stress test to determine a safe level of exercise for you.

If you have had a heart attack or bypass surgery or angioplasty, I recommend getting involved in a supervised cardiac rehabilitation program that includes aerobic exercise, low-intensity weight training, and an educational program to teach you how to manage your heart disease.

Finally, if you have coronary artery disease, you might want to stay off the golf course when the outside temperature is very humid and hot and also avoid playing at high altitudes.

■ COUGH

Question: "I've been coughing a lot lately and don't know why. I don't think I have a cold because my nose isn't stuffy and all that. What's going on?"

Answer: A cough is a protective reflex, not a specific illness. Coughing helps to produce secretions of mucus and phlegm to protect your airways from infections and irritants. These secretions wrap around and flush out viruses, bacteria, and foreign particles.

Basically, coughs have two characteristics: duration and productivity. Duration refers to how long you keep the cough, for example, a minute or two when something is stuck in your throat or a period of several days when you have a cold or bronchitis. A productive cough is one that produces some of the mucus or phlegm that is protecting the lungs.

Coughs can be caused by anything that irritates the respiratory airways. The most common causes are colds, flu, and sinusitis. Coughs can also occur when you accidentally inhale small objects, such as pieces of food, or breathe in irritants, such as dust, cigarette smoke, and noxious fumes.

Any persistent cough might be a symptom of an underlying illness. Coughing is a symptom of some obstructive lung diseases, such as emphysema, certain types of lung cancer, and occupation-related lung diseases. If you have a dry cough along with leg and backaches, a fever above 101°F, headache, and a sore throat, you might have the flu. When a cough is accompanied by difficulties in breathing, wheezing, and tightness in the chest, the diagnosis might be bronchial asthma. If a cough produces blood or pink, yellow, or rust-colored mucus and is accompanied by chest pains, headache, fever, and difficulty in breathing, the diagnosis is likely to be pneumonia. A persistent cough that produces green or yellow mucus could indicate chronic bronchitis, which might be caused by a bacterial infection.

Treatment: Because coughing is a protective response by the body, suppressing a productive cough with cough medicine can reduce its protective clearing action and perhaps hide a more serious underlying problem. I recommend that conventional or alternative cough remedies be used for no more than 7–10 days and preferably only for temporary relief from nighttime coughing.

If the underlying disorder is a bacterial infection, an antibiotic might be prescribed. For a viral infection, however, antibiotics are of no use. Treatment for viral infections consists of bed rest, aspirin or acetaminophen, plenty of fluids, and moist air from a vaporizer. If you are producing a sticky, thick sputum, an expectorant can help to clear your lungs.

Nonproductive coughs can be treated with throat soothers and cough suppressants or with antihistamines if the cough is the result of allergies. Irritating coughs often respond nicely to cough drops, lozenges, and syrups. In some instances, I prescribe a cough suppressant containing codeine.

Tip: See your doctor for any cough that persists for more than 7–10 days. If you are coughing up blood, you should be immediately evaluated. The underlying cause might or might not be serious, but it's prudent to see your doctor.

■ DETACHED RETINA

Question: "The other day, while I was walking up to the first tee, I began to see flashes of light. It scared the daylights out of me. When the flashes subsided, I couldn't see out the sides of my eyes. I had this dark shadowlike image blocking my sight. Then everything was fine after that. Can you tell me what was going on?"

Answer: You might have a detached retina. Although it is not a common occurrence, seniors occasionally acquire the disorder. If you have a detached retina and ignore it, you can either lose your vision or be visually impaired.

A small tear appears in the retina, and fluid seeps into the tear. The fluid drags down the retina until it collapses. The cause of the tear is usually an eye injury or a blow to the head, but a detached retina sometimes results from cataract surgery.

The symptoms that you describe—light flashes, floating dark spots, and peripheral vision loss—often occur.

Treatment: Immediate treatment is essential. Visit an ophthalmologist as soon as possible. The sooner the retina is repaired, the better are the chances of success.

DIABETES MELLITUS ■

Question: "What do I need to do while I play golf to minimize the symptoms associated with my diabetes?"

Answer: There are two major forms of diabetes mellitus (usually referred to simply as diabetes). Type I diabetes is congenital and shows up in youth, sometimes as early as two years of age. The sooner it manifests, the more ominous this disease can be. In type I, the pancreas is not capable of producing enough insulin. Because sufficient insulin is missing, it is difficult for the body to maintain moment-by-moment control of glucose.

If you were unaware that you had diabetes until you noticed some vague symptoms, such as fatigue, excessive thirst, a frequent need to urinate, or blurred vision, or until your doctor discovered high blood sugar on a routine examination, you might have type II diabetes. This type is caused by the resistance of body cells to insulin, which, in turn, increases the level of sugar in your blood. The issue is not a lack or overabundance of sugar as much as a maldistribution. Sugar in the blood does no good to the body. It needs to be in the cells where it can provide nourishment.

Other symptoms of type II diabetes include rapid weight loss and recurrent infection. The most common health problems associated with diabetes are related to the obstruction of small blood vessels. The vessel damage can result in eye problems, including blindness; decreased kidney function or even kidney failure; and loss of sensation and circulation in the feet, which sometimes leads to amputation. Heart disease and arteriosclerosis are among the major possible consequences of diabetes. Because each of these disorders evolves over a period of years, you might have time either to prevent or to assist the process, and all of them are less likely to occur at all if you control the disease.

Treatment: Diet and exercise are the mainstays of diabetes control. Although medications might be required, they will be less effective if you refuse to alter your diet or to maintain a regular exercise schedule.

The appropriate diet consists mainly of foods that comprise a well-balanced diet. It is low in fats and simple sugars and high in fresh fruits, vegetables, breads, and other complex carbohydrates. Protein is important but only in small quantities. Much has been written about diabetic diets and many details offered about appropriate foods and amounts, but a basic truth remains. Fast food and all the other junk food that modern society has foisted on the world's people are not conducive to the health of someone with diabetes or to anyone else, for that matter. While playing golf, however, you have to watch out for extreme blood sugar swings. It's prudent to have some snacks with you (an apple works better than a bag of chips). If you are prone to wild blood sugar swings, you might want to monitor your blood sugar level during the round, but this is not usually necessary for most people.

The more exercise you get, the more efficiently and effectively the body uses its energy (i.e., sugar). Studies show that the person who does more exercise requires less medication to control diabetes. Obviously, playing golf is an ideal mode of exercise for the physically casual athlete. It also can aid in weight loss, which reduces the strain on the energy transfer mechanisms of the body.

Recent studies also demonstrate how diabetes is better controlled by reducing stress or one's reaction to it. I expect that many more studies to come will reinforce this conclusion, but it already appears obvious to me as I see patients with diabetes.

People with type II diabetes can conscientiously follow the prescribed regimen of diet, exercise, and stress reduction, but many of them will require drugs to control the disease if it proliferates beyond the point where this regimen is sufficient. Also, for people who choose *not* to exercise, control the diet, or reduce stress, drug treatment is mandatory.

Oral medications are the first line of drug treatment used to regulate the flow of sugar through the blood to the cells. If they do not control blood sugar levels, insulin, a hormone ordinarily produced by the body, is introduced. It must be injected to be effective. Unfortunately, insulin is only a part of a complex mechanism of glucose control, and the technology is not yet available for injecting the right amount of insulin at the right time in response to the body's ever-changing needs. Efforts are under way to do this, for example, by use of a portable insulin pump, but such devices do not have the feedback capabilities that the healthy body maintains.

Tip: Make sure to carry hard candy with you on the course. Fruits are also helpful in keeping blood sugar elevated. If you begin to feel weak and dizzy, sit down, drink some water, and have a snack. After you finish playing, don't forget to monitor your blood sugar in order to prevent hypoglycemia (abnormally low level of blood sugar).

DIABETIC RETINOPATHY ■

Question: "I have diabetes, but it doesn't seem to be affecting my golf. However, I have been warned that my vision at some point could change. Could you tell me what can happen, what I need to watch, and what I need to do to prevent this from occurring?"

Answer: Diabetic retinopathy can cause loss of eyesight because diabetes can weaken the blood vessels in the retina and cause them to break open and leak. In an effort to continue to nourish the eye, the body builds more blood vessels. If this happens, the vessels will obscure the light getting to the retina and some loss of vision will result. A slight, gradual blurring of vision is usually the first warning sign. Other symptoms are cloudy vision and complete loss of sight.

Treatment: Early treatment can stop the damage from leaking blood vessels. Laser therapy is often used to seal the leaks. Sometimes, a surgical procedure called a vitrectomy is used. This procedure removes the viscous fluid that makes up the posterior portion of the eye (the space where these exuberant vessels are growing) and replaces it with another solution.

Tip: The best way to prevent diabetic retinopathy is to control your diabetes. Also, make sure to have an eye examination by an ophthalmologist at least once a year. Immediate treatment and careful monitoring will help you to keep your eyesight.

■ DIARRHEA (Also see Irritable Bowel Syndrome)

Question: "While on a golfing vacation overseas, I suddenly got weak and had to rush to the bathroom. The attack came out of nowhere. Can you explain to me what might have caused the attack?"

Answer: Diarrhea is diagnosed when you have to go to the bathroom frequently and the bowel movement is very loose. It is the body's way of defending itself by eliminating any organisms or agents that can restrict or prevent it from getting nutrients and fluids.

What you describe is probably *acute diarrhea,* which usually relates to the body's attempt to rid itself of viruses or bacteria that come from food or water or from contact with an infected individual.

When you are on vacation, especially in another country, you can easily develop what is known as *traveler's diarrhea,* which is caused by your inability to resist local microorganisms in water and food. Symptoms often include nausea, stomach cramps, bloating, vomiting, low-grade fever, fatigue, and a frequent need to go to the bathroom.

Treatment: It's important to replace the fluids that you lose in order to guard against dehydration. If a service wagon comes by or a snack bar is on the course, get a can of soda or fruit juice as soon as you can. If you are experiencing traveler's diarrhea, purchase bottled water from a reputable outlet. At all costs, avoid milk and dairy products and eat salted crackers to restore the body's chemical balance. Pepto-Bismol can provide some relief for your symptoms, but use it only as directed. Taking Imodium as directed can also help to reduce the frequency of diarrhea. Usually after a few days, your discomfort resolves itself; however, severe forms of diarrhea can cause dehydration and fever. If diarrhea persists more than a week or if you find blood in your stools, see your doctor right away. You could have a more serious intestinal infection.

Tip: To prevent traveler's diarrhea, avoid consumption of raw vegetables, raw seafood, raw meat, and unpeeled fruit. Stay away from tap water, ice made from tap water, and unpasteurized milk and dairy products. And take my personal advice: Don't buy food from street vendors. I won't go into what happened to me. Look at all the symptoms listed above—they tell the story.

DIZZINESS AND VERTIGO ■

Question: "I was playing my fifteenth hole when I began to get dizzy as I approached my ball. In fact, I had to drop to my knees and wait for a while. When I got up I felt better, but it happened to me again a few holes later. What was happening?"

Answer: The sensation of feeling light-headed occasionally during a round is quite common. Playing on a hot day, not drinking fluids, or drinking too much alcohol can create the dizziness you experienced. Also, bending over to pick up your ball can create temporary dizziness because your blood pressure does not have enough time to adjust.

In addition, dizziness can be a symptom of influenza, a head injury, low blood sugar (see the section, "Hypoglycemia," in this chapter), irregular heartbeats, or a severe allergic reaction. Prescription medications and over-the-counter drugs can also cause dizziness.

Vertigo differs from dizziness. Vertigo means illusion of movement. It's a neurologic disorder involving your body's automatic balance control system. When you are experiencing vertigo, you feel unsteady, as if you or the golf course is moving. This occurs because of a malfunction of your balance sensors in the vestibular part of the auditory nerve inside your ears.

Infection, head injury, or atherosclerosis in the blood vessels leading to the brain can cause vertigo. Labyrinthitis, an inflammation of the inner ear, can also cause vertigo, along with nausea and vomiting. In rare instances, vertigo is a symptom of Ménière's disease, which also causes ringing in the ears, nausea, vomiting, and hearing loss.

Motion sickness and height vertigo cause sweating, nausea, vomiting, and weakness. Positional vertigo often results after you change positions, such as reaching down to pick up your ball. The cause is unknown.

Treatment: An occasional incidence of dizziness or vertigo should not worry you. If the episodes are frequent, however, it is best to make an appointment with your doctor, who might order diagnostic tests of your hearing and nerve function. When vertigo is caused by a bacterial infection, antibiotics are prescribed, but when it's caused by a viral infection, the problem goes away on its own. Remember, there is no need to take an antibiotic for a viral infection. If the blood flow to the brain is impeded because of atherosclerosis, treatment usually consists of anticoagulant drugs.

Tip: If you can't get to the root cause of your dizziness or vertigo, ask your doctor about antivertigo medications, such as prochlorperazine (Compazine), meclizine (Antivert), and scopolamine (Transderm Scōp).

DRUG ABUSE ■

Question: "I'm fifty, a former flower child, and yet I still like to play golf when I'm high. I usually smoke a little marijuana before I play which helps me to relax and improve my play. What do you think?"

Answer: The prevalence of stress has helped to increase illicit drug usage, and illegal drugs are the driving commodity of a major growth industry. There are drugs to get you up and drugs to get you down. Perhaps they offer a different "reality," a vacation from the daily grind. Transcendence is a necessity for humans, which sets us apart from other animals. Illegal transcendence enablers, as one could call them, however, don't seem to be used much by golfers. Still, with the flower children now acquiring the status of seniors, perhaps there are some who seek an occasional chemical transcendence on the golf course.

The drug of choice during earlier years, of course, was marijuana. It does serve as a minor tranquilizer, but it alters one's perception. If you think you can do better on the golf course while under the influence of marijuana, I must insist that you are wrong.

Tip: Try playing three rounds while under the influence and three rounds when you are not. Add up your total strokes for each set of three rounds and divide by three. Compare the results. I'll wager that your overall performance without the use of marijuana will be better. My argument is that you might feel like you're doing better with marijuana, but this test will demonstrate otherwise. Of course, you might unknowingly try to play worse when you're off the drug in order to justify using it. To avoid that, have a friend monitor your round to make sure that you're not fluffing it. The friend might be interested in playing with a little money on the line.

■ EYE INFECTION (CONJUNCTIVITIS)

Question: "My golfing partner came to the course with bloodshot eyes. I kidded him about tipping too many the night before. He told me he hadn't been drinking and couldn't understand what was happening. He also said he had trouble opening his eyes when he woke up. We played a few holes, and then he had to quit. What was wrong?"

Answer: Certain allergens, bacterial or viral infections, or irritating substances can sometimes slip into the thin, transparent mucous membrane that covers the front of the eyes and cause conjunctivitis. The eye has a bloodshot appearance, as you describe. Conjunctivitis is also referred to as pinkeye. Other symptoms are itching, burning, and a discharge that crusts over at night and makes the eyelids stick together.

Treatment: When conjunctivitis is caused by a mild virus, it usually clears up on its own. If the infection is bacterial, antibiotic eye drops or ointments are commonly described to reduce the heavy discharge and swelling of the lids. In either case, a warm compress applied to the crusty eyelids in the morning helps to dissolve the crust and make it easier to open the eyes.

Tip: This may sound harsh, but stay away from your friend. Whether viral or bacterial, conjunctivitis is caused by person-to-person contact and is highly contagious. To prevent the spread of infectious conjunctivitis, I recommend not sharing your towel or eye makeup; also try to avoid touching your eyes. In addition, caution against the use of over-the-counter eye solutions for bloodshot eyes. They can prolong or worsen the infection despite any minor relief from the symptoms that you experience.

Question: "I had the biggest scare yesterday. A friend in our four-some fainted. He regained consciousness a few minutes later, but it left me with a lot of questions. Any tips on what could have hap-pened?"

Answer: Fainting (syncope) is usually a brief and sudden loss of consciousness that occurs when the blood flow to the brain is briefly reduced. It can be caused by fear, anxiety, fatigue, emotional stress, hunger, or pain in people with no known health problems. Some people might faint during prolonged physical exertion in hot weather, after exercising, when they are in hot and crowded rooms, or as a reaction to learning about an accident or another tragic event. Use of certain drugs, such as heart medications that slow the heartbeat, can bring about a fainting spell. Some people have fainted after prolonged straining from coughing forcefully or at-tempting a bowel movement while constipated. You can also faint if you've been ill in bed for several days and try to get up because your blood pressure needs more time to adjust to a standing posi-tion. Symptoms prior to fainting are a feeling of light-headedness, weakness, nausea, blurred vision, and breaking out in a cold sweat.

Treatment: In the future, if you or any of your playing partners have any of the above symptoms prior to fainting, it's best to lie down at once or sit with your head between your knees. Once in that posi-tion, begin to breathe deeply. For future reference, if your friend faints again but is breathing and has a pulse, lay him or her on the ground with both feet raised a little higher than the rest of the body. Loosen any tight collars or constricting clothing. Check again for breathing and a neck pulse. When neither is present, call immediately for an ambulance. If the victim is a child, perform one minute of CPR first. Also call for an ambulance if the victim is breathing but consciousness doesn't return within a few minutes.

Tip: It is important to know that fainting also can be associated with serious health problems, such as abnormal heartbeat, heart disease, low blood sugar, diabetes, and anemia. Therefore, I recommend that you get to know your playing partners and be aware of their medical conditions. Finally, fainting for no apparent reason or fainting that accompanies a head injury or convulsion needs immediate attention. Again, I urge you to carry that cellular phone.

■ GAS

Question: "What can I do about intestinal gas? I get a lot of it while I play and find myself wanting to hit my balls into the woods so I can release a little. Of course, that can affect my score. Any suggestions?"

Answer: It's natural to have some gas buildup in your digestive tract during your daily routine. So, although you can't prevent gas formation, it is possible to reduce the amount of it that can cause the problem you describe.

Abdominal bloating often can be caused by disorders of the intestinal tract (e.g., irritable bowel syndrome) or by what you eat.

The problem that you describe, flatulence or the need to pass gas from the rectum, is usually the result of eating carbohydrates that are not fully digested as they enter the lower intestinal tract. These foods then pass on to the colon where they are invaded by bacteria.

Burping or belching usually results when you swallow air and you are trying to release it. You swallow air while you eat or talk fast. If you belch a lot, it can make the problem worse because you're swallowing more air.

Another common cause of excessive gas is the lactose in milk.

Treatment: Review your diet to see if you eat gas-forming foods a few hours before you play. Obviously, beans bring on gas, as most of us know. Cabbage, broccoli, brussels sprouts, cauliflower, and eggplant are other common foods that can bloat your stomach and cause excessive gas. You might want to cut down on dairy products before a round.

Tip: Check to determine if you have a sensitivity to these and other foods. Keep a log of what you eat prior to playing and even the night before. Taking those foods out of your diet can help to reduce excessive gas. You may want to try LactAid or similar products.

If none of these suggestions works, you might want to have your doctor to rule out the unlikely possibility that something is partially blocking the intestine.

GASTRITIS ◼

Question: "Recently, I've been suffering from a lot of stomach pain and nausea for no apparent reason. It usually lasts a few days and then goes away. Can you tell me what the problem could be?"

Answer: If your doctor has ruled out other possible causes, you could be suffering from stomach gas resulting from the inflammation of the mucous lining of the stomach. Too much coffee or alcohol, foods that cause allergic reactions, infections, and such medications as aspirin, ibuprofen, and some prescription drugs can cause the inflammation. Another major cause of gastritis is stress-related mucosal disease. Symptoms often include pain, nausea, appetite loss, and vomiting (in some cases with blood).

Treatment: No treatment is needed if you have been diagnosed with gastritis, but you could take some over-the-counter antacids for temporary relief. I also suggest cutting down on coffee, strong teas, and/or alcohol. Tagamet, Zantac, Axid, and Pepcid help to control gastric acid secretions, thus reducing gastric inflammation.

Tip: Your best bet to reduce gastritis is to eat little meals of bland foods and to stay away from heavy and spicy foods until all symptoms have disappeared. The mainstay to relief of gastric pain, as with all upper abdominal pains, is avoiding certain things: drinks containing caffeine (coffee, tea, and many soft drinks), fried foods, fatty foods, spicy foods (some people do OK despite eating these), alcohol, and smoking. A significant part of healing gastritis is to reduce stress. (See the section, "Stress Reduction," in chapter 4.)

■ GLAUCOMA

Question: "My golfing partner told me that he was going to have eye surgery for glaucoma. Can you tell me what it is and what can be done for it?"

Answer: Simply stated, glaucoma is a disease causing increased pressure in the eye that goes beyond the eye's level of tolerance. Nerve fibers and blood vessels in the optic nerve become compressed, and the loss of sight can result. Almost all types of glaucoma result from the eye's inability to get rid of excessive fluid; in other words, the eye's draining system does not function properly. Although anyone can develop glaucoma, the disease is more common in adults who have a family history of glaucoma, people who are nearsighted or have diabetes, people suffering from other eye diseases, and smokers. To diagnose glaucoma, an ophthalmologist uses a tonometer to measure eye pressure. If the pressure is high, an examination called a gonioscopy allows inspection of the drainage system inside the eye chamber.

Treatment: If early-stage glaucoma is detected, your doctor will treat it with medicated eyedrops to prevent damage from increased pressure. Two drugs often used are pilocarpine (Pilocar) and epinephrine (adrenaline). Beta-blocker eyedrops, such as Timoptic Ocu-dose, are sometimes used to reduce fluid production. If drug therapy doesn't work, the next step is laser surgery to widen drainage passageways and relieve the pressure. These treatment approaches can help to prevent blindness.

Tip: I strongly recommend that anyone over age sixty-five be tested by annually to detect the early warning signs of glaucoma. By doing this, glaucoma can be treated early before irreversible vision loss occurs. Keep in mind that many primary care physicians do have the training and equipment to test for glaucoma. However, if yours does not, or if you have diabetes which is associated with other eye complications, an ophthalmologist is the one to see.

The following is a self-test to see if you might have the earliest warning signs of glaucoma. It was developed by George Spaeth, M.D., president of the American Glaucoma Society and director of glaucoma services at Wills Eye Hospital in Philadelphia.

1. Sit about a foot from a large TV.
2. Set your TV on a channel without a station. (All you want is the "snow".)
3. Close your left eye, and look at the center of the screen with your right eye.
4. If any areas of the screen are blank or wash out or if they are less visible, especially in the upper left-hand side of the screen, this might be the result of glaucoma.
5. Do the same thing with the other eye.

HEADACHE ∎

Question: "I get frequent headaches. Sometimes I get them when I'm playing. I take aspirin, but they don't go away. Is there a possibility that I might have a serious illness? Also, should I play golf with a headache?"

Answer: My senior patients often tell me that the first worry when they get splitting headaches is the possibility of brain tumor. Rest assured, pain from a headache doesn't mean that.

The most common types are tension headaches and migraine headaches. Other problems, such as teeth problems, ear infections, eyestrain, glaucoma, allergies, and certain diseases, can also cause headache symptoms. Headaches can also result from stress or irregular eating or sleeping patterns.

A tension headache causes steady pain. The pain might be located in the front or back of the head and in both temples. The headache can return daily, usually in the afternoon or evening. It results from maintaining a contracted muscle, usually in the shoulders and neck, for a period of time long enough for the muscle to tire. Not only do tired muscles hurt, but they also call for help from adjacent muscles to bear the perceived extra load. This is called recruitment. I call it the Atlas syndrome because the person is a metaphoric Atlas who is carrying the weight of the world on his shoulders. There are a lot of unknowing Atlases in this world.

Although some estimates indicate that migraine headaches affect about 25 percent of people who have headaches, this is not my experience. I treat an infinitesimally small number of true vascular (migraine) headaches compared with muscular tension headaches. Many people define a migraine headache as a very severe one. Tension headaches also can be severe, cause vomiting, and require rest for recovery. During a migraine attack, the blood vessels that flow to the brain are believed to contract or go into spasm. They then dilate and cause pain and often other symptoms. Migraine headaches have a tendency to occur in families. For unknown reasons, more women experience migraine headaches than do men. One theory explaining this suggests the possibility of shifts of hormones during the menstrual cycle. Weekends, holidays, and vacations can set off migraine headaches, especially in people who have difficulty relaxing. Foods, particularly red wine and other alcoholic beverages, chocolate, aged cheese, caffeine, nuts, and monosodium glutamate (MSG), can trigger them. Bright sunlight, too much sleep, and certain medications (e.g., estrogens and oral contraceptives) can also bring on migraine headaches.

Cluster headaches are much like migraine headaches except that they occur in clusters several times a day. The patient can almost predict when they are going to occur. They are more frequent in men than in women. Symptoms begin with a piercing pain around the nostril or behind the eye, and then it spreads into the forehead. Each attack can last from 30 minutes to as long as 2 hours.

Treatment

Tension Headaches: Treatment is directed toward rest and relaxation. Lying down or taking a hot bath or shower can help to ease tension. Relief often results if you can determine the cause of your stress and take steps to change your behavior or your reaction to or attitude toward external stress-producing situations.

Migraine Headaches: The best treatment is prevention. Your doctor can help to determine the steps that you need to take after you provide a complete medical history and describe the precipitating events or behaviors that precede an attack. For migraines that occur at least once a week, your doctor might prescribe Imitrex (sumatriptan), which works in the dilated artery causing the pain. This action often rapidly and dramatically reduces the pain.

Cluster Headaches: Treatment might include oxygen inhalation, ergot, methysergide, prednisone, lithium, and Imitrex. Antidepressants and calcium channel blockers, such as verapamil, are the main preventive medications when people suffer from cluster headaches. As in tension and migraine headaches, there is a strong emotional component to cluster headaches.

Tip: If you experience severe, recurring headaches that nonprescription pain relievers don't help, see your doctor. Sometimes headaches signal other disorders that require prompt medical attention. See your doctor if you have any of these four symptoms:

1. You rarely get headaches but suddenly experience severe pain.

2. You develop a headache along with a stiff neck, fever, and sensitivity to light, and your headache gets worse when you bend your head forward.

3. You injure your head, and soon after you develop a headache accompanied by nausea, vomiting, and lethargy.

4. You start developing headaches on a daily basis, and they get worse over time.

■ HEARING DISORDER (RINGING/TINNITUS)

Question: "This may sound foolish, but I'm ready to give up playing golf because I hear this constant ringing in my ears that distracts me from concentrating. Also, when we're in the clubhouse after playing and it's quiet, I can hear my heart beating constantly. Is there anything that can be done to get rid of these annoying distractions?"

Answer: Tinnitus, or ringing in the ear, affects an estimated 50 million adults in the United States. It is the sensation of hearing ringing, buzzing, hissing, chirping, whistling, and/or your heartbeat. Tinnitus can either be constant or come and go and can vary in intensity. In most cases, it is more of an annoyance than a serious disorder. When it affects concentration and sleep, however, it can have a profound psychological effect on one's work and personal relationships.

Tinnitus is often associated with hearing loss, but it is not the cause or vice versa. That is, hearing loss does not cause tinnitus. Some cases are caused by infections or blockages in the ear, and the tinnitus often disappears once the underlying cause is treated. Research suggests that the most common cause of chronic tinnitus is prolonged exposure to loud noises. Other causes include certain drugs, such as aspirin, several types of antibiotics, and quinine medications. Deterioration of the cochlea or other parts of the ear as a result of aging can cause the symptoms. In some cases, Ménière's disease, a disorder of the inner ear, or otosclerosis, a degenerative disease of the small bones in the middle ear, can cause tinnitus. Research has also shown that stressful conditions can bring on an attack of tinnitus.

To determine if your tinnitus indicates a medical disorder, your doctor will give you a general physical examination, which includes a careful examination of your ears. If a diagnosis can't be made, your doctor might refer you to an otologist, an otolaryngologist, or an audiologist for hearing and neurological tests. Sometimes, a balance test called an electronystagmography may be ordered along with magnetic resonance imaging (MRI) or computed tomography (CT) scan of your head to reveal any abnormal structural problems.

Treatment: The first step is to treat the underlying medical condition. If the ringing noise continues after such treatment, a number of nonmedical options can be recommended to mask or reduce the unwanted noise. If the noise really annoys you, consider a counternoise generator, which produces a white noise to block out the distracting sounds that is usually not as annoying as the tinnitus itself. Some people prefer the counternoise, but some don't.

Tip: Unless the ringing is a symptom of Ménière's disease, there is no serious medical reason for doing anything about it.

HEARING LOSS ■

Question: "Sometimes I'm sitting in the clubhouse after a round and my friend asks me something, but I can't hear it. The room noise drowns out his voice. How can I tell if I'm a candidate for a hearing aid?"

Answer: Most of us suffer some hearing loss, related to either high-frequency or low-frequency sounds, as we grow older. More than 9 percent of the people in this country have some form of hearing loss, often as the result of heredity, injury, infection, or occupational exposure. Recently, more and more hearing loss has been attributed to environmental factors, such as exposure to loud machines, motors, and music.

The two most common types of hearing loss can be described as follows:

1. Conductive hearing loss results when sound waves can't travel from the outside ear to the inner ear because of blockage, either by ear wax or an infection.

2. Presbycusis, better known as age-related hearing loss, is the decline of the ability to hear high-frequency sounds. It also becomes more difficult to tell the difference between certain sounds in speech, such as b's and p's. Other symptoms include the perception that people are mumbling or slurring their speech, the inability to hear a faucet dripping or musical high notes, and constant noise in the ears.

Treatment: Resistance to acknowledging that one has a hearing loss is the biggest hurdle to overcome. Many people take the attitude that hearing difficulties are the result of the aging process and there is nothing that can be done. Just the opposite is true. Many types of hearing loss can be treated, and most can be corrected through the use of hearing aids. As you probably know, Arnold Palmer and many other senior golfers use hearing aids. Today's technology makes them not only affordable but so small that you have to look quite closely to detect if a person is wearing one. The latest technology also provides excellent sound enhancement.

Tip: If you think you have a hearing problem you should see a doctor who specializes in hearing disorders. Consult an ear, nose, and throat specialist (otorhinolaryngologist) or an ear specialist (otologist). The specialist might refer you to an audiologist for additional testing to determine if you can benefit from a hearing aid. Do not let any myth that you have heard about hearing aids dissuade you from seeing an audiologist. You will be amazed at what hearing aids can do to improve your hearing without affecting your self-image.

HEART ATTACK (WARNING SIGNS) ■

Question: "The other day, I felt this pain in my chest and felt like I was going to have a heart attack. How do you know if you are?"

Answer: Although the risk of having a heart attack while you play golf is low, it's still a possibility. A risk assessment is based on age, sex, cholesterol count, blood pressure, smoking, and presence of diabetes. Cardiac arrest (heart attack), however, can happen to anyone.

Treatment: Give close attention to any of these four early warning signs of an impending heart attack:

1. Angina or chest pain: The pain or pressure occurs first in the chest, then moves up your neck or jaw or moves down your arm. If the pain stops or is relieved when you rest, call your doctor. If the pain continues even while you're resting, get emergency help immediately.

2. Irregular heartbeat: A skipped heartbeat now and then does not indicate anything serious. If you have many skipped heartbeats, however, call your doctor immediately.

3. Shortness of breath. Obviously if you just climbed a hill to get to the next tee, you will have some shortness of breath. If you're

sitting in your cart and you can't seem to catch your breath, however, see your doctor.

4. Other signs: If you feel extreme fatigue after exercising or experience light-headedness and/or nausea while playing golf or other sports, see your doctor.

Tip: Have one member in your foursome carry a cellular phone for emergencies. Time is crucial during a heart attack, not only in reducing the amount of potential damage to the heart and brain but in keeping someone alive.

If you've had a heart attack, you are three to five times more likely to have another one. That's why I recommend walking your round of golf. In fact, walking can reduce the risk of a second heart attack more than it reduces the risk of the first attack.

■ HEART ATTACK FIRST AID

Question: "I was playing golf with a friend who had a heart attack. He died. What could I have done to save his life?"

Answer: It's important to remind yourself that you could not have known at the time that your friend was actually having a heart attack. You discovered this only later. Your friend could have been suffering merely a loss of consciousness (syncope), but he would have looked the same.

If your partner had been conscious, he could have told you about his symptoms, such as, "I have a pain in my left chest. It goes to my jaw, left shoulder, and arm. I feel sweaty and light-headed." Any combination of such symptoms is an indication of a heart attack.

Treatment: It's crucial to keep a heart attack victim still, calm, and covered for warmth while you send for help as soon as possible.

When a person lapses into unconsciousness, the first few moments are critical in making the correct assessment and starting treatment. The proper steps are codified in the well-known procedure called cardiopulmonary resuscitation (CPR). You can learn CPR and become certified in basic life support. You will know what to do to keep a person alive before the ambulance arrives. The four-hour course is taught in almost every city and town that has a hospital or clinic, and the American Red Cross conducts many CPR programs throughout the United States.

Knowing what to do is not that difficult. When a person has a syncopal (fainting) episode, shake him or her gently and shout, "Are you OK?" If there is no response, you perform two "ABC" procedures. The first one is as follows:

A = airway

Is the airway open? If your friend just ate something, it may have blocked the trachea (air tube). A person who is still conscious will look very uncomfortable and probably point to the throat. If the airway is not cleared, the person will lapse into unconsciousness. The airway could be blocked, whether the person is conscious or unconscious, by food, vomit, or the tongue.

B = breathing

Is your friend breathing? You can tell by putting your ear to your friend's mouth while watching the chest for breath movements. If you see no movement, the airway could be closed or your friend could be in such a deep coma that he or she is unable to breathe on his or her own.

C = circulation

Is blood circulating; that is, is the heart pumping blood? You can tell by feeling for your friend's pulse. Place your forefinger and middle finger just below the angle of the jaw to locate the pulse.

This first ABC procedure might seem to take an interminable amount of time when someone is unconscious, but you actually have several minutes in which to work. The entire procedure requires only 5–10 seconds.

The next part of CPR pertains to the actions required to keep oxygenated blood moving to your friend's brain. If the brain is starved for oxygen for 10 minutes, brain damage is inevitable. This ABC procedure is as follows:

A = airway

To keep the airway open, make sure that no foreign particles are in the victim's mouth. If there are any, remove them by sweeping your forefinger through the mouth. For a foreign body in the trachea, you must use the Heimlich maneuver. This is a process designed to expel any mass that is blocking the trachea. Wrap your arms around your friend, place a fist in the solar plexus, and place your other hand over your fist. Then squeeze against the solar plexus with firm, spasmodic thrusts. The force of the thrusts will dislodge the foreign body in the trachea. If that is the only problem, your friend will begin to breathe normally and recover.

If there is no foreign body in either the mouth or the trachea, lay your friend supine and tilt the neck back. This will keep the tongue from blocking the throat and keep the airway open.

B = breathing

If the airway is open, your friend still might not be breathing on his or her own. Refer to step B in the first set of ABC procedures. If the person is not breathing, you must breathe for him or her. Holding the chin back, plug the nose by squeezing it with your fingers, and make an airtight seal of the victim's mouth with your mouth. Breathe two breaths into the other person with enough volume for his or her chest to expand. You can tell that this is working when you see the chest rising and falling with the breaths you are giving. Sometimes, the stomach fills with the air that you instill. If this happens, press gently over the stomach to expel the air.

C = circulation

To promote circulation after you have determined that there is no pulse, you can perform cardiac compression. To do this, place the heel of your hand about three fingers above the xiphoid, the bottom part of the sternum (the long bone between the ribs) and place your other hand over the first hand. Apply smooth, even compressions in displacing the sternum about two inches by pressing straight down. The rate of compression should be 80 to 100 compressions per minute.

If there is only one person doing the CPR, the ratio of resuscitation to compression is 2:15; that is, give two consecutive breaths to fifteen compressions. With two people, the ratio is 1:5. For example, in this situation, the person giving the breaths will count the compressions the other person is doing and give a breath at every five compressions.

Tip: If there is no one else around and you follow these guidelines, you could save a friend's life, even if no one else is there to help you. You will do well to take a CPR course, however, because it's hard to do these procedures smoothly just by reading them a few times. Practice makes perfect. Again, I recommend carrying a cellular phone in your bag.

HEART DISEASE AND EXERCISE ■

Question: "I hear exercise is good for my heart disease, but when can it be dangerous?"

Answer: If you have had a diagnosis of valvular heart disease, you might want to have your exercise program carefully evaluated by a physician. Valvular heart disease is a condition in which the heart valves are either leaking or blocked. The most common valve problem for which folks over age fifty are at risk when exercising is a thickening of the valve separating the heart from the aorta and other blood vessels. It's called aortic stenosis.

Treatment: Valvular disease can cause fainting and even death. If you have heart disease, consult your family doctor or cardiologist before you do any kind of exercising. Congestive heart failure (CHF) and coronary artery disease (CAD) can both improve with careful, progressive exercise.

Tip: None of the several types of heart disease prevents one from golfing, and the health of people with most types is improved with this activity. The more severe the disease, however, the greater the need for professional evaluation before exercising.

■ HEARTBURN

Question: "Why is it every time I eat at the golf course, I get heartburn. What causes it, and what can I do about it?"

Answer: Heartburn, or gastroesophageal reflux disorder (GERD), occurs when digestive juices from the stomach flow upward and back into the esophagus and produce pain and burning. Another condition that causes heartburn is hiatal hernia. It could be that some or all of your upper stomach bulges upward through a weakened opening (hiatus) in your diaphragm. Because of that, acid in the stomach travels up instead of down and causes that burning sensation. Other symptoms range from mild discomfort to painful burning, not only in the throat but in the chest. Very often, the pain is thought to be a heart attack.

Treatment: As with all upper gastrointestinal disorders, control of diet is paramount, as is stress reduction. For temporary relief, take antacids, such as Mylanta, Maalox, or Gaviscon (my favorite because it seems to coat the esophagus longer and more completely). A number of histamine blockers are now available over the counter (e.g., Tagamet, Pepcid, Axid, and Zantac). I prefer not to use these medicines as a substitute to changing one's diet and dealing with the disruptive emotional changes that induce excess gastric secretion. The medicines are of temporary benefit only.

Tip: If you want to control heartburn and reduce the symptoms, I recommend that you eat small, frequent meals rather than two or three big ones. Don't eat snacks too close to bedtime. Avoid acidic foods, particularly citrus juices and tomato products. I also suggest that you stay away from alcohol and cigarettes, both of which increase stomach acid. Also, don't wear tight-fitting clothing around your waist because it increases stomach pressure that can cause heartburn. Finally, I suggest that you lose weight and do crunches (see chapter 3) to reduce stomach pressure on your hiatus (the opening in the diaphragm).

HEMORRHOIDS ■

Question: "At the clubhouse, I noticed blood in my stool. When we started playing, I could hardly sit in the cart. When the round was over, I couldn't sit in the dining room and had to leave. I think I might have hemorrhoids. Can you tell me what causes them and what I can do to prevent going through that agony again?"

Answer: Half of folks who are past age fifty have had at least one experience with hemorrhoids. They occur when blood vessels in the anal canal and rectum experience repeated pressure. As the vessels begin to swell and bulge, hemorrhoids are created. Usual symptoms include bleeding, itching, and protrusion toward the anus.

The major cause of hemorrhoids is constipation (see the section, "Constipation" in this chapter). Frequent bowel movements can also bring on the symptoms. Abdominal pressure during pregnancy and the result of obesity are other causes.

Treatment: Sitting in warm water in your bathtub helps to relieve symptoms. You can also try pain relievers, such as Motrin or Tylenol, and stool softeners. Often, self-treatment is successful with the use of over-the-counter products that both lubricate the area and provide pain relief. Witch hazel applied topically with toilet tissue is a great way to soothe and shrink swollen hemorrhoids. I have found that refrigerated Maalox applied topically is also very helpful.

If you require medical intervention for hemorrhoids that bleed often and protrude, several treatment procedures are available. An injection technique involves the injection of a sclerosing agent into the hemorrhoid that scars and shrinks it, often forever. In rubber band ligation, a rubber band is applied to internal hemorrhoids. After a while, they rot and fall off because they lack a blood supply. This procedure cannot be used for external hemorrhoids because of intensive nerve pain. Photocoagulation is a procedure in which a laser burns away the tissue.

Tip: I tell my patients that they can prevent hemorrhoids by increasing the amount of fiber in their diets. Fiber helps to reduce constipation, thus preventing increased pressure in the anal canal and rectum. I also recommend the practice of good hygiene and keeping the skin around the anus clean and dry in order to control irritation and itching in the area.

■ HIGH BLOOD PRESSURE

Question: "I'm overweight, and my family has a history of high blood pressure. Should I be concerned?"

Answer: Severe high blood pressure is any consistent number of readings above 180/110 mm Hg. Any reading above 140 (systolic—the top reading) and/or 90 (diastolic—the lower number) is also considered abnormal blood pressure. The cause of high blood pressure is arteriosclerosis (hardening of the arteries), which diminishes the elasticity of arterial walls as they contract and expand. Left untreated, high blood pressure can lead to stroke, heart attack, and kidney failure.

Yes, you should be concerned. Even though you don't have any symptoms, it's best to see your doctor because of your family history of high blood pressure.

Treatment: You want to get your blood pressure under control, especially before you start an exercise program. High blood pressure is mainly treated with medication, but remember two rules:

Rule 1: All drugs cause side effects.

Rule 2: If you take a drug that you believe has no side effects, see Rule 1.

Also, remember that many side effects can diminish your well-being and performance on the golf course.

For a long time, the mainstay of modern drug therapy for high blood pressure consisted of a diuretic and a beta-blocker, such as propranolol, atenolol or, metoprolol. The beta-blocker works by interfering with signals from the brain that tell the heart to speed up and the blood vessels to contract. It counters the adrenaline response and works great in this way. Unfortunately, it also slows down everything else in the body. It can contribute to depression, fatigue, sleep disturbances, and Raynaud's phenomenon. The latter disorder includes such features as numbness in the hands and feet, caused by massive constrictions of the arteries, that is followed by reflex dilation, with resultant pain, and limbs that are markedly red in a well-demarcated area. The patient becomes intolerant to cold, which triggers the latter response. Raynaud's phenomenon rules out winter golf as well as golfing in inclement periods during other seasons.

Sometimes people taking beta-blockers don't even notice their fatigue, but they do see a decrease in performance. I golfed with one such person, and he told me how his handicap began to rise slowly over a period of a year. Around that time, he had been diagnosed with hypertension and had tried a beta-blocker. Seeing the connection, he changed to a different type of drug and his game improved. He also noticed how much more energy he had, even though he was not aware that he had lost any energy while he was taking the beta-blocker.

Dizziness and even fainting are associated with all of the sympatholitic agents (medications that interfere with the adrenaline-activated system), such as reserpine, guanethidine, prazosin, methyldopa, and clonidine. These side effects are especially evident on hot days and when one does not consume enough fluid.

Have your doctor evaluate you for one of the newer regimens for treating hypertension. The newer families of antihypertensives are less likely to cause problems, but they are not reaction free. Angiotensin-converting enzyme (ACE) inhibitors work at the level of the kidneys to block the hormone that causes the arteries to contract. Captopril and enalapril are among these. I prescribe them a lot, but patients occasionally have associated dry mouth, fatigue, and rashes. Captopril can also reduce one's ability to taste, but if your normal fare is the typical golf course food, such a side effect actually could be beneficial. Calcium channel inhibitors, such as verapamil, block the basic contracting mechanism of muscles and can cause similar problems.

In addition to medication, your doctor might prescribe a blood pressure–reducing exercise and a diet regimen.

Tip: Consider the side effects of various medications, especially those that slow down bodily functions. Although they can control your blood pressure, they also might affect your gastrointestinal system, with constipation as the result. Therefore, if you feel slower, duller, and less yourself, consider that one of these medications could be the reason.

■ HYPOGLYCEMIA

Question: "I was playing the back nine and began to feel very weak and dizzy. My hands began to shake, and I couldn't putt. Was I experiencing the yips? I didn't get anything to eat at the turn, but I did have a beer before we teed off on ten. What's going on?"

Answer: Hypoglycemia (low blood sugar) is sometimes experienced by diabetics. Usually, however, it is an indication that something else is going on. Please note: Hypoglycemia is not caused, as many people believe, by eating a lot of foods containing sugar.

There are two types of hypoglycemia:

1. Fasting hypoglycemia: This is probably what happened to you. It is diagnosed in otherwise healthy people who miss a couple of meals and then drink alcohol. Other causes include reactions to medications, such as insulin, or oral hypoglycemics; tumors in the pancreas where cells produce insulin; liver and kidney disease; and hormonal and autoimmune disorders.

2. Functional/reactive hypoglycemia: This diagnosis is made when symptoms occur after meals. A major cause of this type of hypoglycemia is recent surgery on the stomach. It's also called dumping syndrome, a disorder in which fluids move too quickly through the stomach.

To diagnose hypoglycemia, your doctor will ask you to describe your symptoms and order blood tests to analyze your glucose levels.

Treatment: Fasting hypoglycemia is treated by correcting the underlying causes. Functional/reactive hypoglycemia is treated by making adjustments to your diet and mealtimes. Instead of eating three times a day, eat six smaller meals in order to maintain your blood sugar levels. You should also eat more fiber and complex carbohydrates. Also, eating less protein helps to slow down the absorption of sugar.

Tip: I recommend that you avoid simple carbohydrates that contain sugar except when you're having a hypoglycemic reaction.

If you have diabetes, you probably are aware of the signs of a hypoglycemic reaction and how to manage it. Your best bet is to carry candy, sugar cubes, or glucose tablets with you.

■ INCONTINENCE

Question: "About a month ago at the course, a friend told a joke and I laughed so hard I actually wet my pants. A few days ago, I sneezed and noticed that I did it again. Can you explain what is happening to me?"

Answer: Incontinence is so common among senior folks and so dreaded that it leads to a number of embarrassing moments, such as the ones you described. Incontinence is the involuntary releasing of urine from the bladder. It's a symptom of some other condition that often can be treated. It is often caused by a local infection of the urinary tract. It can also result from taking certain medications. Women can suffer incontinence from weakened pelvic floor muscles. Some men with prostate problems suffer from incontinence. Not going to the bathroom when you have to can weaken muscles, and, over time, incontinence can develop. Diabetes, multiple sclerosis, depression, and prolonged constipation can also cause incontinence.

The type of incontinence you're experiencing is called stress incontinence, which is usually the result of weakened tissues around the bladder. Small amounts of urine are often released when you cough very hard, sneeze, laugh, run, or lift a heavy object.

Treatment: Treatment depends on the cause of incontinence. If your pelvic floor muscles are weak, exercises are prescribed to help strengthen the area around the bladder and urethra. Biofeedback is sometimes used successfully.

Anticholinergics, such as Urispas and Ditropan, often can be effective in reducing or eliminating incontinence. For prostatic hypertrophy (enlargement) Terazol and Proscar have saved many men from the surgeon's knife.

If these nonsurgical methods fail, surgery is usually recommended to reposition the neck of the bladder and/or to correct an obstruction that is blocking the flow. Urologists can now replace the sphincter, the muscle that controls flow at the bottom of the bladder.

Tip: Most cases of incontinence can be treated. This disorder should not be taken for granted as the inevitable result of a deteriorating body. If you have difficulty holding your urine for more than a few hours or urinate involuntarily or unknowingly, see your doctor who can help in many ways.

Finally, I always make it a point to learn the location of rest rooms on a course and plan accordingly. And I always make certain to use the bathroom before I tee off and to reduce my caffeine intake before I play. If all else fails, I hit a shot near a grove of tall trees.

INDIGESTION ■

Question: "For the last six months, I've been having trouble with my digestive system. I get indigestion even after I have a soft drink. If I eat anything before I play golf, I've got to take an antacid, which helps only a little. Believe me, it affects my concentration. Any suggestions?"

Answer: Indigestion is a global term for various stomach discomforts. Symptoms of indigestion signal that normal digestion has been affected for one or more reasons. For example, if stomach acid gets into the esophagus, heartburn is the result. Swallowing too much air while eating or drinking can distend the stomach and cause excessive belching.

Indigestion can be either occasional or chronic (daily or almost daily). It is mostly discomforting but not life threatening; however, it can accompany serious problems and should not be ignored. In addition to heartburn and belching, symptoms can include gas, mild nausea, and vomiting.

Causes include overeating, too much alcohol intake, excessive aspirin use, eating while under stress, and foods that do not agree with you. The two most common causes of chronic indigestion are obesity, which increases pressure in the stomach, and smoking, which increases the production of stomach acid.

Diagnosis of heartburn is usually done by a physical examination.

Treatment: Unfortunately, no single remedy will help everyone. If your doctor determines that there is no serious underlying disorder causing the indigestion, the treatment is directed toward eliminating the symptoms and suggesting ways to avoid indigestion in the future.

Heartburn remedies, antacids, or other medications that alter the stomach's production of acid are often recommended first. If excessive acid makes ulcer a threat, sucralfate might be prescribed to protect the stomach lining. Painful indigestion is usually treated with a combination of an antacid and the anesthetic lidocaine. If there is an infection (*Helicobacter pylori*), antibiotics are prescribed.

Tip: Indigestion happens to nearly everyone at one time or another, so it's hard to avoid it. You can reduce the frequency of indigestion, however, by watching your weight, avoiding overconsumption of foods that are rich in fat, overindulging in alcohol consumption, and abstaining from smoking.

■ IRRITABLE BOWEL SYNDROME

Question: "I have this embarrassing problem. When we have catered tournaments at our club, I begin to cringe. I usually get cramps, excessive gas, and diarrhea, which make it almost impossible for me to finish a round. Does this mean I'm getting old? Is there anything I can do?"

Answer: You probably suffer from irritable bowel syndrome (IBS), a common disorder. It affects millions of senior golfers, but it is not an exclusive domain of seniors. Also known as spastic colon, IBS produces the symptoms you describe, as well as constipation that often follows episodes of diarrhea. The disorder frequently is related to stress or emotional upset, which causes the nerves in the intestines to overreact. A sensitivity to dairy products can also produce similar symptoms. Also, corn, peanuts and individual foods for certain people cause symptoms.

Treatment: In some medical circles, treatment consists of ruling out the possibility of other diseases, but I hope this is no longer the norm. You should suspect another disease only if you have bloody stools or progressive weight loss. Once disease is ruled out, your doctor and a dietitian will work with you to identify situations or foods that often trigger the symptoms. Behavior modification techniques, such as learning relaxation responses through meditation, can be of some benefit. Your diet should include foods high in fiber and fluids. Also, restrict your spice and caffeine intake.

Loperamide can slow the movement of food through the intestines. Your doctor might also prescribe dicyclomine to calm the gastrointestinal tract and atropine or belladonna to relieve stomach cramps.

Tip: This syndrome is the result of an inappropriately acting intestine. When it should rest, it stops, and when it should move, it gallops. Training the gut to live within the mean is a process of eating balanced meals and avoiding agitation. To calm the gut, you must learn to remain calm overall.

■ MENOPAUSE

Question: "I've passed menopause and I'm concerned about the effects. I also read somewhere that I've also reached an age where I will be losing a lot of bone mass. Any advice?"

Answer: The major concern once you've gone beyond menopause is the risk of developing osteoporosis (see the section, "Broken Bones," in chapter 1). The term *menopause* refers to the end of menstruation, as well as the years prior to and after your final period. At about age fifty, most women stop menstruating, although some stop in their forties or in their late fifties. Temporary symptoms include hot flashes, mood swings, night sweats, painful intercourse, increased nervousness, anxiety, irritability, and the need to urinate more often, especially during the night. Because estrogen levels decrease during menopause, absorption of calcium by the bones is affected, which, in turn, can raise cholesterol levels.

Menopause is caused by the ovaries slowing and stopping their normal functions, including egg production. Because the levels of the female hormones, estrogen and progesterone, are also decreased, other changes occur throughout the body, especially in the reproductive system.

Treatment: The most popular treatment approach to problems associated with menopause is to control the level of estrogen, which is no longer produced in sufficient quantity for the needs of the body. Hormone replacement therapy, however, has side effects that can lead to endometrial and uterine cancer. Irregular bleeding, headaches, bloating, and breast swelling and pain are other complications. My treatment of choice consists of estrogen and progesterone supplements taken in small amounts. Consult your doctor about your personal factors with this type of therapy.

Tip: A new drug (Avista) was recently approved by the Food and Drug Administration for use during menopause. It is supposed to have less serious side effects and cancer-causing agents. Check with your doctor about this medication. I also recommend eating foods high in plant estrogens, such as soybeans and lima beans, which can help to alleviate some of the symptoms mentioned. Other sources include nuts and seeds, fennel, celery, parsley, and flaxseed oil. Also, try to increase your calcium intake, and definitely engage in weight-bearing exercises to avoid osteoporosis and maintain your general good health. Last, consider taking 400–800 IU of vitamin E daily to treat hot flashes and to reduce the risk of cardiovascular disease.

MENSTRUAL PAIN ■

Question: "During my menstrual periods, I have a lot of lower back pain and cramps. Should I be playing golf when I am in this condition?"

Answer: Exercise is one of the best relievers of menstrual pain.

Treatment: I recommend analgesics, such as aspirin and acetaminophen for painful periods. If the pain is really bad, consider ibuprofen, mefenamic acid, or naproxen. You might want to start the analgesic a day before the onset of your menstrual period (if you have regular periods) and continue it for a day or a half day after it subsides.

Tip: Keep in mind that many women athletes do extremely well while they are menstruating. It is really a myth to believe that hand-and-eye coordination or the ability to concentrate is significantly reduced. I recommend eating a balanced diet divided into small meals throughout the day and urge you to avoid sugar, salt, and caffeine, all of which can aggravate cramping.

■ MOLES

Question: "I keep getting these moles on my face, arms, legs, and back. I'm worried about their turning into cancer. Also, playing as much golf as I do, I wonder if being in the sun so much is causing the moles that I get?"

Answer: Most moles are harmless growths made up of pigment-producing cells that can appear anywhere. They range in size and shape and are usually in various shades of brown. Moles can often darken, become elevated, and change in size over time. Frequently, they fade into the skin and disappear, or they rise from the skin and fall off. Moles can grow larger, and hair can grow out of them. Don't worry—these changes are harmless.

Another type of growth called an actinic keratosis can appear on your face and head. It looks like a discrete patch of dry skin that doesn't go away. This precancerous growth can be potentially dangerous. People who are out in the sun a lot, such as farmers and golfers, are prone to the development of actinic keratosis.

A type of mole that can become cancerous is a dysplastic nevus. This type often runs in families. Unlike the common circular or oval-shaped mole, it has irregular borders, color variation, and an asymmetric shape, and it is usually wider than a pencil eraser.

Treatment: If you have a mole that could be a dysplastic nevus or if you notice a new growth or sore that doesn't heal, it's best to see your doctor right away. The doctor will take a biopsy of the area to determine if the mole has to be removed. Usually, the entire mole is removed, and a biopsy done to make sure that it is not malignant. An actinic keratosis is often frozen off, a simple process done in a physician's office.

Tip: If you do notice any skin changes, especially those that grow over a period of time, see your doctor to have them examined and possibly removed. Remember that removing skin lesions is the domain of a physician, but responsibility for their prevention belongs to the individual. People who are most susceptible are those with light skin. Wear wide-brimmed hats and use sunblocks with an SPF of 15 or more.

NAIL DISORDERS ■

Question: "My big toenails have turned blue and black. I also noticed that my fingernails, especially on my ungloved hand, crack and split. It bothers me during my swing, and I end up putting Band-Aids on the affected nails. Is there anything I can do with my nail problems?"

Answer: Your nails are a part of the outer layer of your skin, so they are easily damaged. Hangnails and small cuts can result in infection. Frequent exposure to water can cause brittleness, and contact with chemicals in day-to-day activities can cause splitting or breakage. Nail problems are used to diagnose a number of other disorders. For example, split, brittle, and/or bent nails that you describe on your hands could be an allergic reaction to soap, nail polish, or some other substance. Your toenail problems could be the result of athlete's foot, a fungal infection, or they could be caused by narrow, tight shoes. Heart and circulatory problems related to atherosclerosis and such disorders as diabetes, anemia, and bacterial infections are often determined by looking at a person's nails, but ridges, white spots, splitting, and bumps can occur on normal, healthy nails for unknown reasons. Psoriasis often produces small pits on the nails. Chronic liver disease can cause a white area near the bed of the nail. In chronic lung disease, the nails often turn thick and yellow.

Treatment: An infected toenail that is thick and dull-looking should not cause alarm. If you don't like the way the nail looks, you can treat it with an oral antifungal drug, such as griseofulvin (Fulvicin, Grisactin) or ketoconazole (Nizoral). Be warned, an antifungal drug must be taken orally for a year or more because toenails grow at a much slower rate than fingernails and fungus works its way out of toenails slowly. The newer oral agents, such as Lamisil and Diflu-can, are very expensive and require a prescription, but they have a shorter course of therapy and are more effective.

Tip: Because treating nail disorders with medications can be quite costly, it might be prudent to let the nail work its way out of the nail plate on its own. Try reducing the frequency of cutting your toenails, which often causes ingrown toenails.

Some oral antifungals are a godsend for the person with chronic tinea pedis (ringworm) and/or onychomycosis (fungus of the nails). Sometimes, the toenails can be so thick from this infestation that shoes are painful to wear. I can personally attest to the benefits of oral Lamisil. It eliminated a thirty-year fungal infestation in my feet and toes.

■ OSTEOARTHRITIS

Question: "My doctor told me that I have osteoarthritis. What is it, and how will it affect my golf game?"

Answer: Osteoarthritis (OA) is caused by the degeneration of cartilage in the joints. It occurs after age fifty and causes pain and stiffness in the back, knees, feet, and small joints of the hands. OA can be mild or severe. Whatever its nature, it is always improved by motion that is not too repetitive or associated with too much pressure.

Treatment: A lot of professional golfers have osteoarthritis, especially in their backs. The most effective treatment is regular exercise (e.g., walking, swimming, cycling, strength-building exercises, and stretching). Cutting down on activities that strain the joints, such as aerobic dancing, running, football, and basketball, will help. Acetaminophen, ibuprofen, and/or a prescription pain reliever taken before you exercise helps to reduce pain associated with golfing.

Tip: A physical therapist can help you to determine the best exercise program for your pain and stiffness. If you find that your exercise program is causing a lot of pain in a specific joint, switch to another activity that engages different joints. When you play golf, warm up first.

PERIPHERAL VASCULAR DISEASE ■

Question: "My doctor told me I have peripheral vascular disease. Anything I need to do while I play golf?"

Answer: Peripheral vascular disease is diagnosed when the arteries that carry blood to the legs are blocked and pain in the calves, thighs, and/or buttocks occurs with exercise. This combination of symptoms is called claudication, which can be quite serious. All tissues need oxygen-carrying blood, and the pain indicates that your tissues are suffocating. The blockage can be seen on an X-ray called an angiogram or on a Doppler ultrasound. Coronary heart disease often accompanies peripheral vascular disease.

Treatment: When a person has pain in the calves, thighs, and or buttocks, as described above, he or she should see the doctor to rule out arthritis and nerve damage. If arterial blockage is significant enough, surgery might be needed to open up or bypass the blocked artery. Sometimes, medications called peripheral vasodilators are used, though their success is not something to write home to mother about.

If surgery is not yet indicated, you might still be able to walk a golf course but in a limited fashion. This could be one reason to use a golf cart.

Tip: Do not ignore claudication. A medical evaluation of the legs can save them. That being said, limited walking while playing golf is the best way to reduce the pain and extend the amount of time that you can exercise without pain. If you have to use a golf cart part of the time, do so.

■ PROSTATE CANCER

Question: "A good golfing buddy told me that he was recently diagnosed with prostate cancer. Can you fill me in about this dreaded disease and what can be done about it?"

Answer: Unfortunately, prostate cancer is the most common cancer to plague American men and the third major cause of cancer death in males. Annually, 96,000 new cases are reported. Prostate cancer is discovered during a routine prostate examination, which should occur yearly after age fifty. A prostate-specific antigen (PSA) test also should be part of the screening procedure. If it is indicative of a growth, a prostate ultrasound and possibly a biopsy should be done.

Treatment: Because the risk of prostate cancer increases with age, usually after age fifty, early detection is the best insurance policy you can have to improve your chances of successful treatment. This was the case with Arnold Palmer and Jim Colbert. (At the time of my writing this section, Arnold shot a 68 during a senior tour event, only five months after being treated for prostate cancer.) Rectal examination should be a part of your routine physical checkup. When your doctor inserts his gloved finger into your rectum, he is checking the nearby prostate gland for any abnormal changes. Newer tests include ultrasound probes. When cancer is suspected, a biopsy is usually the next procedure. If cancer is detected in its early stages, the disease is usually confined to the prostate gland. Treatment consists of surgical removal of the entire gland and the adjacent lymph nodes or radiation therapy.

Tip: Before making a decision regarding treatment for prostate cancer, I strongly recommend that you go over the pros and cons of each treatment with your doctor. Both approaches, surgery and radiation, offer cures as well as complications (e.g., painful urination, incontinence, and impotence). Finally, please heed my recommendation: All men over the age of fifty should be examined regularly and have their PSA levels monitored closely. The PSA is a tumor-maker blood test designed to measure a specific chemical that often is elevated in the presence of a specific cancer; however, it is not 100 percent accurate and should not be the sole basis for a diagnosis. A high PSA reading might be the result of an enlarged prostate, rather than an indication of cancer.

At this writing, new therapies are being developed for the treatment of advanced prostate cancer. Researchers are using radiation and hormone therapy in innovative ways and are testing the effectiveness of chemotherapy on patients who do not respond to other treatments.

PROSTATE ENLARGEMENT ■

Question: "I frequently get up in the middle of the night needing to urinate, but I can't. What could be the problem?"

Answer: It could be an enlarged prostate gland. Part of the male reproductive system, the prostate gland surrounds a portion of the urethra that carries semen and urine from the body. As you age, the gland affects the urinary tract and causes a number of symptoms. Most likely, your prostate gland will enlarge at some time during your life. The cause can be infection (prostatitis); benign prostatic hypertrophy, a harmless condition; or prostate cancer. If you have prostatitis, an inflammation of the prostate gland caused by bacteria, symptoms might include fever, chills, and pain in the lower back and in the area between the anus and penis. Often, urinating is painful.

Chronic bacterial prostatitis causes persistent urinary tract infections that can cause burning, painful, and frequent urination. Patients also complain of pain in the lower back and in the genital area.

By age fifty, one-half to three-fourths of all men experience symptoms of benign prostatic hypertrophy (BPH), or an enlarged prostate. After puberty, the prostate gland begins to grow. The reason for this is still unknown. As it enlarges, the gland compresses the urethra and blocks the flow of urine. Symptoms include difficulty in urinating, a weak stream, frequent voiding of small amounts, and dribbling after urinating. One key feature to BPH is nocturia, in which a man might get up four or more times a night to urinate. In rare situations, some patients cannot urinate at all, which can lead to kidney complications if a doctor is not seen right away. Other complications can include kidney infections; cystitis; and an excessive accumulation of urine in the bladder, which causes incontinence.

Treatment: Prostatitis is treated with antibiotics, such as Septra or doxycycline. Nonsteroidal anti-inflammatory drugs (NSAIDs), zinc supplements, and diet changes also figure into the treatment. You should avoid fried, fatty, and, especially, spicy foods; caffeine; alcohol; and smoking. These are all irritants. By avoiding them during treatment, you not only enhance your chances of healing, but you might also prevent an acute problem from becoming prolonged or chronic.

Once prostatitis is ruled out, you should consider BPH. Medical treatments are available before surgery becomes an option. Hytrin, Cardura, and Proscar have been effective in reducing the frequency of urination and in promoting better emptying.

The surgical procedure for an enlarged prostate is transurethral resection of the prostate (TURP). A thin, flexible tube with a fiberoptic lens is inserted into the penis to locate the enlarged area of the tissues. A delicate cutting instrument is then inserted through the tube to sever the diseased part of the gland.

Tip: Be assured, TURP doesn't usually interfere with sexual abilities. In a few cases, however, incontinence occurs. I recommend that you ask your doctor for the latest studies on the pros and cons of this procedure. In many instances, living with an enlarged prostate doesn't interfere with normal functioning.

PSORIASIS ■

Question: "As I get older, I've been getting these patches of scaly skin on both my knees. Sometimes, I'll even get a red patch on my forehead. I'm wondering if this is a result of aging?"

Answer: You could have psoriasis, a disease in which the skin overproduces new cells, that is causing the scaly skin on your knees. About four million Americans of all ages have psoriasis. The cause is unknown, although it does run in families. It is definitely not caused by aging. The belief is that something in the process of skin production doesn't turn off even when no new skin is needed, so you end up with thick skin and scales in the affected areas. Some theories hint that a variety of factors, ranging from emotional stress to a streptococcal infection, can bring on an attack of psoriasis. Alcohol can make psoriasis worse.

Psoriasis is not infectious. A small number of people with the disorder are vulnerable to arthritis in the hands and feet. Symptoms include reddened patches, as you described on your forehead, and scaly skin, usually on the scalp, elbows, knees, and lower back. Other areas affected include the groin, genital area, and fingernails. The course is hard to predict. Plaques may suddenly go away, only to return just as suddenly.

Treatment: In mild cases, no treatment is needed. In others, a dermatologist should be seen to determine a treatment plan and medication that will help to control the symptoms. Treatment varies, depending on the patient and severity of the symptoms. Moisturizing creams and lotions can improve the skin's appearance and reduce itching. Often, topical medications containing cortisone, tar, or anthralin are prescribed. Topical tars are often used, along with ultraviolet light and a drug containing psoralen (a constituent of certain plants). This light therapy is carefully administered while the patient, wearing protective glasses, stands in a booth. In very severe cases, certain cancer chemotherapy drugs, such as Folex or Tegison, might be recommended.

Tip: I recommend soaking in warm water for 10–15 minutes and then applying a topical ointment, such as petroleum jelly, to help your skin retain moisture. In some cases, I have had patients respond nicely to light therapy. Patients get time exposure to ultraviolet radiation several times a week for up to eight sessions monthly. Be warned, however, that although you might respond favorably, light therapy can have serious short- and long-term side effects.

■ RESTLESS LEG SYNDROME

Question: "During the night after walking eighteen holes that day, I find that my legs bother me while I'm resting and particularly when I'm trying to sleep. Is this common for senior folks?"

Answer: You might have restless leg syndrome if you feel creeping and crawling sensations that make you jerk or move your legs to get rid of them. Sometimes, cramps and pain occur. If they persist, you usually end up getting out of bed and standing or walking around to get rid of them, which could make it harder for you to get back to sleep.

If your doctor can't come up with the cause, you might need to get a diagnosis from a sleep specialist. Some restless leg syndrome symptoms are the result of peripheral neuropathy, a neurologic condition that often occurs with diabetes. In many cases, an iron deficiency causes symptoms. Occasionally, the symptoms are the result of pregnancy. In your particular case, if the restlessness occurs after walking a round of golf, you might just be having a transient bout of leg muscle spasms.

Treatment: If your restless leg syndrome is the result of diabetic neuropathy, it can be treated with drugs used for epilepsy, although tolerance usually occurs. If the cause is iron deficiency, a nutritional program is often advised.

The drug of choice is clonazepam, which acts to stabilize the conduction of nerve impulses. Another drug that might bring relief is a combination product of carbidopa and levodopa. If all of these treatment approaches fail, sedatives, such as methadone and codeine, may be prescribed with the warning that they can be habit forming.

Tip: For a mild case, I recommend keeping the legs cold or hot at night to provide relief. Sometimes, my patients respond well to soaking their feet in cool water. Don't use ice water, however, because it can cause nerve damage.

SEIZURES ■

Question: "I have been suffering from epilepsy for years. The seizures are fairly well controlled with medications. Is there any risk to me if I golf?"

Answer: The short answer to this is no. Although overexposure to the sun might trigger a seizure, it is unlikely, especially if the seizures are well controlled. The history surrounding a seizure is significant in making the diagnosis. Although only 0.5 percent of the population has epilepsy, 10 percent of people suffer a seizure once in a lifetime but do not actually have epilepsy. A physical examination is helpful to the diagnosis because skin lesions can relate to internal tissue disorders. Laboratory tests are not particularly helpful. Some doctors order computed tomography (CT) or magnetic resonance imaging (MRI) to determine if calcific lesions or brain masses are present, but they are rarely found.

The most informative test is an electroencephalogram (EEG). Because brain wave patterns can identify different types of epilepsy, an EEG helps the doctor to determine which type of antiseizure medication will be most effective.

The mainstay in the diagnosis of epilepsy is a good history. The timing, nature, and characteristics of a seizure are more informative than any study.

Treatment: Depending on the type of epilepsy diagnosed, various antiepileptics are used. For instance, grand mal seizures are initially treated with phenobarbital and/or Dilantin. The initial treatment for petit mal seizures is valproate or clonazepam. Neurologists are not afraid to mix and match, if necessary, to control the seizures.

Some studies show that as many as half of patients who have not had seizures for more than five years are able to stop their medications without suffering subsequent seizures.

Tip: If you have well-diagnosed epilepsy and are controlled on medications, don't worry about it. The diagnosis of epilepsy carries with it legal and social consequences. Make sure that a diagnosis is made with care and deliberation.

■ SKIN CANCER

Question: "I noticed this sore on my face that hasn't healed. It's been there now for more than a week. I've tried all kinds of lotions, and it still doesn't go away. Any suggestions?"

Answer: The incidence of skin cancer is rising and is about three times more common in men than in women. The risk also increases as you get older. Most people diagnosed with skin cancer are between ages forty and sixty. If you have relatives with skin cancer, you are more likely to be susceptible to the disease. Skin cancer is primarily caused by prolonged exposure to the sun's ultraviolet light. (Please note: Sun lamps, tanning booths, and UV-rays can damage skin and cause malignant cells to grow.) Fair-skinned people are most susceptible because they have the least amount of protective skin melanin (dark pigment). Redheads, blue-eyed blonds, and people with pigment disorders, such as albinism, are at greatest risk. Also, people with many freckles or moles—especially those that appear abnormal—are more vulnerable. For decades, the medical profession has been trying to dispel the myth that suntanned skin is a sign of health. The reality is that suntanning increases the risk of developing skin cancer.

The three types of skin cancer can be described as follows:

1. Basal cell carcinoma—The most common form of skin cancer, it begins with a small, shiny nodule, or collection of cells with raised surfaces. In a few months, it enlarges and blood vessels can be noticed on the surface. Crusts might form over the area and/or it might bleed. If left untreated, the area will bleed, crust over, look like it's healing, and then start bleeding again. Basal cell carcinomas usually occur on the face, neck, arms, and hands.

2. Squamous cell carcinoma—This cancer appears as a reddish lump that later starts to look like a wart or, in some cases, an ulcerated area of the skin. If this type of carcinoma is left untreated, the cancer cells can spread to other parts of the body.

3. Malignant melanoma—Although the least common type of skin cancer, it is the most dangerous. If it's not caught before it penetrates into the skin's second layer, the chances of a cure are reduced. If you have any kind of growth or change in moles, see

your doctor. Appearance can be (a) Asymetric; (b) Border irregularity; (c) Color variegation (black, red, blue); or (d) Diameter enlarges with time.

Treatment: Your doctor will take a skin biopsy to check for cancerous cells. Depending on the location and extent of the cancerous skin, the treatment varies. Growths can be scraped away, frozen with liquid nitrogen, or excised. Topical chemotherapy cream is also prescribed to eliminate cancerous or precancerous cells. The good news is that most skin cancer cases can be cured.

Tip: If you are in a high-risk group for skin cancer or have been treated for it before, it's important that you examine the skin all over your body, front and back, every few months. Use a full-length mirror. Check even your mouth, palms, soles, backs of ears, genital area, and area between the buttocks. If you play a lot of golf, I recommend that you schedule tee times very early in the morning and/or very late in the afternoon. The sun's ultraviolet rays are strongest at midday.) If you do play during the day, wear all types of protection, including a full-brimmed hat, long sleeves, trousers, and sunglasses that completely cover both eyes. Definitely use a sunscreen with a sun protection factor (SPF) of 15 or higher whenever you go outside. To play it safe, call your doctor if you have an existing mole that changes in size, shape, color, or texture; if you develop a very noticeable new mole; or if you notice a new skin growth that does not go away or an open sore that does not heal within a few weeks.

■ SKIN RASH (DERMATITIS)

Question: "I get rashes when I take medicine or eat certain foods. I get to the course, and my skin feels like it's on fire. I want to stop playing, sit down, and scratch everywhere. Any tips on what's going on with me?"

Answer: Dermatitis can be one of the most annoying occurrences on the golf course. Although dermatitis refers to skin inflammation, it can also be related to a range of other ailments. In most cases, the early stages of dermatitis are characterized by dry, red, itchy skin, but acute attacks can result in crusty scales or blisters that ooze fluid. A variety of agents can irritate the skin. Your doctor will try to narrow the diagnosis to a specific category of dermatitis, even though the treatment is similar for most types of skin inflammation.

Your skin might be reacting to a medication, or the rash might occur when your skin is exposed to the sun. Sun-associated rashes are called photodermatitis. Many drugs, cosmetics, and skin care products can cause sun-affected rashes. Even disrupted skin resulting from cuts or scars can be the site of severe sunburns. Plastic surgeons warn their patients to stay away from the sun after surgical procedures, sometimes for months, to avoid this possibility.

Other causes of dermatitis are poison ivy, poison oak, and contact with certain flowers, herbs, fruits, and vegetables. Chemical irritants include detergents, soaps, chlorine, certain synthetic fibers, nail polish remover, antiperspirants, formaldehyde (found in permanent press fabrics), polishes, and particleboard. Wearing rubber gloves, unwashed new clothes, or plated jewelry can also cause inflammation. Cosmetics and skin care products are considered to be quite common irritants, whether or not you expose your skin to the sun.

Diagnosis consists of your doctor's observation of the irritation and its location on the body. Sometimes, a skin scraping is taken for microscopic analysis to determine the underlying cause.

Treatment: The first step in treating dermatitis is to identify and eliminate the cause. Most mild skin inflammations respond well to warm baths followed by the application of Vaseline or over-the-counter hydrocortisone cream. Once the irritants that cause the inflammation are identified, treatment is based on avoidance. For severe cases, a prescription corticosteroid cream, along with an oral antihistamine, can help to relieve severe itching. If secondary infection develops, an antibiotic might be prescribed.

Tip: A rash on your face, neck, lips, or hairline could result from the use of certain cosmetics, skin care products, or other toiletries, including perfume, deodorant, antiperspirant, shampoo, toothpaste, mouthwash, and aftershave lotion. Although it's a tedious process, try to eliminate one product at a time to determine if any of them might be causing the skin irritation.

Finally, consider any fruits and vegetables that you eat on the course. Believe it or not, they can cause severe itching and rashes. Exposure to psoralens found in fruits, vegetables, and some perfumes, along with exposure to the sun, can cause a localized rash. Let me give you an example. One of the most confusing skin rashes that I have treated came from a baby's saliva. The rash went from her mouth down her chin. Mom had the same rash where the saliva got on her. There was nothing unusual about them. Mom walked the baby regularly and did her level best to avoid any medicines unless they were absolutely necessary. The baby was healthy and didn't even get ear infections or colds. The only "therapy" Mom used was actually a food snack. Celery has a mild anesthetic quality, and the baby's chewing on it helped to reduce her teething discomfort.

I had never seen a rash like this. Despite various remedies used to get rid of it, the rash persisted. Referral to a dermatologist colleague also brought up a diagnostic goose egg. I then referred Mom and baby to the university dermatology program, where the rash was quickly diagnosed. Celery contains psoralen, and that was the cause of the baby's rash. Once celery was no longer consumed, both mother and daughter fared well.

■ SLEEPING PROBLEMS (APNEA)

Question: "My doctor told me that I might have sleep apnea and wants me to be tested for it. I can't figure out why he told me that.

I feel fine, except I'm tired a lot during the day and my wife complains that I snore quite a bit at night. Can you tell me what sleep apnea is and what can be done for it?"

Answer: Sleep apnea can be dangerous, which could be the reason your doctor ordered testing. It is characterized by a 10–60-second halt in breathing, loud snores, and gasping for air in order to breathe, and it often prevents a good night's sleep. If you have this condition, you can't discover it alone. Symptoms include daytime tiredness and irritability, and, as you pointed out, your partner complains about your snoring. Other symptoms include difficulty in concentrating and depression. Overweight men past age forty are the most likely people to develop sleep apnea. Not only does sleep apnea cause snoring that is irritating to your wife, but it could trigger cardiac arrhythmias or a heart attack because the halts in breathing result in a lack of oxygen.

Treatment: As you mentioned, your doctor will refer you to a sleep center for diagnosis and to determine the cause of the disorder. Treatment can include medication; weight loss; and, if needed, surgery to eliminate any obstruction to your breathing. Sometimes a face mask can be used to provide a constant delivery of air through the nose to prevent breathing cessation.

Tip: I definitely suggest taking your wife's complaints about your snoring seriously and following your doctor's advice regarding tests for sleep apnea. If your doctor recommends a sleep clinic, you might be asked to check in for a few nights so that a variety of tests can be conducted to measure your brain wave patterns, heart and breath rates, body movement, and level of oxygen in your blood.

SLEEPING PROBLEMS (INSOMNIA) ■

Question: "My golfing foursome loves to get to the course at the crack of dawn. I don't mind doing that except when I don't have a good night's sleep. In fact, I have noticed that I get up more often in the middle of the night and can't get back to sleep. Is this natural as you grow older?"

Answer: In my medical practice, patients often tell me about the difficulty they have in falling asleep or staying asleep. Everyone, at some time, experiences a night of restlessness or very little sleep.

Insomnia can be a passing phenomenon as the result of stress from job pressures, arguments, airplane travel, and/or sleeping in a new place. When the anxiety wanes, so does the sleeplessness.

Short-term insomnia can last several weeks. It is usually caused by stressful situations, such as job loss, death of a friend or family member, or a crisis.

Chronic insomnia can go on for months or years. Persistent sleeplessness is often the result of a deeply rooted problem, such as depression, or it can be a symptom of alcohol use, reliance on sleeping pills, shift work, or sleep disorders. Insomnia also can be caused by stimulants, such as caffeine, appetite suppressants, and certain medications.

Treatment: Here's a step-by-step list of things to do to get back to normal sleeping:

1. Schedule times for going to sleep and waking up, and stick with the schedule even if you don't get much sleep. This holds true for weekends. A schedule programs the inner sleep/wake cycles.

2. Don't drink caffeine beverages before going to bed. Also, before bedtime, avoid taking over-the-counter diet pills and decongestants containing stimulants that can interfere with your sleep.

3. Don't go to bed on a full stomach, especially if you have frequent indigestion problems.

4. Don't drink alcohol after you eat dinner.

5. Get into a regular exercise program, but don't do any aerobic exercises just before bedtime.

6. Make a list of the busy day ahead so that you won't toss and turn trying to remember "things to do." Just tell yourself that they're on your list.

7. Avoid taking naps during the day unless they are beneficial for you.

8. Finally, if you're not sleepy when it's time to go to bed, don't go. If you toss and turn once you get into bed, get out of bed and read or do something until you get sleepy. Don't try to fight it.

Tip: If the above suggestions don't work, you might ask your doctor for sleeping pills. They are best used sparingly, however, because it's easy to develop a tolerance to these pills and become dependent on them for sleep. Over-the-counter sleeping aids usually have an antihistamine that can make you drowsy, but some people react to the antihistamine by getting stimulated. There is also the possibility of serious side effects, such as confusion, dizziness, disorientation, double vision, and fatigue.

If at all possible, abstain from alcohol before bedtime. Although it might make you drowsy, alcohol withdrawal while you sleep can interfere with deep sleep and often lead to disturbing dreams.

If you still can't get back to a normal sleeping pattern, you might want to reset your inner clock by moving your bedtime forward three hours each day until you find a time that suits your schedule. This technique is called chronotherapy (time therapy). For example, if you're used to falling asleep at 1 A.M., stay up until 4 A.M. on the first day and sleep your full eight hours. The second day's bedtime would be pushed up three hours to 7 A.M., and you'd sleep your full eight hours. On the third day, bedtime would be 10 A.M. From there, you go to 1 P.M., then 4 P.M., and so on until you arrive at your preferred bedtime, such as 10 P.M.

(I recommend that you use this approach with the help of a specialist, or check with your doctor for the name and address of the nearest sleep laboratory. Also, you can obtain a list of accredited sleep disorder centers by writing to the American Sleep Disorders Association, 604 Second Street S.W., Rochester, MN 55902.)

■ SMOKING

Question: "I know that I smoke too much, and yet it's one thing I look forward to when I play golf. Can you tell me what the risks and hazards are and what I can do to give it up?"

Answer: No book about health would be either complete or appropriate without a detailed discussion on smoking. Like many other people, golfers smoke. It is not rare to see any number of professional golfers on the senior tour smoking. Among the greats who have smoked are Chi Chi Rodriguez, Arnold Palmer, and Jack Nicklaus. And as much as I would like to say otherwise, the games of golf pros who smoke are probably not diminished by their tobacco habits. Golf, like baseball (baseball greats, such as Lou Gehrig, actually appeared in cigarette ads), is not so much a game of strength or even endurance as are many other sports. By contrast, you probably will not find many professional soccer players or runners who smoke because smoking would seriously diminish their chances for success.

Admittedly, smoking does not decrease your ability to hit a long, straight shot or reduce the accuracy of your putt. If you continue to smoke, however, you will cut short your golfing years. Depending on the source, deaths from tobacco are estimated to be 400,000 to 450,000 per year in the United States alone. To put this statement in perspective, these numbers exceed the combined number of deaths related to motor vehicle accidents, suicide, homicide, alcohol, cocaine, heroin, fire, and AIDS. Smoking causes 30 percent of all deaths in the United States.

In addition, smoking contributes to the deaths of 21 percent of those who die from coronary artery disease and 90 percent of those who die from chronic obstructive pulmonary disease (emphysema, chronic bronchitis, and asthma). Smokers with cancer comprise 35 percent of total cancer patients. Lung cancer patients, of course, are in the lead at 90 percent. Smoking is also involved in other cancers of the oral cavity, esophagus, kidney, bladder, and pancreas.

A living smoker is sometimes not much better off. Smokers have a higher incidence of peptic ulcer disease; gastroesophageal reflux; allergies; and respiratory diseases, including perennial rhinitis, bronchitis, and pneumonia. Smoking also complicates the control of diabetes, and it causes skin to age more quickly.

Deaths caused by smoking are increasing among women. The aggressive advertising aimed at women thirty years ago (e.g., "You've come a long way, baby") have dramatically increased their tobacco consumption. As the death rate for male smokers increased by 18 percent during this period, the death rate for female smokers increased by 118 percent! Female smokers have more cervical cancer and osteoporosis. The babies of mothers who smoke suffer from low birth weight, and they enter into menopause more quickly.

Even bystanders are not immune. Some three thousand deaths from lung cancer occurred among "passive" smokers, non-smokers who live with smokers. Children who are passive smokers have more bronchitis, pneumonia, fluid in the ears, and asthma than do children who are not living with smokers. They're also passively addicted to nicotine. Adult smokers have more lung and other cancers and cardiovascular disease. So, is it worth the consequences to enjoy smoking during a round of play?

Treatment: A caring doctor will constantly lecture, plead, beg, reprimand, cajole, reason, argue, scream, rant, and persevere in order to convince you to stop smoking. It's hard for me to understand a person who comes to my office repeatedly with numerous bouts of wheezing, some of which require hospitalization, and yet continues to smoke.

The first step in giving up smoking is to accept that you are addicted. Tobacco is an addictive substance, regardless of what tobacco companies tell you. Former Surgeon General C. Everett Koop said that tobacco addiction is worse than that caused by heroin. He was met with much derision and ridicule for that statement, but he is correct. Try to get off cigarettes during the next week. You will no doubt experience the craving as hunger, irritability, insomnia, anxiety, and abdominal discomforts. The body is rebelling as it tries to return to normal; however, most withdrawal symptoms peak forty-eight hours after you quit smoking and are completely gone in six months.

Smoking cessation drugs and behavior modification appear to be the best ways to quit smoking. I recommend a smoking cessation program that might include a nicotine-based chewing gum or a skin patch to reduce the symptoms of withdrawal. After a month or two, I get my patients off the gum or patch since their intent is to help modify behavior, not to allow a smoker to maintain their nicotine habit.

The makers of a new prescription medication, Zyban, claim that it is more effective than the patch, hypnosis programs, and behavior modification. Recently approved by the Food and Drug Administration, Zyban is an antidepressant formerly known as Wellbutrin and the first nonnicotine antismoking drug. It works in the brain by reducing cravings and the symptoms of tobacco withdrawal. I suggest that you ask your doctor about it and see if it's something you can use.

Tip: It wasn't until the clinical years of medical school that I found the impetus to quit smoking for good. I saw people who had so little lung function that the space between the mouth and the lungs, called dead space because there is no exchange of oxygen in that area, was shortened by putting in a tracheostomy. They would smoke through the tracheostomy between breathing in concentrated oxygen. Kind of makes you struggle for air just thinking about it.

What finally convinced me to quit was my own conflict, which I count as a pivotal cognitive dissonance. I knew all the facts then. How was I going to be able to tell anyone to quit smoking if I continued to do so? It was a turning point in my life and career.

This is what I did. I prepared for more than six months. I knew I was leaving Mexico after that time, and I resolved to have quit at the time I crossed the border. From the moment of resolution to a week before I left, I did not buy another pack for myself. Instead, I bought cigarettes for my smoking friends and bummed off them. They were willing to put up with my annoying behavior because I bought more for them than I consumed. One aversion "benefit" was that each request for a cigarette was met with a scowl, thus reinforcing the negative approach I wanted toward smoking.

The last week, I bought the cheapest cigarettes Mexico could offer. That was a brand called Faros. By way of quality (if such a term can apply to a product that kills people), this was the comparison. Marlboros and Winstons sold for 5 pesos at that time. A reasonable facsimile was a Mexican brand called Commander, which sold for $2\frac{1}{2}$ pesos. Faros cost 80 centavos and consisted mainly of stems and roots. They had the flavor of burning trash. I smoked four times my usual consumption—four packs of Faros—with the intention of doing this for one week and stopping cold turkey, forever. I did not get to the seventh day. By the fourth day, I was so sick of smoking this burning debris that I stopped in disgust. I smoked only once after that. It was on a day when I received some very discouraging news. I was at my father's office and took a cigarette from his secretary. After lighting up and taking a few puffs, a thought occurred to me. Did I want to get beaten twice in one day? I put out the cigarette and never picked up one again. That was in the summer of 1975.

I also offer a simpler, but similar, plan to quit. All you really need is the desire to quit. I don't mean a vague desire that flies away with the wind. Have a bold desire, worthy of a great leader and warrior. Arm yourself. Strengthen your resolve by thinking about the bad things you get with smoking: the nagging cough; the diminished endurance; the frequent colds; the smelly clothes, car, and house; the taste of ten dead mice in the morning; the discolored teeth; the concerned friends and loved ones; and the expense, a thousand bucks a year or more. Think about what you could have: fresh smells wherever you go, an enhanced ability to taste, and a subtle but distinct difference in how you approach the world with optimism and clarity.

Next, set a date to quit. I used six months. That was probably too long, but I wanted it to coincide with leaving Mexico (I have returned many times since without resuming this noxious habit). Make the date an event. Publicizing it can enforce your resolve—perhaps a party or a dinner out to commemorate the event.

From the time of your resolution to the final event of quitting, put the butt of each cigarette you smoke into a jar containing some water. Smell the jar before lighting a new cigarette. You don't have to collect all your cigarettes. Just make sure that you have a hefty supply in the jar and that your last cigarette is in there. Don't diminish your smoking.

A week before the end, quadruple your intake. When you reach the date—QUIT! And don't look back with nostalgia. Remember, this is a demon pursuing you. By using the resolve and concentration that serve you so well on the golf course, you will succeed. Like all great successes, this one will carry over to many areas of your life.

■ STROKE

Question: "A golfing friend was told he had a stroke but didn't even know it. Can you educate me as to the warning signs of stroke?"

Answer: There are four warning signs of a stroke:

1. Sudden weakness or numbness of the face, arm, and leg on one side of the body.

2. Loss of speech, or trouble talking or understanding speech.

3. Dimness or loss of vision, particularly in only one eye.

4. Unexplained dizziness, especially when associated with other neurologic symptoms.

Stroke is the third leading cause of death behind heart attack and cancer. A stroke results when blood vessels to the brain become blocked and rupture. This lack of blood getting to the brain can lead to irreversible damage, not only to the brain but also to the nervous system. If nerve cells in the brain don't get oxygen, they are destroyed and cannot be replaced. The same warning signs of a heart attack (see the section, "Heart Attack (Warning Signs)," in this chapter) apply to a stroke. Immediate treatment is crucial to reduce the possibility of permanent disability.

Most strokes are the result of a blood clot, or cerebral thrombosis, that gets stuck in an artery narrowed by atherosclerosis. Blood flow to the brain is blocked. A clot can also originate in the heart and travel through the arteries until it can't move any farther because of narrowing or blockage. This is called an embolism. High blood pressure can damage small blood vessels and block the blood from passing through the arteries, as well. Stroke can also result from a hemorrhage. This is called an aneurysm, which is a weakened section of a blood vessel that balloons outward.

Seven factors can increase the likelihood of stroke:

1. Age—The rate of incidence in people age fifty-five and older doubles with each upcoming decade.

2. Sex—Men have a 30 percent higher incidence of stroke than women.

3. Race—Blacks have a 60 percent greater risk than whites.

4. Diabetes—When hypertension is also present, the risk for stroke is higher.

5. Prior stroke—The likelihood of subsequent strokes is greater.

6. Heredity—Your risk increases if your family members have a history of stroke.

7. Carotid bruit—This is an abnormal sound made by the blood flowing to the brain through a narrowing in the carotid artery of the neck. It has no outward symptoms.

Treatment: Stroke treatment has changed dramatically in recent years. The goals of treatment are to halt the progression of the stroke and to prevent subsequent strokes. It is now known that all nerve cells in the brain do not die immediately upon being deprived of oxygen and that partial recovery can occur if blood flow can be promptly restored.

Treatment of stroke during the acute phase is focused on maintaining fluids and electrolytes (e.g., sodium, potassium) in the blood, avoiding low blood pressure, and preventing secondary complications and paralysis. A stroke victim also receives heparin, which helps to prevent subsequent strokes.

After the acute phase of a stroke has passed, treatment emphasis is on recovery, rehabilitation, and prevention of another stroke. Therapy is often a combination of drugs, surgery, and a reduction of risk factors, which include high blood pressure, diabetes, smoking, being overweight, high cholesterol, and immoderate alcohol intake.

Be careful about believing all the hoopla about taking aspirin to reduce the risk of stroke. Aspirin might not be appropriate for some people. A person with abnormal blood pressure should not take it to reduce the risk of stroke without first consulting a doctor.

A newer medication called ticlopidine appears to be about 15 percent more effective than aspirin in reducing the risk of those who have had a minor stroke. Its side effects, such as rash, diarrhea, and lowered white cell counts, and its cost, however, should be considered before using it.

An anticoagulant often used is Coumadin (warfarin) when aspirin therapy fails or when the source of the clot is the heart. Coumadin must be carefully monitored, however, because bleeding complications can occur if the dosage is too high. Also, leafy green vegetables, such as spinach and broccoli, and certain medications can alter its effectiveness.

Finally, surgery is used when it is essential to provide a pathway for blood to get to the brain. Studies show that carotid surgery can play a key role in preventing recurrent strokes.

Tip: Rehabilitation should begin as soon as possible after a stroke. Early attention to weak limbs can have a significant effect on recovery. I recommend frequent changing of the patient's position in bed and exercising of paralyzed legs and arms by physical therapists, nurses, or family members to improve circulation and to maintain joint flexibility and muscle tone.

Recovery from a stroke can be a very slow process, and both family and patient should take time to acknowledge improvement. Also, keep in mind that a stroke victim might have some loss of emotional control because of damage to the area of the brain that controls emotions. As a result, the patient can have unusual emotional reactions, such as suddenly crying or laughing. Depression is another common reaction to a stroke. Antidepressant drug therapy can be prescribed. Ultimately, support from family and health professionals is important during these difficult times.

ULCER ■

Question: "I recently was told I have an ulcer. What caused it, and what can I do to keep it from affecting my play?"

Answer: An ulcer results when a small portion of the stomach's lining becomes eroded and inflamed. The raw area causes a burning or gnawing that can certainly affect your concentration during play. The cause is not known. One theory suggests that an ulcer results from bacterial infection caused by *Helicobacter pylori*, which has been associated with stomach and duodenal ulcers in humans. This theory has led some researchers to believe that this bacterium is the cause of the ulcer; an analysis of the evidence has led others to different conclusions, such as *H. pylori* being an opportunistic infection. One observation is that the number of people who have *H. pylori* but no symptoms of ulcer is greater than the number who have both *H. pylori* and symptoms. Nevertheless, treatment with antibiotics tends to eradicate the ulcer more often than other types of treatment. It is also known that ulcer formation is the result of an excessive amount of pepsin and hydrochloric acid, as well as a reduced capacity of the mucous layer of the stomach to resist ulceration.

Symptoms vary with each person. Some people experience pain on an empty stomach, and others have pain after they eat. Most experience symptoms 1–3 hours after eating. Pain can vary from a few minutes to a few hours. Appetite loss, weight loss, and occasional vomiting occur.

Treatment: If the pain in your stomach lasts more than 2 weeks and you don't get any relief from the usual antacids, you need to see your doctor. Treatment often includes eating less irritating foods and eliminating coffee, tea, and alcohol from your daily routine. Tagamet (cimetidine) or Zantac (ranitidine) is prescribed at higher doses than normal to decrease the large amount of acid in your stomach. Tetracycline is also prescribed to combat an *H. pylori* infection.

Tip: Try to watch what you eat prior to a round. In fact, what you eat the night before can make a big difference in how you feel the next day. Try bland, nonspicy foods, and reduce the amount of coffee or tea that you drink. Smoking and alcohol should be avoided, if not eliminated altogether.

Regarding the gastrointestinal tract, many patients choose cimetidine over a good diet. If you're among them, pay attention to the drug's side effects. Cimetidine is among those medications called H_2 receptor antagonists, which inhibit the secretion of gastric acid, thus reducing stomach pain. Although they are the single most significant cause for the dramatic reduction in gastric surgeries, such medications also contribute to headaches, dizziness, decreased white cell counts, joint and muscle pains, rashes, and diarrhea. I suppose that the risk of having these problems is a small price to pay for the joy of eating whatever you want and the thrill of having a high-stress lifestyle. Actually, golfing more and eating properly will significantly diminish the need to take an H_2 receptor antagonist. I'm not so sure that high stress is as exciting as it's cracked up to be. If you have had enough of it, you might want to take cimetidine to reduce stomach pain.

URINARY PROBLEMS ■

Question: "The frequent need I have to go to the bathroom at night also occurs when I play golf. During a round, I'm usually looking for a rest room as much as I spend time looking for my ball. What can I do about this?"

Answer: Kidneys can shrink in size by as much as 10 percent each decade. As a result, the urinary system is usually affected around your forty-fifth birthday. Bladder size decreases, which makes it harder to keep from urinating. Urinary flow decreases, while frequency increases. Nocturia, an excessive need to urinate at night, is normal as you get older. In women, control of the pelvic muscles usually declines after menopause and can contribute to incontinence. In men, the prostate gland enlarges and can impair emptying of the bladder. In some rare cases, however, frequent urination could be a symptom of kidney disease or congestive heart failure. In the case of professional golfer Terry-Jo Myers, it could be the result of suffering from interstitial cystitis, a chronic inflammation of the bladder wall, that forced her to go to the bathroom as often as every 30 minutes. Interstitial cystitis afflicts 450,000 Americans, 90 percent of them women. Diagnosis of this disorder requires a cystoscopic examination.

Treatment: Sometimes, physical activity strengthens the pelvic muscle that helps to control your bladder. Ditropan and Urispas can relax the bladder in order to keep it under control. For interstitial cystitis, the treatment of choice is the drug Elmiron and elimination of acidic, spicy foods.

Tip: For a man with urinary problems, I recommend asking your doctor about the drug Proscar, but remember that many urinary symptoms, such as frequency of urination, are caused by spasm of the bladder muscle and not by an enlarged prostate. Frequency and urgency might not be helped by Proscar, which tends to shrink the prostate but does not affect the bladder muscle.

If a urinary problem is the result of bladder spasm, I recommend Hytrin and Cardura; however, they have side effects. These medications lower blood pressure, which can result in lightheadedness and dizziness. If you're already on high blood pressure medication, your doctor might have to make adjustments in the dosage.

■ VISION LOSS (MACULAR DEGENERATION)

Question: "As I get on in years, I often worry about my vision. My dad lost his sight when he was seventy. I don't see the golf ball like I used to. Are there any eye diseases that I should be aware of?"

Answer: A common loss of vision for folks past fifty years old is macular degeneration. The macula, which is the central part of the retina, loses cells. This causes a reduction in the sharp central vision that we count on for following the flight of a ball. As the disease progresses, there is a loss in the ability to see fine details. You lose visual field in the center but not on the periphery.

Symptoms vary from person to person and include straight lines that look distorted, blurred print, or an empty spot in the center of your vision. The disease affects more women than men. If there is a history of macular degeneration in your family, your risk of getting it is increased.

Treatment: Unfortunately, there is no cure for macular degeneration. Vision aids usually consist of magnifying glasses and large-print books and newspapers. There are two types of macular degeneration. In the first type, the tissues of the macula thin out and irreversible deterioration occurs. The second involves degeneration of the blood vessels behind the retina. If the latter type is detected early enough, laser therapy can halt the deterioration.

Tip: I strongly recommend that you use the following test on a regular basis. Select an object with a straight line, such as the words on this page. Cover one eye, and see if the line is still straight. Then do the same with the other eye. If there seems to be a bent line or if you notice a blank spot, see an ophthalmologist.

VISION PROBLEMS (FLOATERS) ■

Question: "While playing golf, I often see these little balls floating around that make it difficult to follow the flight of my golf ball. Does it mean I'm losing my eyesight, and is there anything I can do about this?"

Answer: You describe floaters, a common concern among golfers. Floaters are small specks that float into your vision field. They consist of tiny clumps of debris cast off from the gelatinous transparent fluid (vitreous body) that fills up the inner part of your eyeball.

When a floater crosses in front of the light-sensitive retina at the back of your eye, a speck of fine line shows up. Floaters are mostly a distraction and not something to worry about. No, you are not losing your eyesight, nor do floaters indicate that you will lose it.

Another concern is a streak of flashing light that appears across your field of vision. These flashes are caused by shrinking vitreous gel pulling against the retina. This happens more often as one gets older.

Treatment: If floaters drift into your field of vision while you are playing golf, you can move the specks out of the way by moving the fluid in your eyes around. You might have a lot of floaters if you have had cataract surgery or are nearsighted.

Some floaters can be eradicated with laser surgery. Vitrectomies are also performed to deal with floaters. This is a procedure in which the vitreous humor, the posterior gelatinous part where the floaters reside, is removed. Because floaters can be associated with diabetes, it is important to screen for this disease.

Tip: See an ophthalmologist right away if you suddenly experience a group of floaters. They might signify a torn retina, which can develop into a detached retina (see the section, "Detached Retina," in this chapter). Also see an ophthalmologist as soon as possible if you suddenly experience spots and flashes.

■ BLURRY VISION

Question: "I abhor glasses, and yet I had my eyes checked and was told I have to correct my vision. I wore my glasses on the course, and I hated it. Yet I need them. What can I do?"

Answer: As one ages, the eyes have a decreasing ability to focus on close objects. This is particularly apparent to those whose arms eventually prove to be too short for reading the newspaper, thereby prompting a reading eyeglass prescription. Eyes undergo decreasing accommodation, which is the ability to focus on various distances. For example, it could be more difficult to read a book if you periodically look up to view the TV screen across the room (and this isn't just the body's subliminal way of telling you to stick with the book and skip the TV program). The reason for the change is found in the eye's lens and connecting muscles—the ciliary bodies—that become stiffer. In later years, the change might prompt a need for surgery to remove cataracts. For many people in their forties, however, it calls only for corrective reading glasses or for tricky-to-master bifocals.

Treatment: Glasses are still inexpensive and effective. They are still the treatment of choice for those who need correction of near and far vision. The latest in surgical care called PRK can refract for one condition per eye. Some people opt to repair one eye for near vision and the other for far.

Tip: Try glasses first.

VOMITING ■

Question: "I was playing golf and, while walking to the tee, I got nauseated and began to throw up. I canceled my round and returned to the clubhouse. After resting, I felt better. What happened?"

Answer: Vomiting can be caused by many things, including viruses, bacteria, food poisoning, motion sickness, alcohol, medications, and even emotional distress. Pregnant women often experience nausea and vomiting, especially during the first trimester.

If the cause is too much eating or drinking, you need not worry. If you continue to vomit, however, there could be a problem in another part of your body. Prolonged vomiting can be caused by appendicitis, cancer, intestinal obstruction, kidney disease, liver disease, brain tumor, or head injury. If vomiting recurs often or is followed by severe stomach pain, or if the vomit contains red blood or dark granules resembling coffee grounds, call your doctor immediately.

Treatment: If you are vomiting, it is probably a good idea to get off the course because the discomfort alone will make for a bad round, that is, unless you are attempting an exercise of mind over matter to reach a higher spiritual plane. That being said, hydration is the most important thing you must do. Hot decaffeinated teas, such as chamomile, peppermint, and anise, are both soothing to the stomach and good sources of fluid.

Often, medication is needed to reduce the vomiting. Although some oral medications can do this, they are often less than perfect because they might come back up. I recommend antiemetic suppositories, such as Compazine and Tigan. If you can keep them in for 10–15 minutes, enough medicine will get to where it is needed.

Tip: As much a pleasure as it is to golf, you are better off to refrain at this time. You need fluids and antiemetics. Above all, you must rest.

EXERCISE 3

Just as we started to write this chapter, an article in the Rocky Mountain News reported both good news and bad news. The good news is that just a modicum of exercise can reduce the risk of heart disease, high blood pressure, diabetes, and even cancer. All that is required is burning an extra 150 calories per day. To put this into perspective, the body uses up about 100 calories while you walk one mile. Imagine the benefits from walking eighteen holes rather than riding in a golf cart. Other ways to burn 150 calories include stair climbing for twenty minutes, bicycling four miles, and jumping rope for fifteen minutes. Thirty minutes of fast dancing works, as does shooting baskets at a modest pace for the same amount of time. Even washing or waxing a car for forty-five to sixty minutes consumes 150 calories. They don't even have to be sustained minutes. Ten minutes at a time will also work.

The bad news is that the proportion of overweight adults and children in the United States (with body mass index more than 27 percent above ideal) rose substantially between 1988 and 1994. Data show that 33 percent of men, 36 percent of women, 12 percent of teens, and 14 percent of children are too heavy. These figures translate into a 3.5 percent increase in six years. The article indicates that 60 percent of Americans do not exercise regularly and 25 percent don't exercise at all.

The relationship between this sedentary activity (a deliberate oxymoron) and disease is evident. The incidence of obesity has risen from less than 25 percent of the population in 1960, when President John F. Kennedy began a national fitness program, to 33 percent today. This increase in obesity contributes to a related increase in illness. At the time of this report, Vice President Al Gore sent a message to the American public: "Take a walk!"

Research demonstrates that as your fitness level rises, your chances for longevity increase. The best health gains were recorded by golfers who moved from a sedentary group to a regular exercise program. Staying fit is also beneficial for your emotional well-being. Exercise boosts your self-esteem, relieves tension and stress, provides enjoyment and fun, and stimulates your mind.

No one can prescribe the perfect fitness plan for you. You have to figure it out based on what you enjoy doing and what you will continue to do. This chapter can help you to decide what works best for you. Whatever you decide to do, consistency is the most important, the most basic, and the most often neglected part of fitness.

If you're like many golfers, you probably don't do any warming up before you begin play. You might consider taking your clubs out of the trunk of your car all the warm-up that you need. The reality is that you're increasing the likelihood of shooting a higher score and increasing the chances of injuring yourself. Consider the strokes you lose on the first few holes because you haven't warmed up. Warming up prior to teeing off enables your body to perform to its full potential. It also enhances your mental acuity, which a lot of us need on the first tee anyway. What warm-up exercises are for you? Read on. Look over the questions and responses to choose the ones that are right for you. Our goals here are to help you lose weight, improve flexibility by helping your muscles work at their optimal length or tension, reduce the risk of injury, reduce emotional stress, and ultimately help you to play better golf.

We highly recommend getting a physical examination before beginning any exercise program. Your doctor can also help you to plan your program according to your health status and goals.

Unfortunately, there is no gold standard for telling you how

WARNING

Consider the following warnings before using any of the exercise recommendations in this chapter:

1. Violent and/or extreme stretching can cause injuries (e.g., damaged joints and bones).

2. If you have a medical condition, such as high blood pressure or heart problems, it is especially important to see your physician before you begin to exercise.

3. Do not overdo it.

4. If you feel any discomfort, stop what you are doing.

---

much physical activity you should engage in after you have been screened. To play it safe, we recommend a screening that evaluates risk factors for coronary artery disease. These risk factors are high blood cholesterol levels, high blood pressure, diabetes, cigarette smoking, obesity, and a sedentary lifestyle. Golfers at risk will have two or more of the above.

As soon as you get the OK from your doctor, we urge you to implement the tips in this chapter. Its underlying theme is that seniors who are physically active have aerobic capacities far greater than those of similarly aged or younger sedentary persons. Moreover, your game will not only be better, but your enjoyment of it will improve too.

AEROBIC EXERCISE ■

Question: "I hear a lot about the benefits of aerobic exercise. Would you define it for me? Is golf an aerobic exercise?"

Answer: An aerobic exercise is one that is strenuously performed, which causes marked temporary increases in respiration and heart rate. It's dependent on your body's capacity to circulate oxygen-rich blood to the muscles. All major organs are involved (e.g., heart, lungs). A fit golfer requires about 25–30 percent of maximal effort when walking the course. (If you are a sedentary person, walking might require 100 percent effort.) In a way, then, golf isn't really an aerobic activity that raises the heart rate to high levels, which is the main factor in making the exercise helpful to the muscle groups. Walking an eighteen-hole golf course, however, can help to control high blood pressure and to lower cholesterol levels. It's also good for weight control because walking a round burns an estimated six hundred to eight hundred calories.

Tips: To benefit from exercise, I subscribe to a program called FIT that scientists have formulated for improving fitness:

F = frequency—how many times you exercise each week
I = intensity—how hard you exercise
T = time—how long each exercise session lasts

I recommend an activity that lasts for 20–30 minutes.

The research suggests that you might have to exercise at an intensity that raises your heart rate to a level where you reach 60–80 percent of your maximal heart rate. *Maximal heart rate* is defined as the highest rate at which your heart can pump safely while you work out.

Keep in mind that some studies suggest that you don't have to complete your exercise session in one shot. Shorter exercise periods that add up to 30 minutes each day will give you the same benefit as a single 30-minute session. Also, recent research shows that the exercise doesn't have to be intense. Raising your heart rate 50 percent is recommended as a starting point for those of you who have led sedentary lives; however, the sooner you can move up to 60 percent of maximal heart rate, the better.

You can easily determine your heart rate. Remember, the goal is to exercise so that you increase your heart rate to 60–80 percent of your maximal heart rate.

After you stop exercising, take your pulse immediately. Use a timer with a second hand to count heartbeats. Place the first two fingers of one hand on the inside of your other wrist near your thumb. Once you locate your pulse, watch the clock. Start counting heartbeats for 15 seconds. Multiply the sum of your count by four to calculate the heart rate that you have reached.

If you are a woman, use the following formulas to determine what your specific maximal and target heart rates.

Maximal heart rate = 220 minus your age

For example, if you are fifty years old:

$$
\begin{array}{r}
220 \\
-50 \text{ (your age)} \\
\hline
170 \text{ is your maximal heart rate}
\end{array}
$$

To determine your target heart rate:

$$
\begin{array}{r}
170 \text{ (maximal heart rate)} \\
\times 60\% \\
\hline
102 \text{ is your target heart rate}
\end{array}
$$

If you are a fifty-year-old man, your predicted maximal heart rate would be 205 minus half your age. For example, at 50 years of age, a man's predicted maximal heart rate would be:

$$205 - 25 = 180$$

The next step is a simple calculation. Just take 80 percent of 180, and you get 144 beats per minute. If your heart rate goes beyond that figure for a minimum of 20 minutes, four times a week, then you are getting an aerobic training effect. Actually, if you get a heart rate of 130 beats for 30 minutes or, say, 150 beats per minute for 10 minutes, four times a week, you are still getting a healthy workout.

ANAEROBIC EXERCISE ■

Question: "A friend told me about anaerobic exercise. I have no idea what it is. What's the difference between anaerobic and aerobic? Is there any advantage to using anaerobic exercise to help my game?"

Answer: An aerobic exercise makes the body use oxygen, which creates energy. An anaerobic exercise gets the body to create energy without using oxygen. The energy comes from chemicals that are released throughout your body. You get aerobic exercise from jogging, treadmills, exercise bikes, and, to some extent, playing golf, whereas anaerobic exercise is derived from resistance exercises, such as lifting weights. Anaerobic exercise works by fatiguing and breaking down some of the muscle and stress bones, which cause them to rebuild and become stronger.

The best results from an anaerobic exercise is one that offers proper resistance and proper movements against resistance. That's one reason to spend a few dollars with a certified training consultant to get the most from all of the resistance equipment on the market today. Resistance equipment includes free weights (i.e., dumbbells and barbells) and weight machines. Some of the exercises that we recommend apply an anaerobic approach.

You're never too old to benefit from anaerobic exercise. In fact, a study shows the muscles and bone density of nursing home patients increased considerably through anaerobic exercises. I suspect that muscles that are toned by using resistance weights correctly will help you to put a few more yards on your drives (see the section, "Longer Drives" in this chapter).

■ ANKLES AND FEET

Question: "My feet hurt me and get sore after I walk a round. My ankles also bother me. I'm wondering if there are exercises to help me reduce the soreness and pain in my ankles and feet?"

Answer: Assuming that you have seen your doctor to rule out other possible causes of your pain, we suggest the following exercises for the ligaments, muscles, and tendons around the ankle and calf:

Exercise 1. Sit in a chair or sit on the ground and move one foot and ankle slowly in a circular motion. Do this in one direction, then the other, until you get tired. Rest and then repeat with the other ankle and foot.

Exercise 2. Again, in a sitting position, draw the letters of the alphabet with one foot but move only the ankle. Do the entire alphabet with each foot daily.

Exercise 3. With your feet flat on the floor and sitting back in a chair, try to slide forward while keeping your heels on the floor. Push down on your knees to help make the move.

Exercise 4. To strengthen the muscles in the foot, sit in a chair and put one foot on a towel. With your heels on the floor, use your toes to pick up the towel, then release. Then use your toes to fold the towel into a heap.

Exercise 5. To strengthen the muscles in both the foot and the ankle, stand on one foot next to a chair and try to keep your balance for 30 seconds or more. Do this with the other foot. Go back and forth between feet several times.

Exercise 6. This is an exercise that we both do. While walking on the course, walk on your heels for 10–20 yards. Play a few more holes, and then do it again.

Exercise 7. To strengthen your calf muscles, raise your heels off the floor while walking in a clockwise circle. Repeat in a counterclockwise circle.

BACK (LOWER) ■

Question: "The pain in my back gets so bad when I practice putting, I have to stop and rest every 10 or 20 minutes. Anything I can do for the pain in my lower back?"

Answer: Assuming that you have seen your doctor to rule out other possible causes of your pain, we suggest the following exercises for the muscles and the joints of the lower back:

Exercise 1. Lie on your back on a firm surface with your legs flat on the floor. Slowly pull one knee in toward your chest with your hands and arms. Hold your leg near your chest, hold for 20 seconds, and then return it to the floor. Repeat several times with each leg. (Avoid straining.)

Exercise 2. Assume the same position as in exercise #1. Pull both knees up toward your chest, hold for 20 seconds, and then return them to the floor. Repeat this exercise six times. (Avoid straining.)

Exercise 3. Lie on your stomach and place your hands, palms down, next to your shoulders. Slowly press up while keeping your pelvis on the floor. (You're trying to create an arch in your lower back.) The object is to go up a little bit more each time until you have fully extended your elbows. For example, your first press up is one fourth, then you return to the resting position. For your next press up, go a little higher, say, one half and then return to your starting position. Repeat several times.

Exercise 4. Syd likes this one. The goal is to assume a position like an angry cat with its back arched. Start by keeping your back flat. Position your hands and legs as though you are standing like a cat, and raise your back repeatedly 10–20 times.

Exercise 5. To help your back, it's important to strengthen your stomach. Do this by lying on your back with your knees bent and your feet flat on the floor. Press your lower back to the floor, and hold it there for a count of 15. Do this 12 times.

Exercise 6. Another way to reduce lower back pain is by doing crunches, which strengthen your stomach. See the section, "Crunches" in this chapter.

Exercise 7. Lie on the floor again, face down with your feet under some immovable object. With your arms by your sides and without straining your neck, lift your head, shoulders, and upper back off the floor, hold, and then return to your resting position. Repeat 12 times.

BACK (UPPER) ■

Question: "I get this terrible soreness and pain in my back around my shoulders whenever I play golf. As a result, I have to restrict my shoulder turn during my backswing and lose a lot of distance off the tee. What can I do to increase my turn and strengthen my back muscles?"

Answer: Assuming that you have seen your doctor to rule out other possible causes of your pain, we suggest the following exercises for the muscles and the joints of the upper back:

Exercise 1. Put your arms straight to your sides, and stand facing in against the corner of a room. Bend your arms up ninety degrees so that your upper arms are parallel to the floor and your lower arms are pointed straight up. Place your hands on the wall, and put one foot and knee in the corner. Once in that position, press your chest into the corner. Then, with your chin tucked in, breathe deeply and hold the posture for 30 seconds. Return to your starting position. Repeat 3 times.

Exercise 2. Roll a bath towel tightly, and wrap some tape around it. Sit on the floor, and place the towel across your shoulders. Then lie down on the floor with the towel acting as a cushion between the floor and your shoulders. You might want to use a pillow to support your head while you do this. Now, breathe in and with each inhalation, let your shoulders press into the floor. Hold in this position for several minutes. Repeat 3 times.

Exercise 3. To strengthen the back muscles, lie face down on the ground with your arms at your sides. Squeeze your shoulder blades together and, as you're doing so, attempt to reach toward your feet with your hands. When you have reached as far as you can, hold that stretched position for 6 seconds and release. Pause and repeat 5 times.

Exercise 4. Again, to strengthen your back muscles, lie face down with your feet under some immovable object. With your arms placed at your sides, lift your head slowly. While lifting your head, allow your shoulders and upper back to lift off the ground. Then return to the starting position. (Be careful you don't put undo pressure on your neck.) Repeat this movement 12 times or so.

■ BEST EXERCISE PROGRAM

Question: "OK, I'm resigned to getting into an exercise program. Which one do I choose? In other words, what's best for me?"

Answer: The best, in our opinion, is one in which there is aerobic activity that increases heart rate (see the section, "Aerobic exercise," in this chapter). A good program also involves warm-up exercises and, if possible, exercises that build muscle. If you hate to exercise, the least you can do for yourself is to walk briskly around the neighborhood a few times a week and choose not to use a power cart at the course.

In terms of exercising to play better golf, you need to involve the muscles of the back, legs, forearms, and stomach.

The secret to the success of any exercise program is simply getting into the habit of doing it. As Sol tells his students, the first secret about making it through medical school is to show up. For them, that means picking up the texts and reading them, going to class, and studying. This easily attainable discipline also applies to an exercise program. If you have never exercised on a regular basis and are just now starting a serious exercise program, it's best to allow yourself attainable goals by limiting the session to 15–20 minutes. Remember, however, that an exercise session must last for more than 20 minutes before it starts to benefit your heart.

Tip: To get started, choose two of the exercises in this chapter and stay with them. Make the first a warm-up exercise and the other an aerobic exercise. Remember, if you do some kind of vigorous exercise, such as jumping rope, you don't need to hop into a pool and swim half a mile on the same day. Instead, go to the warm-up exercises right away and you'll be through for the day. Don't feel compelled to increase the time after a week or even a month. The larger goal is to develop the habit of exercising so that it becomes a part of your daily ritual. If you jump the program into high gear and increase your requirements too soon, you might get up the following day and find every reason to procrastinate. In no time, you'll lose all motivation to work out.

Another common mistake made by beginners is the refusal to "listen" to the body. Once your muscles tell you that they can't do much more, you should listen, continue for a few more seconds, and then stop. Also, don't throw out a training program just because, for some reason, you failed to exercise one day. If you miss a day, make it all the more reason to exercise the next day. Life's vicissitudes will creep in now and then. Accept them. No one is keeping tabs. You won't get into trouble by skipping a workout. You are your own best taskmaster, and you needn't jump on yourself for missing a day. But, remember, once you develop the habit of exercising, you'll find changes in your life that you never could have foreseen.

■ CRUNCHES (ALSO SEE BACK [LOWER])

Question: "I hate to do crunches. What are the advantages? I mean, how can they help my game?"

Answer: If there were only one exercise you wanted to do to help your game, I'd tell you to do crunches. Crunches help to develop more torque during your backswing, which is one way of hitting longer drives. By keeping your abdominal muscles strong, you are also helping to reduce the risk of developing lower back problems.

Briefly, a crunch is a variation of a sit-up, but instead of lifting your back all the way off the floor, you lift only your head and shoulders and keep the small part of your back on the floor. Also, you make this movement with your feet elevated and with your knees and hips flexed. Cross your arms over your chest. Raise your back off the floor as you would during a sit-up, but come up only a few inches. Hold this position for a few seconds, and then return to the floor. To work all of the abdominal muscles, alternate bringing your shoulders toward, but not all the way to, the opposite knees.

Tip: Start doing 10 crunches a day for a week so that you can develop the habit of doing them and not get discouraged. After that, go to 15 and so on until you can do 200 at a sitting. Believe me, 200 crunches take no more than 3 to 5 minutes of your time and do wonders for your abdominal muscles. Many senior professional golfers spend a few minutes before a round in lifting their heads to their elevated knees, back and forth, sometimes doing 300 crunches at a sitting.

Question: "I took a golf lesson, and my teacher told me to curl up my wrists during my backswing. It produced wonders for my ball striking but caused a horrendous pain in my elbow. What can I do to strengthen my elbows and increase the range of motion in them?"

Answer: Assuming that you have seen your doctor to rule out other possible causes of your pain, we suggest the following exercises for muscles surrounding the elbow. (Note: If you have lost motion in your elbow, approach these exercises with caution. That is, if you feel any pain, it is better to stop and let the area heal completely.)

Exercise 1. To increase your elbow's range and motion, put your arm with the affected elbow at your side. Slowly bend your elbow; if necessary, use your other hand to bend it. Hold it in the bent position for 30 seconds or so. Repeat 3–4 times.

Exercise 2. Sit in a chair. Lean forward so that the upper and lower parts of your arm is flat on a table. Lift the lower part of your arm until you have straightened the elbow. Hold in that position for 30 seconds. Repeat 3–4 times.

Exercise 3. To strengthen the biceps surrounding your elbow, stand and hold a weight or other object that's no heavier than 1–2 pounds by your side. Your palm should be facing toward the front. Slowly begin to bend the elbow and move the weight or the other object toward your shoulder, but move only a foot or two forward. Then return to your initial position. One round consists of 12 repetitions; do the exercise for a total of 3–4 rounds with breaks between rounds.

Exercise 4. To strengthen the triceps surrounding the elbow, stand and bend forward, with the affected elbow bent, while holding a light weight (e.g., a hardcover book) in your hand. Slowly straighten the elbow, hold it in a straightened position for 2 seconds, and then return it to a bent position. Repeat this exercise 12 times to complete a round, and do 3–4 rounds with pauses between them.

■ EXERCISE MACHINES

Question: "There are so many different products that help people to exercise at home. Can you review these machines and what they can do for my golf game?"

Answer: Excellent question. I meet so many golfers who spend hundreds of dollars on exercise equipment that does not correctly benefit their games, let alone their health and fitness. Also, many folks don't use their equipment effectively. They often fail to support themselves on treadmill handrails or improperly grip their weight machines. Make sure that you purchase equipment to fit your particular exercise needs.

If you want to improve cardiovascular fitness, a motorized treadmill is recommended. By increasing the incline of the treadmill, you can increase your aerobic exercise activity. In addition, a treadmill helps to improve lower body muscles, but it doesn't do much for muscles in the upper body.

A stationary cycle is a nonimpact exercise machine that works the hamstring muscles. It is an excellent choice for a golfer with back problems.

A cross-country ski simulator offers much the same aerobic and muscle toning benefits that you get from cross-country skiing. You get an excellent workout of your arms and legs, which is crucial for longer drives.

A stair-climbing machine improves cardiovascular fitness and leg muscle strength because you stay on your feet and push down on levers.

Weight machines and home gyms offer a variety of strength-building programs, but so do inexpensive handheld weights. The machines apply resistance through the use of stacks of weight plates, thick rubber bands, flexible rods, hydraulic or pneumatic cylinders, and centrifugal brakes.

Tip: Before you buy an exercise machine, try out one. Better, go to your local club or YMCA and ask to use the type of machine that you're thinking about buying. Also, get help on how to use it correctly. If you feel discomfort during the tryout, switch to another type of machine. You don't want to spend hundreds of dollars for a machine that is not beneficial to your particular needs, so continue to try out machines until you find one that works for you.

Keep in mind that many people buy exercise machines and quickly discard them. If you haven't developed or don't develop a habit of exercising, a machine in your home will not motivate you in that direction. One way that Sol maintains his motivation is by watching television while he exercises. In fact, he catches up on his continuing education classes. Syd motivates himself by watching videotapes of his golf swing. There are dozens of things to do in order to counter the monotony and boredom of exercise.

FITNESS TEST ■

Question: "I seem to have my weight under control, and I walk the golf course where I play every once in a while. So how do I know if I'm fit?"

Answer: Fitness has four components:

1. Aerobic fitness. If you are out of breath after walking to your car, lifting a few items, or cutting the lawn, you might not be as fit as you can be. In other words, fitness can be defined as your capability of utilizing more oxygen or your heart's capacity to pump blood to your muscles.

2. Flexibility. This is your capacity for range of motion during an

activity. If your muscles are too tight or too loose, you can be more prone to injury.

3. Muscle strength. Simply put, muscle strength refers to the number of crunches and push-ups that you can do in 1 minute.

4. Body composition. This is the percentage of muscle to body fat in your body. The standard is 19 percent body fat for men and 22 percent for women. A simple test is the skinfold thickness test. Ask your doctor to recommend a caliper that measures skinfold thickness and show you how to measure your own body fat.

To test your aerobic fitness, take your pulse now for 1 minute and take the same reading a month after you've been in a regular exercise program. Most likely, your resting pulse will drop as your body gets more efficient doing the same amount of work. To take your pulse, find your carotid artery. It's located at the base of your throat and runs up the front of your neck toward the back of your ear. If that is too hard to understand, locate the artery in your wrist and press your fingers on it, just below your thumb. Count the number of times your heart beats during 60 seconds, or count it for 30 seconds and multiply by two.

There are two tests to determine your range of flexibility. For the first test, sit on the floor with your legs extended in front of you. Try to touch your toes without bending your knees. If you can, your flexibility fitness is fine. This is a good test for golfers with low back pain, which is sometimes caused by tightness in the muscles of the lower back.

The second test is for your shoulders. Reach one arm up and back and the other arm down and back. In other words, pretend that you're trying to shake hands with yourself behind your back. If you get your thumbs pretty close to each other, you're doing fine.

You can determine muscle strength by the number of crunches and push-ups that you do in 1 minute. The acceptable standard is thirty crunches for women and thirty-five crunches for men between the ages of thirty and fifty. For people over age fifty, fifteen crunches are fine for women and twenty-two crunches are acceptable for men.

Twenty push-ups for women and twenty-three push-ups for men between the ages of thirty and fifty are excellent. Over age fifty, the acceptable rates are thirteen push-ups for women and sixteen push-ups for men.

Tip: To get into shape, we recommend using the easiest exercises in this chapter and consulting chapter 5 for nutritional information. If you see an exercise program that you can do, by all means give it a try.

FLEXIBILITY AND WEIGHT TRAINING ■

Question: "I'd like to develop an exercise program to strengthen my muscles, but, years ago, I heard that getting into a strength-building program would tighten my muscles and restrict my golf swing."

Answer: Just the opposite is true if you combine a strength-building routine with stretching. You will actually become more flexible. In addition, well-conditioned muscles recover faster and are less likely to be injured. You will not only develop a more consistent golf swing, but you can avoid soreness, aches and pain, and injury.

Use a light warm-up session (e.g., running in place, a brisk walk) before stretching. Consider the use of minimal weights during stretching. You can be the judge of a minimal weight. Just don't overdo it. At the beginning, repeat the stretch 8–10 times. After a week, do an additional 8–10 repetitions, and so on, or make small increases at your own rate. If you don't want to use weights, just apply muscle contractions and hold them longer over time. Remember to do both sides of the body. For example, first stretch the right arm, then the left arm.

Finally, take a look at Gary Player, who probably heard the same things you did when he was younger. Fortunately, he ignored the myth that strength training causes a restricted golf swing. I suspect Gary's success over the years is due to the rigorous exercise program that he has been following since the age of eighteen. He still does eighty-plus push-ups a day and manages at least one aerobic activity before playing golf. (Rumor has it that he lives in the exercise trailer facility that is housed at each tournament. Whatever, it paid off in 1997 when he won the Seniors British Open at the age of sixty-two.)

■ HANDS AND FOREARMS (ALSO SEE WRISTS AND HANDS)

Question: "Is there any benefit from doing exercises that strengthen my hands and forearms? And what are the best exercises? Please, make it simple."

Answer: Your hands and forearms are instrumental in maintaining control of your club throughout your swing. The benefit of exercise for your hands and forearms relates to reducing the risk of injury to your elbow and wrist.

Exercising your hands and forearms is very simple. You merely have to squeeze a rubber ball or use one of those tension-relieving hand huggers that you can buy at a drugstore. Carry the ball or hand hugger with you, and start squeezing whenever you get the chance, even while driving. You'll be surprised at how quickly you can build up strength.

Tip: Spend more time on exercising your weaker hand and forearm. If you're right-handed, exercise your left hand and forearm.

■ HEART ATTACK: FEAR RELATED TO EXERCISE

Question: "I sometimes read about people dying from heart attacks while exercising. My reason for not exercising is the result of what I read. What are the facts about exercise causing a heart attack?"

Answer: Physical activity rarely leads to death. Unfortunately, when someone dies while exercising, the media usually blow the story out of proportion. Let's face it, it's newsworthy because it suggests irony, and most of us are fascinated with irony. Studies demonstrate that in any five-year period, fewer than forty people died while exercising, and those individuals were suffering from congenital heart problems or advanced heart disease. The few basketball players who have died from sudden cardiac arrest during play had cardiomyopathy, or thickened heart walls.

The fact to keep in mind is the risk of heart attack is directly related to your level of physical exertion. So, high levels of physical exertion, where your heart is at maximal capacity, can increase the risk of heart attack.

Tip: I strongly recommend that you engage in moderate exercise, rather than not doing any at all. It will help you to stay healthy and reduce the risk and your fear of having a heart attack. Moderate activities include walking on the golf course and bicycling. You want to make sure, of course, that you know how healthy your heart is. Before you engage in any exercise program, consult your doctor.

HIPS AND PELVIS ■

Question: "I suffer from a lot of hip pain when playing golf. As a result, I have to restrict my hip turn, which, of course, affects how well I swing at the ball. Any exercises to help me increase my hip turn? Any exercises to help me strengthen my hips and pelvis?"

Answer: Assuming that you have seen your doctor to rule out other possible causes of your hip and pelvic pain, we suggest the following exercises for the muscles and tendons of the posterior thigh, groin, and hamstring:

Exercise 1. To increase the range of motion in your hamstring and the back of your thigh, sit on the floor. Stretch out one leg as you bend the other leg and bring the heel close to your groin. Lean forward slowly. The idea is to pretend to put your stomach on the thigh of the leg that's forward. Hold the position for 20 seconds. Reverse leg positions and repeat.

Exercise 2. Use this exercise when you're getting ready to practice or play. Stand on one leg and hold the ankle of the other leg with one hand as you try to bring your foot behind you. While doing this, contract your buttocks as you try to position your knee to face the ground. Hold for 30 seconds or so, and repeat with the other leg.

Exercise 3. For a really simple exercise, lie on your stomach and lay your head on one of your arms. You can hold your head up if that's more comfortable. Raise one leg about 3–8 inches off the ground, hold a few seconds, and then lower it. Repeat 15–20 times for each leg.

■ KNEES

Question: "My knees kill me after playing, especially when I walk. I'm all ears. What can I do?"

Answer: Assuming that you have seen your doctor to rule out other possible causes of your pain, we suggest any of the following exercises for the ligaments surrounding the knee:

Exercise 1. To increase the range of motion of your knee, lie on your back with your feet propped up against a wall. Slowly slide one foot down the side of the wall until you feel a stretch that reaches your knee. Hold each stretch for 1 minute or so. Repeat several times for each knee.

Exercise 2. Sit in a chair with your feet on the floor. Bend forward while keeping your feet flat on the floor, and stay in that position way for 1 minute or so. Then bend back to your original sitting position. Repeat several times.

Exercise 3. To strengthen the area around your knee (quadriceps), lie on your back with your legs completely stretched out. Tighten the muscles by trying to press the back of the knees into the ground. Hold for 10 seconds or so and repeat 10–20 times; this is 1 round. Repeat for 10 rounds, with brief pauses between rounds.

Exercise 4. Another knee-strengthening exercise that can also impact your hamstrings is to sit in a chair with the knees straight. Then lower your legs and push your heels into the floor. Hold for 10 seconds. Repeat several times to complete one round. Try to perform 4–6 rounds with a brief break between each round.

Exercise 5. To strengthen the hamstring area around the knee, hold the back of a chair or place your hand on a wall and stand on one leg. Keep the knee of the leg that is off the ground pointed toward the floor. Bend the knee by taking the heel and pulling it toward your buttocks. Do this 12 times to complete 1 round. With short breaks between rounds, complete 3–4 rounds.

Exercise 6. While standing, spread your feet shoulder-width apart and squat. Keep your heels on the floor and your knees directly over your feet. Hold the squat position for 15 seconds or so, then return to your standing position. Do 10 or so repetitions for one round. Pause, and then repeat the rounds 2 times. Eventually, you might want to perform this exercise on one leg at a time.

LEGS ■

Question: "I heard that Jack Nicklaus has had so much success playing golf because he has strong legs. What can I do to build up strength in my legs?"

Answer: Get out of the cart, and walk. Park your car a distance from where you are going, and walk. Stay out of the elevator, and walk a few flights of stairs. In other words, the easiest and best exercise for strengthening your legs is walking.

If you already walk a lot and still want to build up leg strength, I recommend a jogging program or riding a bike. Running, however, can cause foot, ankle, and knee stress and injuries. Stationary bikes are a good substitute if you don't have a place to ride a regular bike.

Skiers frequently practice what is called the wall sit. It's also a great way to build up leg strength. Place your back against a wall, and position your feet 1–2 feet in front of you. Then slowly lower your buttocks until you get your thighs even with the floor. Once you do, hold that position until you can feel the pressure building in your thighs. Do this a few times a day, and you'll be amazed at the results.

■ LONGER DRIVES

Question: "I bought a new driver and thought it would help me get length off the tee. It didn't. My pro told me that I need to do some exercising to build body strength that can help me with length. Please tell me what I can do to get a few more yards off the tee."

Answer: To get more distance, clubhead speeds at impact must increase. Your legs, hips, arms, and shoulder turn on the backswing are the main factors that determine clubhead speed. Of course, if you have a lighter club, you can increase speed that way, too. The reason that most of us lose distance off the tee as we get older is not being able to swing as quickly with the club as we once did. (Please note: We don't mean swinging fast and throwing your tempo to the wind.)

To increase speed and strength during a golf swing, consider weight training. Because the speed of your clubhead face (assuming you are right-handed) is affected by how quickly you can swing your left arm back to the ball. At the gym, use pulley weights. Hold the pulley rope much like you would hold your club at the top of your backswing. Then pull down like you are swinging at the ball and feel the tension and resistance created by the pulley. Another strengthening technique is to make the same movement with a heavier club. Have your pro put extra weight in one of your old clubs and swing it back slowly until you reach the top of your backswing. At that point, just hold the club there and slowly begin your downswing.

Tip: If you don't want to spend a lot of time on building arm strength, we recommend getting a lighter driver. Did you know that, during his prime, Jack Nicklaus used a driver with a weight of C-9? Most of us have clubs that are too heavy. Check to see if your club is a D-2 or heavier. If it is, get a lighter one.

You might want to change from a stiff shaft to a regular shaft. You might lose a little control at first, but you will eventually get those few extra yards.

Finally, don't overlook technique. If you are not getting most of your weight shifted on your backswing and downswing, your distance off the tee will be affected. That's also the case with movement of your head during your swing. Again, we emphasize a lesson here so that your pro can assess your swing to see if your mechanics are causing the loss of distance.

NECK ■

Question: "Whenever I play, I end up getting a sore neck. Please suggest some exercises that I can do to reduce this soreness."

Answer: Before doing any exercises focused on reducing neck pain or soreness, you would be prudent to have your doctor examine you for any kind of neck injury or neck pain, especially if you are experiencing numbness or tingling in your hands.

The following exercises are designed to treat the muscles and joints in the neck:

Exercise 1. You can do this exercise anywhere, even while you're having breakfast in the clubhouse. To exercise the muscles and joints in the neck, slowly look toward the ceiling and then down toward the floor. Each time you look up or down, try to move your head a little higher and a little lower. Hold each motion for a few seconds and then move your head in the opposite direction.

Exercise 2. You can also do this one in a chair. Instead of looking up and down, turn your head to look as far as you can to the left, then to the right. Each time you do this, try to extend the range a bit more. Hold each stretch for several seconds, then repeat the exercise.

Exercise 3. Again while sitting in a chair, place two fingers on your chin and push it back until you sense tension under the back of your head. Hold for 15 seconds, then repeat 12 times. Variations of this exercise consist of placing a hand on your forehead, on the sides of your head, and/ or in the back of your head and pushing in the opposite direction.

■ SHOULDERS

Question: "My shoulders hurt me after I play. Before I play, they feel stiff and sore. What exercises will help me?"

Answer: Assuming that you have seen your doctor to rule out other possible causes for the pain and soreness, we suggest the following exercises for the muscles and ligaments surrounding the shoulder. (Please note: If you have lost motion in your shoulder, approach these exercises with caution. If you feel any pain, it's better to stop the exercises. Let the area heal completely and/or seek medical attention.)

Exercise 1. To increase range of motion, stand and bend forward. Put one arm on a table or the back of a chair. Hold a book or a light weight in the other hand and let it hang toward the ground. Move your body back and forth to create momentum so that the arm with the weight will swing. Do this for 2 minutes.

Exercise 2. Get on your hands and knees and slowly move back onto your heels. Hold in that stretched position for 1 minute or so, and repeat 6 times.

Exercise 3. While at the course, lie on your back, with both hands holding one of your long irons. With your arms straight out, lower the club backward over your head toward the ground; hold it there for a few seconds; and, with your arms straight, slowly return the club to its original position. Do this again, but lower the club to your right side, hold, then straighten up, and to your left side, hold, then straighten up. Repeat 6 times. (Note: If your buddies think you're crazy, just remember the benefits that you are obtaining to reduce the risk of shoulder pain and injury.)

Exercise 4. With your arms at your sides, lie on the floor face down. Squeeze your shoulder blades together while making a reaching movement toward your heels with your hands. You might want to raise your head while you do this. During the stretch, count to 10, rest, and then repeat. Do this several times with brief pauses in between.

Exercise 5. Establish a modified push-up position. Keep your elbows straight and push up toward the ceiling and then lower your body by bending your elbows. It's best to do this daily by starting with 5–10 push-ups. After a week, increase to 15 push-ups and so on.

Exercise 6. The muscles that make up the rotator cuff in your shoulders can be strengthened in the following way. Stand with a book or a light weight (1–2 pounds) in the hand of the sore shoulder. Slowly raise your arm in front of you. Hold for a few seconds when you reach eye level, then slowly lower your arm to your side. Repeat this at least 12 times with short breaks in between.

■ STRETCHES

Question: "What's the easiest stretching exercise that doesn't take too much time?"

Answer: Stretching helps to maintain your suppleness and reduce the possibility of injury when you do your strength-building exercises. It is important, however, to warm up your muscles and tendons by a little light exercise before you stretch. This ensures maximal benefit and reduces your risk of injuring yourself while stretching. Try jogging in place or walking at a brisk pace. Stretching is where you can be creative. Just acting like a cat stretching for a bowl of milk can be beneficial.

With any stretching exercise, the secret is to do it consistently and regularly. If you set up a time to do it, say in the morning, stick to that time. The benefit will not be apparent right away, but, within a few weeks, you'll start feeling better and looking better.

Consider one of these stretching exercises:

1. A simple stretching exercise is to sit on the floor and hug your knees. Roll yourself back until your toes are behind your head, then roll forward to the starting position. Repeat 6 times. The purpose of this stretch is to loosen the muscles around the spine.

2. Syd's favorite, which he uses every day, is what he calls the "Syd Harriet crunch." He named it after himself because he cheats on it a little, but it gets the job done. The best part is that it takes no more than 15 minutes. Lying on your back, put your hands behind your head and bend your knees so that your legs make two arches. Push your head toward your knees, and keep it there for 3 seconds before returning to your original position. You have to do this exercise regularly to get results. Syd started with 10 per day. After a month, he extended the number to 20. He's now doing 200 daily and feeling great. Syd boasts that his flat stomach is the result of this exercise.

3. If you wake up late and don't have time to exercise or stretch, a simple movement during play can loosen you up. Take any club and reach a position during your swing. Then abruptly stop and pose. Once there—say you've stopped at the top of your swing—stay in position and try gently stretching your large and small muscle groups.

TREADMILL TEST ■

Question: "All my buddies are telling me since I reached fifty that I should get a treadmill test. What is it, and what will it tell me?"

Answer: If you are age fifty or older and have more than one of the risk factors related to coronary artery disease—high blood cholesterol levels, high blood pressure, diabetes, cigarette smoking, obesity, sedentary lifestyle—or if you experience chest pain or discomfort, shortness of breath with mild exertion, dizziness or fainting, swelling of the ankles, skipped heartbeats, or leg pain with walking, it's a good idea to get a Bruce Protocol Stress Test (an exercise stress test). The test consists of walking on a treadmill at increasingly higher levels of exertion as your heart rate and blood pressure are continually monitored.

Exercise stress test results indicate that people who have electrocardiographic abnormalities during the test are more likely to have heart disease or heart attacks during the next few years. It's a bit more sensitive way to indicate heart disease than the standard electrocardiogram. The test is also useful to determine your exercise endurance level. Low endurance can suggest other chronic diseases, such as cancer, obesity, and diabetes.

Keep in mind that the test is not foolproof. Sometimes, it erroneously suggests heart disease by giving a false-positive reading or indicates that a person does not have heart disease when, it fact, he or she does have it by giving a false-negative reading. A false-positive test can generate a lot of worry and lead to expensive follow-up testing and unnecessary drug therapy. With a false-negative reading, necessary treatment for undetected abnormalities is either not given at all or not given soon enough to prevent or forestall serious disease.

Tip: The American College of Cardiology, the American Heart Association, and the American College of Sports Medicine advise healthy individuals not to engage in stress test screenings, which are time-consuming and expensive.

We also recommend that you don't need the test if you engage in moderate exercise and have none of the risks and symptoms described above. If you do have any of these risks or symptoms and/ or have a chronic disease, it's a good idea to have the test. Also, if you plan on a vigorous exercise program, we recommend the test even if you are apparently healthy.

■ WARM-UP

Question: "When I get out of my car, I'm as stiff as a board. Because I don't have time before I play to warm up, I usually get into the flow after I've played a few holes. What can I do to get rid of that tightness I feel before I tee off?"

Answer: The tightness you describe is caused by restricted tissue around the joints. All of us have a tendency to be stiff in the flexors and extensors of our legs and hips.

Correct warm-up before stretching helps you to avoid injury and pain. Muscles and surrounding tissue shorten with time unless they are stretched on a regular basis. If you don't stretch those parts of the body involved in the golf swing, you will lose full range of motion as you get older. The tight feeling that you describe will force you to hurry your swing because of the short turn. Obviously, this will cause you to mis-hit. Stretching only before you play is not going to do it either. The treatment of choice is daily stretching so that you keep all of the major muscle groups loose.

Tip: Just swinging a club is not a proper warm-up. This is a myth. You are loosening up a lot of muscle groups, but it's taking too much time during a round to get the maximal benefit and you are not giving your back the warm-up that it needs.

If you do want to exercise with a club, try the following. Take any club and position it on the ground at twelve o'clock. Lift and hold it at eye level for 10–15 seconds, and then slowly lower it to two o'clock, then four o'clock. Return to twelve o'clock, and go counterclockwise. Getting a friend to hold the club while you pull on it at different clock positions also helps to loosen muscle groups.

The point here is that you want to stretch your body into as many different positions as you can. Syd's favorite is taking a posture and freezing on it. For example, he likes to bend forward as though he's bowling and hold that position. Or, he pretends he just kicked a field goal and holds his leg in the air. (Of course, taking either of these postures might make you look a bit silly.) Whatever you decide to do, make sure that you stretch lightly and hold your position. Finally, if none of these tips seem right for you, we strongly recommend that you park the car as far from the club-house as you can so that you can benefit from the extra walk. Also, if you are going to hit practice balls, walk to the farthest section of the driving range and carry your bucket of balls at eye level in front of you.

■ WRISTS AND HANDS (ALSO SEE HANDS AND FOREARMS)

Question: "My wrists get sore after I practice putting and especially after I hit a bucket of balls. What can I do to strengthen my wrists and hands so that I can get rid of the soreness?"

Answer: Assuming that you have seen your doctor to rule out other possible causes for the pain and soreness (e.g., carpal tunnel syndrome), we suggest the following exercises for ligaments and tendons of the wrists. (Please note: If you have lost motion in your wrists, approach these exercises with caution. If you feel any pain, it is better to stop exercising and let the area heal completely and/ or seek medical attention.)

Exercise 1. Put your forearm with the sore wrist on a table so that your hand is hanging over the edge. Keep your wrist relaxed, and then flex it by tightening the muscle. Keep the hand stretched for a minute, and then repeat the exercise 2–3 times.

Exercise 2. Place your sore wrist flat on a table, palm down. With the wrist flat, gently pull on the thumb and the little finger toward your elbow with your other hand. Hold the stretched position for a minute, then repeat several times.

Exercise 3. Sit down with your sore wrist at your side and your elbow bent to 90 degrees. Turn your palm toward the floor with your other hand. Hold the stretched position for a minute, then repeat 3 times. Repeat the exercise with your palm turned toward the ceiling.

Exercise 4. To increase the range of motion in your fist and hand, make a clenched fist. Hold it for 1 minute, then release. Repeat several times.

Exercise 5. To strengthen the wrist and fingers, hold a tennis ball or anything that's small. Grip and squeeze, count to 10, then repeat. Sol squeezes a little rubber ball whenever he gets the chance. Also, drugstores and golf shops sell little colored bags filled with a firm substance that you can squeeze.

Exercise 6. To strengthen the wrist and forearm, sit at a table and hold a light weight in your hand. Rest your wrist on the table with your hand off the edge. Slowly raise and lower the weight by curling your wrist up and down. Repeat this exercise 12 times at one sitting with short breaks in between.

4 Psychology

As people age, they often tend to become preoccupied with physical problems, but these are scarcely their only concerns. Their cognitive functions go through tremendous changes. For example, short-term memory declines; the ability to learn oral material decreases; they make more errors in verbal learning; and visual memory, measured by the ability to reproduce geometric designs from recollection, declines slightly between ages fifty and sixty and drops off greatly after about age seventy. But the good news is that performance in mental tasks does not decline. Yet, most golfers of all ages share a nearly uncontrollable affliction of living in the past. To recall how they think they played golf at age twenty and lamentingly compare it to the way they play now can seriously diminish appreciation of the game. My favorite advice to aging golfers pining about lost youth is: "When is old?" Miller Barber and Arnold Palmer obviously don't swing the way they did during their prime years, but who would conclude that they're too old to play well and—more important—enjoy the game?

To the reader of this book, I must point out that the book won't help you to twist your body on the backswing the way you could at age twenty. It won't put you in position to stay out late, have a few drinks, catch an early tee time and play a brisk thirty-six holes the next day prior to another evening party. The truth is that a lot of people couldn't—or didn't—do that at twenty, either. Just as physical exercising can have significant positive effects by giving the body a semblance of youth (e.g., increased energy, more flexibility, added strength), mental exercise and concentration can keep you young at heart and in spirit.

The initial step in any mental conditioning program is to realize that golf takes just one minute and thirteen seconds to play. The rest of the time invested in the game is mental—what the golfer thinks about before and after hitting the ball. A little-known fact is that a lot of mental toughening is done not during the round but before the golf game—long before, for that matter. In fact, all of the suggestions that I make in answer to the questions that follow should be discarded while playing. A contradiction? Not to worry— I'll explain and also demonstrate how to do this. For now, keep in mind the infamous cliché: Analysis creates paralysis.

ACCENTUATE THE POSITIVE ■

Question: "I read somewhere that Jack Nicklaus believed that 90 percent of golf is mental. He claimed that your attitude had a tremendous impact on the outcome of your performance. Any truth to that for a senior like me who shoots in the 90s?"

Answer: You bet. Mental attitude can make a difference in terms of getting the maximum performance out of your game regardless of your handicap. I calculated that, during a round of golf, eighteen thousand thoughts rush in and out of the average brain. Most of these thoughts are negative and accentuated by "should" statements: "I should have kept my head still." "I should have aimed more to the left." "Should" statements are negative because there is nothing you can do about them. All they do is put you down with the false belief that they will help you to change your approach on the next shot. You can react to them angrily and let them fester while you walk to your next shot, or you can recognize what you did wrong, see that you are "should-ing" on yourself, and then let the thoughts go. Unfortunately, most golfers allow their negative emotions to continue. By doing that, they fuel the tension in the body with other negative emotions, such as disgust, worry, and fear.

Because you will be dealing with these thousands of negative thoughts during a round, the secret is to recognize that it is your choice as to how you handle them that will impact your performance. Dismissing negative thoughts allows you to approach the next swing in a more peaceful state of mind.

Tip: Think of a negative thought as a thought and nothing more. It will have no impact on your play unless you keep it going. In other words, the more you scold yourself with "should" statements, the longer the emotion will remain. If you recognize that you have control of how long you hold onto a negative thought, you can choose to let it go.

■ ACCEPT LIMITATIONS

Question: "I love playing golf, but I don't like my swing. I've tried everything to get rid of this terrible loop that occurs when I start my downswing. I can't. Every time I play, I'm always thinking about it and it takes a little away from my enjoyment. Any advice?"

Answer: Most golfers are programmed to believe that they can be perfect wives, husbands, fathers, sisters, brothers, employees, or employers—and golfers. If any imperfection sneaks into their self-images, they are programmed to eradicate it at all costs. The truth is, every golfer is probably plagued with some aspect of the game that is seen as flawed.

For golfers who are middle-aged and beyond, it's crucial to start accepting every bone in your body and what these bones can do on the course. If you feel nervous, accept your nervousness; it will allow you to be more self-accepting. If you can't get rid of that so-called terrible loop, accept it and be more compassionate toward yourself. By doing that, you allow yourself to enjoy all the other wonderful things about playing (see the section, "Why We Play Golf," in this chapter). Acceptance is the best way to move and grow beyond negative thinking. After a while, the loop will fail to have its control over you and you can play and loop all you want. Ironically, you will then be free to observe and enjoy parts of your game that are special but that you didn't make the time to see previously because you were so busy putting yourself down.

Tip: If you have a swing flaw that can't be fixed after trying everything, say to yourself, "What the heck. I may not have a perfect swing, but so what. I'm playing this game for the bigger picture, to enjoy the moment, to be with my golfing buddies, to derive pleasure from an occasional birdie, and so forth."

ALCOHOL ABUSE ■

Question: "My friends tell me I have a drinking problem. I don't think they're right. I drink socially and could do without drinking. So how do you know if your drinking is a problem?"

Answer: There are more than eighteen million alcoholics in this country, and I suspect that many are not aware of being alcoholics. Alcoholism is often called the disease of denial because alcoholics strongly believe their drinking is not out of control. Although there is no definitive definition of alcoholism or criteria to make a diagnosis, four stages are used in determining the severity of a person's drinking problem.

1. When one's drinking interferes with work, health, one's social functioning, and family life, it is called problem drinking. The drinking has become the source of such negative situations as problems at home, missed workdays, and problems with the law.

2. A problem drinker becomes an alcohol abuser when daily consumption consists of large quantities, with occasional periods of

not drinking. Sobriety is often followed by heavy drinking sprees that might last for months.

3. Alcohol dependency occurs when the abuser develops an increasing tolerance for larger amounts. Eventually, this leads to medical complications, such as problems with the liver, stomach, and heart. Neurologic and psychiatric changes, including loss of control and personality changes, also can occur.

4. The fourth stage is characterized by poor physical health, impaired thinking, and a complete loss of control over one's drinking. Without help at this stage, the alcoholic has a greater risk of premature death. Reports indicate that more than one hundred thousand Americans die each year as a result of alcohol abuse.

Symptoms of alcohol abuse include temporary blackouts, memory loss, recurring arguments or fights with family and/or friends, and the use of alcohol as a way to relax, lift one's mood, get to sleep, and cope with problems of everyday living. Physical symptoms include headache, anxiety, insomnia, and nausea when the drinking stops. Flushed skin and broken capillaries on the face, trembling hands, chronic diarrhea, and drinking alone, especially in the mornings or in secret, indicate that the abuse has become chronic.

Treatment: Numerous treatment programs exist, but unfortunately there is no known cure for the disease. The most effective way to treat related social, physical, and emotional problems is to stop drinking.

Treatment programs for alcoholism combine a variety of techniques focusing on behavior therapies that help the alcoholic to learn how to deal with situations that create stress and anxiety. They also stress ways of staying sober. Some programs also offer a variety of psychological treatments, such as individual counseling, group therapy, marital and family therapy, and psychologic intervention in conjunction with the drug Antabuse.

Organized treatment programs, such as Alcoholics Anonymous (AA), are also available. Reportedly, more than half of the alcoholics who complete an AA program stay sober; however, recent studies contradict these statistics and propose that relapse is much greater than had been previously reported.

Tip: The problem of alcohol touches home because I lost a dear friend who couldn't control his drinking. The only recommendation that I can make is to take the first step—accept the fact that you have a problem and become committed to overcoming it. Motivation is crucial in any treatment program for alcohol abuse because recovery is often difficult to maintain. The literature suggests that continued therapy, motivation, and social support often can prevent a recovering alcoholic from returning to drink. Also, relapse can be prevented by changing routines, accepting a new set of values, and avoiding activities or people where drinking is involved.

Let me offer you Syd's acid test:

- If you're not sure whether you have a problem, ask a family member or a close friend if you drink too much. If that person says you do, you might have a problem.
- If you don't believe the person, ask yourself if it's hard to stop drinking after you have had a couple. If it is, you have a drinking problem.
- If you can't remember what you did during a drinking escapade, you have a problem.
- If you get into fights when you're drunk, you have a problem.
- Finally, if you've been arrested for driving under the influence or have been hospitalized because of your drinking, you are definitely at risk and have a severe problem. Get help.

ANGER: FIVE STEPS TO CONTROL ■

Question: "Anything I can do without a therapist that will help me control what I say to myself so that I don't get so mad?"

Answer: The most exciting approach to dealing with anger that I use with most of my clients is a concept called rational emotive therapy (RET). RET is based on the premise that what you are feeling is caused by what you are telling yourself. And what you're telling yourself is usually something that isn't true, is irrational, or is based on a myth.

To move beyond your anger, you simply dispute these irrational beliefs. Again, the premise behind this method is to change how you feel by changing what you think.

The following five steps can help you to gain control of anger that doesn't let up:

1. Recognize what that little voice inside your head is saying to you when you feel anger. For example, a senior golfer, whose foursome had played every Monday for years, screamed at all of his partners one morning when they showed up late, which resulted in a missed tee-off time. Later, he became depressed about this temper problem that he's had for years. In therapy, he learned to recognize that, right after raging away, he would tell himself, "I'm a terrible person for not being able to control my temper." He learned to become aware of that kind of self-talk.

2. Dispute or challenge the self-talk by focusing on alternative evidence. The senior golfer learned to say to himself that when he gets angry at his buddies the next time, he will sympathetically listen to their explanations for showing up late (He objectively gathers evidence to contradict his belief that he is a terrible person for raging about his buddies' lateness.)

3. Make additional explanations and use them to dispute the self-talk. The senior golfer taught himself the following self-talk: "Sometimes I get angry at my buddies for showing up late. That's okay, it doesn't mean that I am a terrible person. More so, it's best to listen sympathetically to why they were late. They could have a reason. Even if they don't, they're human and it's

so much easier to forgive them. They win. I win." By rationally observing himself this way, he does not attack himself by thinking that he is a terrible person. He learns to interrupt or dispute the belief that he is terrible by changing what he thinks to a different explanation: "So I get mad. It's illogical to say to myself I am terrible because I get angry. It's okay to get angry, and when I do, I try to give my buddies the chance to tell me why they were late. Even if they have no excuse, they're my buddies. I'll forgive the old rascals. Hell, they're only human."

4. Stop the flow of negative thoughts. Or, stop ruminating. Rumination, particularly if you are thinking about how you have to birdie the next hole to win, will make the situation only worse. As I've been stressing all along, in order to do your best, you should not set yourself up like that. In other words, it's crucial to control what you think and when you think it. So the senior golfer might remain mad at his friends for showing up late, but he decides to forget it for the time being and enjoy the round with them. In the clubhouse after the match, when everyone is having a good time, he decides to use a very calm voice to bring up his disappointment. His partners are then less likely to become defensive.

5. Question the anger-generating beliefs that dictate so much of what you end up doing. For example:

   ■ I can't and won't play golf anymore without shooting in the low 80s.
   ■ Unless I hit solid drives and make 3-foot putts like I used to, I'm no good at this game.
   ■ Unless my buddies like my jokes, I'm no good to them.
   ■ There must be a way to play golf the way I used to. I've got to find out how, or I'm giving up this game.

   That kind of self-talk is a sure way to end up getting upset. If you choose to live by those beliefs—as so many senior golfers do—your life will be filled with a great deal of anger. You can, however, choose self-talk based on more reasonable and forgiving hypotheses to live by. For example:

- Shooting in the low 80s is great, but let's face it. That's rare for most people at any age. If I don't shoot in the low 80s, I don't. I had fun just being out there.
- Success is doing my best even if that means hooked drives, erratic putting, and so on. Success is leaving the course after having had the chance to embrace several hours plugged into the present.
- If my buddies don't like my jokes or who I am, such is life. The fact remains, only half the people I know or meet will like me regardless of how wonderful I might be. Anyway, if they don't like me for whatever reason, it's their loss.
- Things change. My game changes. Life consists of learning how to live with change. Ah, so I don't play like I used to. Now I can learn how to surrender to that reality. Let's see if I can find other reasons to enjoy the game.

Again, the skill of getting out of your anger state is to dispute some of those habitual negative-thinking patterns that can so easily creep into your thoughts. Remember: They are not facts but beliefs, which are often false and inaccurate. By grabbing onto the little defense attorney you have inside and using your ability to argue against so-called unimpeachable beliefs, you are on the road to gaining control of that feeling of emptiness. The more you do this, the better you become at disputing all those energy-eating beliefs that rob your golf game of its wonder and ultimate purpose: living every moment to the hilt.

■ ANGER (ON AND OFF THE COURSE)

Question: "I usually find that when I get upset after hitting a bad shot, I come back and hit a good one. Is there such a thing that anger can help your golf game?"

Answer: Perhaps you are an exception to the rule. Granted, getting upset with your game can provide a healthy impetus for improving your swing through more practice, lessons, and so forth. Often, however, anger that you can't "shake" will prevent effective action.

Anger that lingers will immobilize you in two ways: (1) The anger will keep you from thinking clearly. (2) Intense anger will lead to an urge to act, to do something—anything—to make the problem go away. Because you're not thinking clearly, the resulting action might cause more trouble and thus more anger. Expressing anger by tossing clubs will cause additional problems, not the least of which is the possible loss of equipment. Imagine the compounded anger were a golfer to break or lose, say, a 3-wood early in a game. Think of Paul Azinger at the 1996 British Open. Although he's a great player and a former Grand Slam tournament winner, "Zinger," like many golfers, couldn't control his emotions when he broke his putter. The result was having to putt the remaining holes with the blade of his sand wedge. During every putt, Azinger and people throughout the world saw the consequences of unbridled anger.

There is another drawback about anger and rage. When you stay upset about a missed hit or some other problem, such as a verbal slight or a wrong inflicted long ago, you forfeit any chance of getting into a golfing zone and jeopardize your ability to have an enjoyable round. Just as important, if not more so, is the fact that anger allowed to "eat" at you can cause a number of physiological problems.

Again, remember that physiological anger, regardless of the source, courses through the body for no more than three seconds. Thinking about the source of your anger is what keeps it alive and festering for days, weeks, or even longer.

Emotional well-being can be achieved through rational emotive therapy (RET (see the section, "Anger: Five Steps to Control," in this chapter). One myth in our society is that emotions have lives of their own. Other people make us angry. Say that a careless driver makes you angry. What happens? You feel forced to get the other driver's attention by driving recklessly yourself. Or, say that a partner audibly chewing gum while you try to putt makes you angry. This seems obviously true, but it is false. Other people don't make us angry. Careless drivers don't upset us, and golfing partners smacking gum don't fuel our rage. Consider the following activating events and their consequences:

Activating Event	Consequence
Bee sting	Physical pain
Hooked drive out of bounds	Anger
Missed putt and loss of match	Rage

If you believe that emotions occur as the result of cause and effect, then you certainly can believe that you have little control over how you feel. The causal relationship between physical pain and emotional discomfort isn't as great as it seems. Doctor Albert Ellis, who conceived RET, argues that the events (hooked drives, missed putts) do not cause you to become upset, but rather the beliefs that you hold about the events are the cause of your anger. In other words: *What you are telling yourself* when someone drives recklessly or when your partner chews gum loudly is what generates the anger, not the event itself.

Ellis tells a wonderful tale that makes this point:

Imagine yourself walking past the home of a close friend and that friend opening the door and suddenly screaming the most intimate things that you had disclosed to him—matters that he had promised to keep confidential. There's no question that your immediate response could be a number of feelings: hurt, disappointment, betrayal, definitely anger, and perhaps rage.

Now, run this same scene again, but this time, instead of walking past the house, you're walking by a mental institution when your friend screams the same intimate things that he did the first time. Most likely, your reaction will be quite different; instead of anger or rage, you will feel sadness or pity. Why is this? Inasmuch as the same words have been screamed by the same person, nothing has externally changed from the first situation to the second. But internally the change that makes the difference is what you are telling yourself about the event. The reason for two entirely different emotional responses has to do with what we call "erroneous self-talk." In the first instance, you probably were saying to yourself: "How dare he disclose what he said he would keep confidential? He has no right to say those things." But, in the second situation, you were probably saying to yourself: "Poor old Bill doesn't know what he's saying. Too bad Bill's emotionally ill." The point, then, is that what you say to yourself about the situation, rather than the situation itself, causes the emotional reaction that you have.

So the external details of missed putts, hooked drives, noisy conditions, bad weather, slow play, and so forth are all events that are unconnected to you unless you erroneously interpret them by what you say to yourself. Once you think something negative, such as, "He should know better than to chew gum while I putt," the emotional paralysis kicks in. You become upset not by your playing partner's gum chewing, but by what you are telling yourself about it.

The following is a more accurate approach to determine how emotions are triggered:

Activating Event	Thought or Belief	Consequences
Friend chewing gum.	He should be more considerate.	Anger.
Friend chewing gum.	He must not be aware of it.	Understanding = nonanger or less upset

So here it is in a nutshell: The key to understanding, controlling, and ultimately changing feelings on and off the course lies in what you are saying to yourself. The trick is to get in touch with the little voice in your head that speaks to you nonstop throughout all of the events that you encounter daily.

Tip: Take a second and try this: Listen to what your voice is saying to you right now. You might even react to what you just read by saying, "What is this shrink talking about?" That, friend, was your little voice. It talks to you as you read; while you drive; while you sit and talk with someone; and, especially for our purposes on the golf course, before, during, and after every shot. Golfers have countless thoughts, and most of them can cause irrational responses that turn a fun adventure into a sickening and heart-wrenching event. Learn to recognize this little voice that coughs up negative, erroneous commentary. It's that buzzing away in your head that's hazardous to your emotional well-being.

You can feel worse, then, after accepting irrational self-talk, which is based on false beliefs. Irrational beliefs, in turn, lead to illogical conclusions, which cause physical and emotional immobility. Think of that little voice again. You hook the tee shot out of bounds. The little voice says, "That's really awful." But "really awful" is an illogical conclusion that can take such an emotional toll as to paralyze your play.

Maybe your little voice is now saying, "Where is he going with this?" But stay with me. Consider the fact that golfers are notorious for self–put-downs: vulture attacks on themselves. Perhaps this is a face-saving measure, although many golfers chastise themselves for mis-hits even when there's nobody else around. And, to some degree, all golfers verbally beat up themselves and sometimes even refer to themselves in the third person. But, hey, let's call time out here. Let's apply some perspective. Did golfers genuinely intend to go out to the golf course just so they can curse at themselves? If so, then why don't they save the greens fee and spend the afternoon standing in front of a mirror screaming "idiot" at the person staring back? If self-abuse is what they're trying to accomplish, then the mirror-image confrontation certainly would be a lot cheaper and easier. Obviously, however, nobody in his or her proverbial right mind would do such a thing. Then why beat yourself up just because you mis-hit a ball at a golf course?

The trick is to learn how to counter the little voice when it starts to beat up on you. Using rational self-talk will minimize, perhaps even eliminate, self–put-downs which are often caused by the following myths.

The Myth of Perfectionism: Much of the self-loathing experienced on a golf course stems from the utterly irrational belief that, to be a worthwhile player, you should be able to handle any situation on the course with complete confidence and skill. Although perfection *might* (note the emphasis) be a goal worth pursuing, it's completely unrealistic for the most part. Ask professional golfers, and they will tell you that, during a given round, they will have hit a maximum of eight shots the way they intended. That means, on average, sixty-four strokes were mis-hits of varying degrees. What if the pros were to beat themselves up for each of those sixty-four errors? Obviously, their negativity would distract them to the point where they'd be too paralyzed to compete. We have, of course, seen pro golfers speak sharply to themselves from time to time, but it's unlikely that the successful ones dwell on negativity. Indeed, after a round, the best golfers tend to dwell not on what they did poorly but what they did with success. Jack Nicklaus, for example, is only too willing to tell commentators and reporters, "I thought I played well today." Not only is that statement usually a fact rather than a boast for Jack, it also places the emphasis of the game where it belongs—on the positive. For both the pros and the rest of golfers, perfection on the golf course is nonexistent. To expect it is sheer folly, which sets you up for perpetual failure and completely unfounded self-loathing.

But let's dig a little deeper. What's that little voice saying that is causing all the inner rage? Listen, and you'll hear "should" statements creeping into your thinking: "I should have used a different club." "I should have kept my head steady." "I should have played earlier in the day." Your anger and rage result from "should-ing" all over yourself. Consider examples of these "should" statements:

- "I should have used a 7-iron." It's the thought, rather than the supposedly (but not necessarily) incorrect club selection, that fuels your anger. But suppose you had said, "Oh, well, I took the wrong club. I will keep that in mind next time." The absence of "should-ing" generates a feeling of control and resolve. That, in turn, can actually become a feeling that borders on satisfaction because you realize that you have learned something as you approach the next shot.

- "I should have kept my head steady." No question that you should have, but you didn't. No matter how angry you are for moving your head, it won't change the fact that your head moved and you mis-hit the shot. But that's all in the past. Your anger can't possibly change, much less reverse, the event, nor will anger help you to keep your head steady the next time.

Perhaps you're now asking, "All right, Doc, so what's the cure? What can I do to gain control of my anger?" You simply talk to yourself and dispute whatever it is that your negative little voice is trying to tell you. Note in the above examples how "should" statements are reworded to become "will" statements and disputes we used are devoid of "should-ing." "Should," which dwells with the past, is replaced with "will," which looks to the future. Moreover, by seeing the situation for what it is, rather than what it "should" have been, frees you to go on to the next shot with much more confidence and calm. On a higher level, it allows you either to stay in the zone or, at least, to get back to enjoying your game.

The Myth of Helplessness: A feeling of helplessness can result from posing an irrational feeling of hopelessness. This can come from making such absolutist pronouncements to yourself as the following:

■ "I never can hit my driver," the oft-heard golf course lament. The rational dispute is to say to yourself: "I have trouble hitting the ball with my driver. Maybe I can get some lessons that will help me with this."

■ "I'm always lifting my head when I putt." Note here how the "should" is implied, as in: "I'm always lifting my head when I putt—but I shouldn't." True, you shouldn't, but you did. Now all that remains is to relegate the head lifting to the past. Resolve not to do it the next time you putt, and then let the thought go.

■ "I can't get any better at this game." Again, consider the implicit "should": "I darned well should be getting better at this game after all I've done to improve myself." The error here becomes clearer when considering that few obstacles in golf are completely insurmountable. To overcome the anger resulting from "can't-ing" all over yourself, tell yourself that you'll replace your "can't" statements with something less absolute, such as, "I don't know how to improve my putting stroke." Many problems associated with putting—and golfers as great as Johnny Miller have found them career threatening—really do have solutions. The secret is allowing yourself to be patient enough to find a reason for your putting woes. Instead of saying, "I can't get any better at this game," say, "I don't know how to get better at this game" or "I need to look for a way to get better at this game." The last two statements provide possibility, whereas the first one expresses hopelessness. Moreover, "can't" statements become rationalizations to excuse yourself from doing the work required for a change. Such statements also can be subtle ways of justifying an unwillingness to change. Once you conclude that there's no hope for your putting, it's easy to throw in the towel and say, "I'll never be a good putter."

The Myth of Overgeneralizations: When you say to yourself, "I'll never be a good putter because I'm always three-putting when I should be two-putting," you base your belief on patently limited evidence. You focus on a limited technique flaw as though it represents everything. By doing that, you're conveniently ignoring that, despite your three-putting episodes (and the pros have those, too), you've also had many occasions of two-putting and one-putting. By exaggerating your shortcomings, you set yourself up both to anticipate three-putting and to distract yourself with the kind of anger that carries over to poor drives and fairway shots.

It needn't be that way. On closer examination, it becomes obvious that statements including the absolutist terms "never" and "always" not only are usually false but are inclined to set us up for anger. What to do? The next time the little voice makes such a pronouncement, counter it by saying, "Sometimes I don't putt well" or "I try not to, but I've been known to three-putt." Then, resolve to practice more. Heed Arnold Palmer's timeless advice to those with putting problems: Try to lag every approach putt within a 3-foot radius of the hole; then concentrate on making putts that are 3 feet or less.

The Myth of Approval: Another mistaken belief is that it is vital to play well so that your golf partners will approve of you. Golfers who succumb to this notion go to unbelievable lengths to gain approval from their partners. Perhaps they buy expensive equipment, wear designer clothing, and/or take lessons not merely to improve but to be able to say they've taken lessons. The lessons become more a talking point than a learning experience. Moreover, the trappings of golf can make up part of an irrational approval myth that sometimes leads to ridiculous situations. This can set the stage for some unfortunate emotional outbursts when expectations presented by the trappings meet the actual level of play on the golf course.

My advice? In the words of the psychologist played by Judd Hirsch in the movie "Ordinary People," why not let yourself off the hook? You've spent a lifetime getting to be who you are and where you are. To go out of your way to gain acceptance is irrational. Your golfing partners have already accepted you. Moreover, soliciting further approval suggests that you believe you will be likable because you try to please others. Not true. How respected is a golfer who dresses a certain way and buys special clubs to win approval? If you buy designer clothes and this year's hot TV-ad clubs because they bring you joy, then fine. But if you buy these things to gain acceptance, then watch out. If your expectations are met with indifference (and it's inevitable that they often will be), your dashed hopes can easily set off anger. You'll be back to "should-ing" yourself, as in: "My golf partner should be signaling appreciation of my Payne Stewart knickers" or "He should be acknowledging that I'm hitting with the clubs Fred Couples used in that commercial with Jim Nance."

Don't get me wrong. I'm not advocating selflessness, such as using garage-sale forged clubs that haven't been washed, much less regripped, in years. I don't suggest that you wear sweaty tank tops and cutoff jeans when other apparel would be more appropriate. Nor am I saying that a golfer shouldn't consider the needs of playing partners. The point is that it's futile and can even become quite embarrassing to try to impress with style, rather than with substance, in order to gain acceptance. Moreover, if all your playing partners can easily afford the latest fad shirt or fantastic alloy driver, where's the prestige in owning one? Shouldn't ownership serve your own satisfaction instead of a need to seek someone's approval?

The Myth of Causation: Approval seeking is closely linked to the myth of causation. This myth is a false belief that you should do nothing that can hurt or inconvenience others in any manner because it will cause them to feel a certain way. Such faulty thinking leads to resentment and anger. Let's say you're a single player placed by the timer with a threesome lacking in the observance of etiquette. They putt out of turn or talk while you're trying to tee off. You can play the round with a feeling of frustration and your little voice grumbling, "These folks should respect the rules of the game." Or, you can thank them, return to the timer, and try to get with a group more suited to your sensibilities. You might not want to do this, but why? Most likely, it's because of the myth that you will hurt the other players' feelings, but the reality is that no one can cause another person's emotions. They cause their own emotions by what they say to themselves about your behavior. This is the reverse of what is covered in Anger (Recovering from a Bad Shot) which follows. It is just as false to say that their feelings are affected by what you do as it is to say that your feelings are caused by them. Other golfers might not be offended by their out-of-turn putting and talking that upset you.

The following four steps can help you to control your rage:

1. **Monitor your emotional reactions:** Because golfers often carry their anger without even noticing how it affects the game, tune into your anger by focusing on physiological responses, such as increased heart rate, tension, and/or sweaty palms. Also, be aware of your own behavior, such as stomping off the green, keeping to yourself, feeling hostile toward a playing partner, or using sarcastic commentary. You can't gain control of your anger unless you recognize it.

2. **Identify the activating event:** Select the event(s) that triggered your emotional outburst. Perhaps there was an obvious cause, such as a partner talking while you were putting; another group taking "forever" to putt out in front of you; or the group on the prior hole hitting into you. Keep in mind that a series of small events during a round can build until they unleash your anger. Keeping mental notes of events that lead to your anger and rage takes a little practice, but it's worth it to become aware of them.

3. **Focus on your self-talk:** As mentioned earlier (see the section, "Anger: Five Steps to Control," in this chapter) get in touch with the little voice talking to you. See how you are interpreting the activating events with that voice. Are there any subtle "shoulds" being heard? What, for example, are you saying to yourself about the rain that halted your round? Did you interpret it as the rea-

son you're angry? Remember, it's only rain; there's nothing you can do about it. The self-talk about the rain is causing your anger. Your little voice is the key to understanding not only how you feel but ultimately how you can change the way you feel.

4. **Dispute your irrational beliefs:** Recognize how you're relying on "shoulds" and "can'ts." Note that you're overgeneralizing, seeking approval, and insisting that you be perfect. This will help to discover how your little voice's self-talk is based on faulty reasoning, which, in turn, causes anger.

Studies show that golfers increase their chances of maintaining golfing prowess well beyond age forty if they control anger. Never deny that anger exists. It does. But by using the tools for controlling anger, you can go a long way toward ensuring that you don't immobilize yourself on the golf course. It is also much less likely that you'll need to spend a lot of money for replacement of lost or deliberately broken clubs.

ANGER: RECOVERING FROM A BAD SHOT ■

Question: "Usually, when I hit my ball out of bounds, I blow up, get mad, and end up throwing my game to the wind. Am I too old to learn how to control my anger?"

Answer: Your out-of-bounds ball should trigger anger with a physiological life expectancy of three seconds, but your anger lasts longer than that because of what you are saying to yourself about the triggering event.

A quick lesson in rational emotive therapy (RET) might do the trick. RET is one of the most effective ways of keeping your emotions from controlling you. Dr. Albert Ellis, a psychologist, points out that anger is not caused by an event, but rather by what you are saying to yourself about the event. In other words, the self-talk about the shot causes you to blow up, not the bad shot. That ball out of bounds is just that, a ball out of bounds, nothing more. For example, if you win the lottery and then go out and hit a ball out of bounds, you will probably not get upset. Why? Because you're saying to yourself, "So what? The ball is out of bounds. Big deal. I've got millions now, what difference does it make?" That type of thinking causes you not to get upset. If you beat up on yourself, however, and say, "I should have been more careful with my setup before hitting" or "I should have played the shot more to the left," the "should" self-talk, not the ball out of bounds, can end up fueling your temper. Again, the ball out of bounds is merely an event, a ball rolling and coming to rest, but what you say to yourself about the event is crucial.

You want to learn to recognize what you do to hit the ball out of bounds and then not to dwell on it. The trick to this is to learn how to stop "should-ing" all over yourself. With RET, you can reduce the time and intensity of an anger outburst controlling your play by using rational self-talk. In other words, try thinking of rational self-statements about a bad shot. Instead of saying "I should have taken the time before I hit it out of bounds," try "The ball is out of bounds. There is nothing I can do other than see what I can learn from this." or "No matter how angry I get, the ball will stay out of bounds. And all I can do is go from there."

I suspect Jack Nicklaus is one of the great RET thinkers in golf. When he mis-hits a shot, Jack probably visualizes what he has to do next. Imagine Jack "should-ing" all over himself. Do you think he could concentrate so well if he did? Now imagine what would happen if you could retain control by getting rid of your "shoulds."

By applying RET to your game, I suspect that the overall effect will improve not only your score but, even more important, the events that you have to deal with in life.

Tip: I strongly recommend a tiny book by Gerald Kranzler, *You Can Change How You Feel* (see Bibliography). It's helped hundreds of my clients and students to gain control of their anger. Remember, anger is a choice—you choose to continue feeling upset by what you are saying to yourself.

ANTICIPATORY ANXIETY (SEE CHOKING) ■

Question: "Whenever I start figuring what I need to score well or try to imagine birdieing the next hole, I end up getting very anxious. Why does this happen, and what can I do about it to keep calm so I can maintain my composure while facing pressure situations?"

Answer: Anticipation takes most of your small muscles and tightens them to prepare you for battle. Actually, there's no battle to be fought other than in your mind, but the mind doesn't know that. So, when you say to yourself, "All I need is a birdie to shoot a good score," you're actually setting yourself up for a less than optimal performance, at least physically as your muscles in your hands and shoulders tighten. That's why telling yourself to keep your head down is one way to set yourself up for not keeping your head down. You'll end up tightening the muscles in your neck and shoulders and turning into a stiff board. Then, you will be able to swing at the ball only by moving your head. In more technical jargon, when you give yourself anticipatory instructions to keep your head down, you actually interfere with the kind of concentration you need to keep your head down.

Work hard at trying not to give yourself an order just prior to swinging at the ball. The order will only interfere with your swing, not make you swing the way you want. Try to practice this, and become aware that when you do give yourself an order, you set yourself up for not doing what you want to do. Instead, practice mental rehearsals without using such affirmations as "Do this" or "Do that." If you are going to say anything to yourself, use a positive statement like "Feel how your hands are gripping the club," rather than a negative statement like "Don't grip the club too tightly." In other words, you simply want to describe what it will feel like to execute a swing, and you will become more conscious of what you are going to feel without forcing yourself to do something. The positive statement doesn't create anticipatory anxiety, but the negative statement does create it.

Tip: I recommend that you break your swing into component parts: the backswing, the club at the top of your backswing, the downswing, and the finish. Within each part of the swing, there are smaller components. When you observe these components without giving yourself demands to execute them, you'll reduce anticipatory anxiety that is often the cause of mis-shots and poor results. I admit, it's going to be hard to keep the little voice from offering demands during your swing. By practicing this approach, however, you will have the best chance of avoiding or, at least, reducing anticipatory anxiety.

■ ANXIETY DURING COMPETITION

Question: "I've got a low handicap and can pretty much hold my own until I'm competing. Then things seem to happen. I miss 3-foot putts for the win, or I may be shooting a subpar round until the last hole when I'll knock the ball out of bounds. Are these signs that I am getting old?"

Answer: You might not like my advice, but your problem has nothing to do with aging and everything to do with your attitude toward winning. That is what you might need to look at. You have an irrational fear of winning. Pros whose games backfire on them often have the same problem.

If I could get into the heads of players who falter or "choke," I'm certain I'd find that they carry around an unknown belief that winning will cause something terrible to happen. For example, a pro who blows a chance to win might have an ongoing fear that springs up at just the right moment, say, when a 3-footer is needed. The choke could be the result of an irrational fear of all the publicity and attention that would take place. Or, the pro could feel that the extra money might mean that he or she would acquire a new social status, and that would become scary for someone who had always felt uncomfortable in such a setting. It's also possible that some pros unknowingly set themselves up to fall short because of an intense irrational fear of generating resentment and jealousy among friends, family, and other players. They could be afraid of losing these relationships if their success made these people feel uncomfortable with them. Of course, they can avoid this by not winning.

The truth is that you could win as many tournaments as Sam Snead and you would still be the same person. In other words, nothing really changes when you win a tournament other than what you say to yourself about winning. The trick is to get that fearful part of you to understand that winning is just that. Life goes on, and most people forget. For example, do you remember who won the majors in 1985?)

Tip: I recommend that you ask yourself what is the worst, most ridiculous, and most terrifying thing that would happen to you if you did make all those putts to win in competitive situations and/ or if you did end up shooting a subpar round? Then, write down your two best answers and see what you get.

If you discover that your fear has to do with possible loss of family and friends, try disputing that fear by asking yourself if your relationships are simply based on whether or not you win at golf? If you find that you're fearful because you would have a different social status as the result of your newly acquired success, challenge that belief by objectively looking at what it would really take to enter a new social world.

The point is, whatever answer you come up with, dispute it so that you can see it for what it really is—just a fear, something based on nothing. Finally, rather than hating yourself, which does no good at all, improve your mental game the healthy way. See the missed 3-footer as an opportunity to improve your putting technique.

■ ATTITUDE

Question: "I'm amazed at how the seniors on tour can keep their competitive edge week after week. Any tips on how I can do what they're doing?"

Answer: Of all the successes of professional sports gambits, perhaps those of the Senior PGA Tour are the most amazing. Consider this: Some fifteen years ago, most events were hardly noticed and rarely televised. But with the coming of age of such legends of the game as Jack Nicklaus, Gary Player, Lee Trevino, Raymond Floyd, Hale Irwin, Dave Stockton, and others, television and corporations have made the senior tour big business. Even the prize money has increased threefold.

My joy through all this hoopla is found in recognizing that athletic skills are not lost after one reaches a certain age. It's a great opportunity for all seniors to model the pro golfers as they slip into their forties, fifties, and sixties. When they watch the senior pros perform, other senior golfers realize that they can do the same.

Your question about how the pros do it fascinates me, as well. The tour, after all, is a rigorous grind that demands both mental stamina and physical stamina. The myth exists that people lose both kinds of stamina as they age. Yet, in the face of time, these players are showing up every week to play competitive golf. Most of them are playing enviably well, and some are performing beyond the spectators' wildest expectations.

My belief is that playing golf successfully after the age of forty has to do with one's mental stamina. Or, to be more succinct, attitude is everything. As people age, it's natural for them to accept their limitations and to perceive the need—realistically, perhaps—to surrender to those limitations. In most cases, however, these limitations are really disguised self-defeating behaviors. They are not limitations at all but only perceived as such.

Self-defeating behaviors can be either external or internal. A self-fulfilling prophecy—something that becomes true because you predict it and help it to happen—is another way of describing thinking or behavior that can defeat you. It can occur when your expectations of a round make its outcome more likely than would otherwise have been true. On the course, as well as in life, self-fulfilling prophecies occur all the time, although you probably don't use that term. For example, think about any of these situations that you might have encountered:

- You expected to become nervous and botch your first tee drive, and you did.
- You anticipated having problems while playing golf at a new course, and your expectations came true.
- Your golf pro explained a new swing mechanism to you and said that you probably wouldn't do well at first. You did not.
- A golfing friend described someone whom he invited to join the foursome and said that you might not like the person. His suggestion turned out to be correct.

In each of the above examples, it is likely that the event happened because it was predicted to occur:

- You needn't have botched the drive on the first tee.
- The new golf course might have had problems only because you chose to look for them.
- You might have done much better with your golf lesson if your pro hadn't spoken up.
- You might have enjoyed the new golfer if your friend hadn't given you preconceptions.

In other words, what helped to make each experience happen was your expectation of it. Senior golfers often attribute such events to "being too old." Nothing could be further from the truth.

Keep in mind that there are two types of this self-fulfilling behavior: The first type is a self-imposed prophecy that takes place when your own expectations influence your behavior. More than not, you've probably "psyched" yourself into shooting a round of golf better or worse than usual, so the only explanation for those extreme scores was your attitude. How else can you explain shooting 80 on one day and 96 the next? Similarly, you've probably faced the award ceremony after a round with some apprehension and forgotten what you wanted to say only because you said to yourself, "I know I won't know what to say."

At one time or another, you've probably had the experience of driving to the course in a bad mood and saying to yourself, "My golf will be awful today." Once you made such a decision, perhaps you neglected to follow your preshot routine or rushed your swing. Such behavior made your prophecy come true. On the other hand, if you had approached the game with the idea that it would be a good one, you might have ignored any unpleasant moments and focused on the pleasant ones. Your attitude toward golf has a great impact on how you approach a round and how your actions during the round respond to your attitude.

The second type of self-fulfilling prophecy is imposed by someone else. That is, the expectations of a friend or your pro can govern your actions. So when your pro or playing partner communicates that you have a smooth swing or a good tempo, for example, you accept that evaluation and change your self-concept by absorbing the evaluation. In turn, your swing will probably stay smooth with a good tempo. As Sol can attest, patients who unknowingly receive placebos often react as if they had received the actual drug. Because they believe that they have taken something to help them feel better, this belief actually brings about some relief. Studies in psychotherapy show that patients who make appointments to seek emotional help start to feel better about their situations when they merely plan to seek treatment. In other words, patients who believe that they will benefit from seeing a therapist usually do, regardless of the type of treatment they receive.

A good example of a self-fulfilling prophecy that came partly from others involved John Daly a few years back when he arrived as an alternative at the PGA Championship. The probability that he would win this major event was very low. When he took the lead after the first round, he and thousands of others began to believe that he could win and perhaps that was the primary reason that he won. Just the opposite holds for those players who falter during the last thirty minutes of play on Sundays. It is also my strong conviction that this often happens because soothsayers of the press make insurmountable odds that those players will lose. Either that, or their own expectations of their ability to play goes south.

Prophecies, then, whether made by yourself or by others, can help or hinder you in almost every situation on and off the course. But please put this information into perspective. It does not explain all successful and unsuccessful golf outings. There certainly are times when the expectation of a great round of golf won't bring it about. Your hope of acing a par-three hole because you've fixed your swing, pounded a thousand balls, and/or purchased new equipment won't much affect the odds of making a hole-in-one, which is a fluke that usually eludes the greatest of golfers. Hoping that the ominous dark clouds dissipate before you tee up won't stop the rain. In the same way, believing that you'll break 80 when you're clearly not grooved with the mechanics is unrealistic. Similarly, on the course or at your club, there will be golfers you don't like and golf outings you won't enjoy, no matter your attitude toward them. At best, then, only to a limited extent can you conclude that what you are is what you believe you are.

Tip: I can offer the following four suggestions to help you break through to a new attitude and get more enjoyment out of your game:

1. *Ground your expectations in reality.* It's crucial to see that some of your dissatisfaction with the game might come from expecting too much of yourself as a golfer. For example, if you learn that your high scores are the result of using a fairway wood that you

duck-hook repeatedly, try curing the problem with a 3-iron. Of course, the distance you get might be 20 or 30 yards less, but you'll be in the fairway and not in any trouble. That's a worthwhile trade-off. And so what if you have to take out a 4-iron, rather than a 7-iron, for the next shot?

Wanting to hit fairway woods perfectly can become one sure way of guaranteeing disappointment. Nobody who plays golf for pleasure is capable of handling every high-percentage shot productively. Expecting to hit shots that take years to control is dooming yourself to an attitude of dissatisfaction, which, in turn, will take much of the joy and pleasure out of your game.

Also, consider other "substitute" shots. For example, say that you're a few feet off the green. In this situation, you've seen the pros hitting wedge shots close to the pin. Sometimes, they even hole out with their wedges, but you know that you tend to skull your wedge in such situations. Leave the wedge in the bag, and use either a putter or a choked-up 7-iron to approach the hole. Remember the adage: "The worst putt can get you closer than the best chip."

Of course, I know it's easy to dump on yourself after a poor shot when your partners seem to be handling themselves so much better than you are. Yet, it's important to recognize that much of what seems to be ability and self-assurance in others is simply their way of masking insecurity. They could be dealing with the same self-imposed demands for doing everything right as you are. In any case, whatever they're thinking might remain unknown to you, so why waste your time worrying about it?

Even when other players seem more confident, it's essential to judge your game in terms of how it's improving and not compare it to how your buddies play. Rather than generating a sense of despair because you might not have as much talent as someone else, realize that you are a better, wiser, and more skillful golfer than you once were, and that is the focus for your self-satisfaction. Playing solid golf consistently is a fine goal, but you're only beating yourself up by expecting to attain it. Remember two points: (1) Don't feel that you have to match the professionals with by-the-book shot selections. (2) Don't worry about what's going on in the minds of your playing partners.

2. *Accept yourself as you are.* Oh, how hard this is, but one reason why golfers dump on themselves is because of inaccurate appraisals of their games. As I stress throughout this chapter, such unrealistic portraits of how you play result from being overly critical. Perhaps you believe your game is worse than the facts indicate. What seems to be a terrible swing fault is hardly noticed by others and is, after all, only one swing. Likewise, if you have a terrible round, it is only one round. Obviously, it would be folly to ignore the possibility that you could play better, but it's also important to endorse your strengths; for example, you might be a fine putter, even though you can't hit drives as far as you would like.

I call this the nonforgiveness syndrome. Rather than forgiving yourself (forgiveness is a form of acceptance), you focus on the weak part of your game and chastise yourself for that. I urge you to spend a few seconds a day "strutting to yourself" how good a putter you are (a positive self-fulfilling prophecy). Private sessions to savor your strengths is a good way to put your whole game in perspective. In short, accept your limitations and acknowledge your whole game with joy.

Remind yourself, too, that an unrealistically poor self-concept of your swing can come from inaccurate feedback from others. Perhaps you are playing with partners from whom you get, maybe only in jest, a bunch of critical messages. Many of the remarks you hear are put-downs and offer a minimum amount of encouragement. For example, your partner might toss one-liners at your missed putts but say nothing when you make a 30-footer. In the same way, employees with overly critical bosses, kids with cruel friends, and students with negative teachers are all capable of suffering from negative self-evaluations that result from excessive criticism. The solution is to try to do what I tell my clients. Next time, say to yourself: "Others are entitled to their opinions even though the opinions are dead wrong."

3. *Desire to change your attitude.* You want an attitude change, but—. Ah, clients who see me regarding their golf games always tell me during the first session that they desperately want to approach the game differently. The only problem is that all this desire jumps out the window when I get down to assigning homework. At that point, harsh reality sets in—changing an attitude takes work, and most people aren't willing to do it. Regardless, the responsibility for not growing rests solely on an individual's own shoulders. Or, clients maintain the myth, "I can't be the kind of golfer I want to be," when, in fact, they're simply telling me that they are not willing to practice what's required. They can change their outlooks in many ways, but only if they're willing to make the effort. (See the section, "Practice Pressure Situations," in this chapter.)

Trying is often not enough, especially if you are unaware of what needs to be done. Maybe that's the reason for reading this book. You can get great help from sports psychologists, instructors, and friends. Of course, not all the advice you receive will help, but if you read widely and talk to enough people, you increase your chances of developing the skills to change.

4. *Adopt a role model.* An effective method of learning how to unleash a new attitude is to gravitate toward models, such as Jack Nicklaus, Arnold Palmer, Lee Trevino, Gary Player, Dave Stockton, and Chi Chi Rodriguez. Good models are golfers who handle themselves in the particular ways that you would like to imitate. I'm not suggesting that you strive to perform at their levels but that you emulate their attitudes toward the game and how

they adjust and compensate for age-related problems. Research demonstrates that most people learn more from models than from anything else. By using this principle, you too will discover that the world is full of senior golfers who can show you how to approach the game more successfully. I urge you to become a careful observer. Watch what your favorite golfers say and do, not so that you can imitate their speech patterns or even their swings, but so that you can take some tips from their styles of approaching the game and adapt them to your own approach.

For example, take a tip from Nicklaus, my own role model. In order to compensate for his gradual, inevitable decline in distance, Jack changed his attitude and made adjustments that helped him to maintain his level of play. Once, because of his tremendous power, he had been able to hit three-fourths of greens in regulation. As he became a Senior Tour player, he found himself hitting them with 15–20 percent less frequency. So Jack's attitude toward approaching a round had to change.

What he did was to work harder and longer on his short game and on putting, aspects of the game for which great distance and raw power don't matter. He also changed the clubs that he carries. During some rounds, his trusty 1-iron that brought fame and fortune over the years might be left home in favor of a fairway wood. Jack has also changed his attitude toward increased exercise (see chapter 3) and improved diet (see chapter 5). Moreover, he doesn't complain about his age. He continues to win on the Senior Tour and has been in contention several times on the regular tour.

Other role model possibilities are Orville Moody and Charles Coody, who developed the yips while putting and switched to long-shafted putters. These clubs reduce the need to use some of the small muscles that twitch during the stroke.

Jack, Orville, and Charles are all excellent models. By their behavior, they teach us that there's nothing wrong with dealing with declining muscle tone and agility by taking an extra club.

Kret, my good golfing buddy, recently made this very clear to me. His ball was lying 3 feet from the pin on a par-three hole. He shouted, "I did that with a 3-iron, partner." Boy, he was bursting with pride. I had used a 6-iron and was putting from about 50 feet. Kret won the hole and the match. It didn't matter to him or, for that matter, to me what club selection he found useful. Moreover, his enjoyment became a source of my own satisfaction.

A change in attitude requires new ideas; new philosophies about living, on and off the course; and the use of technology that allows you to continue playing at more acceptable levels. Along with attitude adjustment comes a wonderful gift of patience and self-acceptance, which make the arrows of outrageous fortune in life, on and off the course, easier to endure.

Yet, you can remain a bit frustrated by the difficulty of changing your attitude about your physical and emotional limitations. I do not claim acquiring a different outlook is easy, although I have many clients who affirm that it is. Golf has hazards at every age, and the secret to coping with such challenges is to develop an openness to change. This kind of attitude not only helps to extend the pleasure you get from playing, but it also can resonate on a deeper level off the course. Striving to learn self-acceptance and continuing to grow can bring more richness to all of your experiences in life.

■ BAD PLAY CAUSED BY OTHER PLAYERS

Question: "When I go out alone and join a threesome or a twosome, I notice my round is affected. If the players are bad, my round suffers. Another thing is that sometimes a player has some quirk about him that drives me crazy. Then, before long, I get so distracted that my game falls apart. Is there such a thing as other golfers affecting your play?"

Answer: Most golfers would say, "You bet!" A well-known myth per-
petuated on any tour is that performance can be affected by (1) how
fast other members play, (2) swing quirks, (3) ritualistic gestures or
postures, and (4) what a playing partner says or doesn't say. I've
heard of one pro who prays that he won't be paired with a certain
player. He claims that the last time this happened, a really good
tournament was literally destroyed.

The key is to understand the myth about causation that most
golfers believe. The effects that others have on your play has everything to do with what you are saying to yourself and nothing—
let me repeat, *nothing*—at all to do with the other players' quirks,
comments, or bantering.

Another golfer's slow play can't cause you to hit poor shots.
Your saying to yourself that he or she should play faster is what
affects your game. The sooner you recognize this, the quicker you
can gain control. You create options to respond in a number of
ways, including not at all.

For example, you might think "He shouldn't be playing so
slowly!" and get upset. Or, you can choose, "Well that's how he
plays. I'll just focus on how glad I am to be out here." In the first
example, your emotions rule and bad play is the result. In the second one, you take control by choosing to accept a slower round.
The payoff? You reduce the possibility of your own bad play.

The exception to this might relate to a golfer who breaks etiquette (e.g., talking at the top of your backswing). There's little likelihood that this person will recognize what he or she is doing unless you point it out. If you don't mention the transgression, your
resentment is likely to remain and build up, so it is better to express, in a polite manner, how you feel than not to say anything. If
the golfer continues to ignore your request, there's nothing in the
rule book that's keeping you in that group.

Tip: Choose to accept the fact that some golfers will be selfish, arro-
gant, and inconsiderate. No matter how much you try to change

their behavior, they'll rarely get the point. After all, the purpose of playing golf is to have a little fun.

In summary, you can choose who controls your emotions by what you say to yourself, or, like many players, you can buy the myth that slow play, swing quirks, and/or comments will inevitably make a good round go sour. When a player lacks etiquette, seek your peace of mind by departing. You don't need to explain—your nonverbal departure can be your revenge.

■ BOREDOM

Question: "I get so easily bored when I practice. I just don't know what to do about it because I know how important it is. Can you offer some advice?"

Answer: Most people have many demands on their time because they engage in numerous activities, but I believe that these folks pursue all of these activities in order to distract them from being bored. There are more than a hundred television stations; if your program becomes boring, you can channel surf to something else. The payoff for all of these so-called boredom busters is that people have lost the fine art of using their boredom to grow. Yes, you are correct when it comes to improving your game. The only way it's going to happen is by spending quite a number of hours in performing repetitive actions in order to fine-tune your swing, whether or not you are bored.

See boredom as a gift, an opportunity to learn more about yourself. Or, see it as a necessary evil to get to where you want to be with your game. The cliché "no pain, no gain" can be changed to "no boredom, no gain." Better still, if you are truly phobic about becoming bored, I would actually insist that you spend time practicing boredom. By doing that, you will soon see that the so-called side effects of boredom will be replaced by getting into a zone (see the sections, "The Zone (Part 1)" and "The Zone (Part 2)," in this chapter). If you don't want to practice beyond boredom, consider sitting and doing nothing for fifteen minutes. You will be amazed at how much joy can come from developing the art of being bored.

Tip: I just love to sit sometimes and do absolutely nothing. I have a million and one things to do and many distractions, yet I still allow myself to get a boredom fix. My best ideas for working on my game often come during such times, but the best payoff is that I find myself completely relaxed.

Give boredom a try. Sit and do nothing. This will be hard at first, but if you stay with it, you will soon experience your mind and body relaxing and a flow of incredible creativity seeping through them. Practice it while you work on your game. Stay with the practice session even after you've grown bored. You will be amazed at how much you will learn to better your game.

BURNOUT ■

Question: "I've been playing golf three times a week and practicing when I'm not playing. The other day, I woke up and had no desire to play. Nonetheless, I went out and joined my foursome. I played horribly. I went to the practice tee, and I had no desire to work on my game. Any tips on what's happening to me?"

Answer: You're probably burned out or, as some pros say, "golfed out." It's time to put the clubs away for a bit.

Burnout happens to everyone in every aspect of life, especially if what you're doing becomes repetitive and boring. There are all kinds: job burnout, relationship burnout, and travel burnout to name a few. The sad fact is that few people realize that they have it and what it is telling them.

Burnout can be loosely defined as loss of the ability to keep an interest in doing something. The symptoms include feeling frustrated, fighting with friends and family, withdrawing emotionally, and/or getting depressed. Ironically, these same symptoms can set up a vicious circle and the burnout syndrome takes on a life of its own. Health problems can ultimately occur, and they, in turn, can affect performance, which can lead to a greater sense of futility and depression and more burnout.

Burnout from playing too much golf is a signal from your mind and body that you need a rest. The good news is that you can used it to help you work on playing better golf. Let me explain.

Technically, by getting away from the game, you're allowing your mind to assimilate some of the new swing information that you have learned. At the same time, your brain is getting the time it needs to trash those subtle swing flaws that have crept into your swing.

For those reasons, you might play the round of your life after laying off for awhile. Your mind will have had a chance to process and assimilate the work that you did on your swing while un-learning bad habits or swing flaws.

Tip: See golf burnout as a great chance to improve your game by taking a leave of absence for a bit and doing other things. The worst thing you can do is to fight it. In other words, surrender to it. Stop playing. The golf course and your foursome will be there when you decide to start playing again. Who knows, your playing partners might even give you a stroke a side because you haven't played for awhile.

■ CHANGE

Question: "I'm not the golfer I used to be ten years ago. I am trying everything to get back my 250-yard drives, but nothing helps. I read your chapter about how we lose muscle mass and as a result don't have the same strength as we did to hit the long ball, but I don't like that. Any tips on how I can change my perspective on all the changes that are taking place as I get older?"

Answer: Everything in the world is in a constant state of change. Everything begins and ends. That holds for your game. The way you used to drive a ball had its own beginning and ending—this fact is inevitable. Nothing can be done, and there is no cure. For some folks, that stark reality is easy to accept; for others, it can be life threatening.

The secret is to see the lesson that change is teaching you and learn how to accept that change happens. A sense of quiet and calm occurs when you expect the inevitable. When I realized I could do nothing about a swing flaw after spending years of practicing, the inner peace and the greater joy of playing with my limitation became an opportunity to shorten my backswing and replace distance with greater accuracy.

Tip: Accept the changes that you notice in your game as opportunities and challenges to learn new and different approaches. Chances are that the technique you use to compensate for the loss will lead to a greater joy in knowing that you are never too old to learn new tricks. The joy and fun in just accepting changes and learning how to compensate for them will be reward enough.

CHEATING ■

Question: "For some time, we have had one player in a weekly foursome who cheats. He gives himself 4-foot putts, betters his lie, doesn't count his out-of-bound shots, and so forth. It doesn't matter too much to us because we don't play for money or drinks. I would like to know what motivates someone to cheat. Any suggestions on how to deal with a cheater?"

Answer: Your friend might cheat to protect himself from embarrassment or to save face. For example, he might cover up his errant shots by blaming them on outside forces: "Oh, I'm hitting another ball. Somebody moved during my swing."

Another reason might be to avoid tension or conflict. A bad score could erupt into a barrage of jokes that your friend would prefer not to confront. "Better to avoid the nineteenth-hole ridicule with some creative coverup," he might say to himself.)

Enhancing his interpersonal relationships with the rest of you could be another motive. He might believe that he's on the same playing level, thus reducing the risk of being rejected. For example, he might think, "If I don't play well, they won't invite me back."

The most likely motive is your friend's need to achieve personal power. Cheating or lying during a round of golf might give him the feeling of being in a one-up position. The irony is that everyone knows he's cheating and the so-called one-up position is only in the eye of the beholder. In other words, he "ain't foolin' nobody," is he?

In my twenty-five years of golfing, I recall once having kicked my ball into a more favorable position. I figured no one would see it and what difference would it make because we were just playing for lunch. That night, when I woke up and couldn't sleep, it made all the difference in the world. I won the bet but "lost my soul." The next day, I told my buddies and proceeded to make amends. I realized that respecting the integrity of the game is the best way to add to the joy of playing. So the next time your buddy cheats, think about how it will be a thorn in his side during the wee hours. Sooner or later, if he comes to terms with his self-deception, he'll be a better person for it. If he doesn't, then what your partner does on the course is a great predictor of what he's capable of doing elsewhere. In that case, heaven help him.

Tip: Depending on how well you know your playing partner, it might be best to bring up the issue right away. Because denial is a frequent reaction to a charge of cheating, however, it may be better to bring it up only if your partner is caught in the act. If that doesn't stop him from cheating, begin to make plans to avoid playing with him until he asks why. At that point, you can let him know how you feel about someone being dishonest during play.

In a gentle way, tell your friend how much you appreciate getting together with him but that you don't like it when he fudges his scores. Tell him it doesn't matter to you what he shoots, it's the getting together that's most important. Avoid making such statements as "You are not playing according to the rules." That puts him on the defensive. Instead, express how his cheating affects the way you feel about playing with him. Try saying, "I like playing with you a lot, and it bothers me when you don't put down the score you actually got. I really respect honesty. That's more important than shooting in the 70s."

CHOKING ■

Question: "I had a 7-iron to hit over a pond and a chance to win the seniors club championship. My whole body felt like it was filled with cement, and my mind felt like mashed potatoes. Swinging at the ball, I resorted to an old bad habit of moving off the ball and coming over the top. My ball went into the water and I started thinking all these negative thoughts and began to get even more tense. When I got to the green, I four putted. On the next several holes, I continued to choke and eventually lost the championship. What can I do when I start choking to keep the damage under control?"

Answer: A phrase in psychology is called regression under stress, which means that when people are under any kind of stress, they will resort to a more elementary level of skill as a way of protecting themselves from what their minds believe are life-threatening conditions. Obviously, there is nothing life threatening about a 7-iron shot to win a club championship, but the emotions that you experienced are similar to those that one feels in a life-threatening situation.

Your body grabs all of its defenses, and the sympathetic division of the autonomic nervous system takes over, thus freezing your body and mind. Pulse rate and blood pressure increase, and you breathe faster. Although you are being prepared for physically defending yourself with a lot of strength, that does little good for the looseness needed to execute a good golf swing. So your skill level is blocked, and your mind's only course of action is to revert to a more primitive swing that was programmed within your brain and muscles over the years.

The best way to prevent this reaction or to reduce the chance of its occurring is through repetition so that you can overlearn your new swing; however, you need to see your failure in this situation as an opportunity. Take the elements of what happened to you and go to the practice tee. Pretend you have that same shot to do over again. Imagine the water in front of you, and try to simulate all of the same conditions so that you actually begin to feel the tension once more. Believe me, this works. Once you have worked up a simulated version of what happened, take out the same club and hit the shot. Then do it again. And again. And again. The secret is to do it dozens of times. This will prepare your mind and body to be ready for the next bout of stress without regressing to an earlier swing flaw.

In other words, although you will still feel paralyzed, the mind will be familiar with the condition and allow you to complete the shot successfully. In psychology, this is called overlearning. In layman's terms, you are teaching your muscles and your mind that the situation that you're in is not life threatening and all you need to do is use the swing that you have been practicing.

Tip: As you might notice, I am a firm believer in the healing power of repetition. I strongly suspect that the mind and body abhor repetition because it produces boredom. That's how long you need to practice—until you're bored silly with the exercise of visualizing the scene that cost you the championship. Do it even beyond the point of your boredom and you will have more success the next time you are confronted with pressure-packed situations.

Finally, choking is nothing more than the body and mind trying to protect you from the myth that something awful and life threatening is about to happen. Sometimes, it helps to ask yourself before you make the match-winning swing, "What's the worst thing that will happen if I hit this ball into the water?" You'll be able to reason that you might lose the match. Then you ask, "And what's the worst thing that will happen if I lose the match?" And you'll be able to reason, "I won't get my name on the trophy." Then you keep asking such questions until your mind finally recognizes that the worst won't really happen. You'll still have your health, and you'll still be playing golf.

CONCENTRATION ■

Question: "I can concentrate just fine when I'm ready to swing. My problem is what to do with my thoughts before and after. I'm like a roller coaster walking up to the ball and worrying about this and that. Any suggestions?"

Answer: I think most golfers talk themselves out of winning or hitting solid shots. Research shows that successful players know how to orchestrate their inner dialogue. If you use a lot of "should" statements or self–put-downs, such as, "What an idiot I am," you have a good chance of preparing yourself for additional failure. Why? Because what you tell yourself determines how you feel and how you feel can creep into your golf swing. For example, if you say to yourself, "I'll never be able to hit it over that pond," you are looking at the shot as a burden. If you say to yourself, "Hey, what fun. Let's see if I can hit this one over that pond," you are looking at it as a challenge. Imagine the impact of each statement on your score.

The trick is to keep in touch with your self-talk while you play. If that's not possible, do it after the round while you're savoring an ice-cold drink. I have my clients run through a five-point program:

1. Identify a negative thought used during the round.

2. Think about another thought you could have used to replace the negative one. In other words, while sipping your drink, say to yourself an alternative positive thought.

3. If you think of something positive but still feel the energy of the negative thought, do some disputing of it by using facts, figures, and/or reasons. One way of doing this is to ask yourself, "What's the worst thing that would happen if I stopped thinking this negative stuff?"

4. Assess to see if you were thinking negatively because you equated worth with achievement. Professionals sometimes tell me that they are worthless as human beings unless they shoot under par. Or, one might say: "If I screw up and shoot over par, other pros will think I'm a pushover." Other golfers tell me, "Syd, I must be perfect when I play if I want to succeed." All of these negative comments are irrational and need to be disputed.

5. Construct some favorite affirmations, for example, "I'm a great putter," "I'm a smart player," and "I'm a good pressure player," then use them to replace the sudden attacks of negative thinking. Remember, golf takes only a minute and thirteen seconds to play. The challenge is what you do in your head the rest of the time.

■ CRITICISM

Question: "My playing partner has this habit of pointing out what I have done wrong when I mis-hit a shot. After the round, he continues his diatribe. What's going on here, and what should I do with his nonstop criticism?"

Answer: When your friend criticizes you, it says more about your friend than it does about you. Essentially, your friend is telling you that he has this need to be critical, even though he thinks he's helping. What he says to you is probably what he is really saying to himself—about himself.

Consider that your friend might be projecting criticism of his own actions onto you, rather than using it to work on his game. You cannot point this out to him, however, because, in a way, you would be criticizing him. Most likely, he would become defensive and who knows what else.

Tip: The next time your friend gets into his mode of criticism, I recommend reminding yourself that he is making a statement to you and to himself that he has a need to be critical. That is the message, not his words. Of course, I also suggest that critiques of a partner's swings are sometimes done out of a genuine willingness to help. If they are nonstop, however, chances are that they have more to do with a need to criticize.

DEPRESSION (GENERAL) ■

Question: "I used to love playing golf twice a week. Lately, I've lost the desire to go out and play. Is there something wrong with me?"

Answer: You could be experiencing one form of depression. There are probably as many forms of depression as there are golf swings, but all of them have a common characteristic. They turn a person away from living in such a way that, during later years, it can be life threatening. That alone is reason enough to seek help. Another consequence of depression is a vicious cycle: The more you *don't do* anything, the less you *do*. The depressed person does less and less and consequently becomes even more depressed.

Consider that depression does not mean sorrow, sadness, or repressed anger. It means emptiness, or as my colleague Dr. Christopher McCullough states, "It's the feeling of running on empty. The faint puffs of vapor hanging over sodden fairways no longer register. The glory of a tulip, a bed of red roses, cornfields in a cover of whispering gray chaff mean nothing. If it's not treated it can destroy long-term friendships, families and ultimately any interest to play golf. Golf has nothing to offer; friends and family cannot give anything to an 'empty' person."

Keep in mind that nobody—not Pollyanna, not even Lee Trevino—thoroughly escapes depression. It visits everyone at one time or another. Some people have better defenses against it than others. They stay down for a three count and then bounce back up and go on with a sustained zest for living.

Depression is composed of a great many feelings that most of us have experienced. Keep in mind that feeling "down" is normal. It becomes a major concern only if it interrupts your personal, social, and professional functioning and if it persists.

Depression manifests itself in many ways, depending on a person's reaction to it. A depressed person can be either very active or inactive. One individual might sit alone in the coffee shop and not play golf whereas another person might talk someone's ear off after playing twenty-seven holes. One symptom that I check when working with depressed patients is how much time they spend on blaming themselves. They might use statements about how worthless they are as friends, as golfers, as husbands or wives, or this or that. The opposite holds as well. They may also regard their predicaments and depressed states as results of cruel turns of fate. This is the "victim" role that can be extrapolated all the way to nation-states that collectively embrace victimization as a means of describing why it's difficult to get ahead in the world. Rather than looking at how they might be responsible for their reactions to bad luck, they turn and blame it on others (see the section, "Attitude," in this chapter).

Some depressed folks also suffer from poor physical health. They often have little appetite and can hardly sleep, which, in turn, can lead to a deeper depression. On the other hand, some become obsessed with their health. They exercise and play golf or other sports until they drop.

Other people react to depression by eating, and they're often overweight. Obesity has been shown to be associated with depression. Other behaviors, including long periods of sleeping and difficulty in getting up in the morning, are also symptomatic of depression.

Many depressed people complain that their sex lives are zilch. Then again, promiscuous sexual activity also can be the result of depression. The link to all of these symptoms is an underlying feeling of emptiness. Even when someone is active and busy, emptiness exists below the surface and drains the joy that usually results from pleasurable endeavors.

Keep in mind, too, that sorrow and other strong negative feelings are not necessarily signs of depression. Such feelings often reflect grief, loss, disappointment, concern, or other sad responses. If the feeling is acute and very intense, it is not considered to be depression.

One of my clients said to me, "I don't feel anything. I just feel numb, indifferent, void of any feeling whatsoever." That's what a depressed person might say.

Sometimes depressed people are not even aware of their "empty" state. They feel only physical lethargy. Their legs and arms are tired, and they often come up with such excuses as: "It's too hot to play a round." "It's too cold to play golf." "It's too much trouble to play."

One clue I look for to detect depression is withdrawal. Depressed persons will begin to give up responsibilities and cut off relationships. If they don't reach out and show interest in another person, they're pretty much making a statement of not having any concern for themselves.

Treatment of depression for the senior golfer can have a tremendously positive outcome. The first and most serious undermining of this treatment is the failure of golfers to recognize their depression. Both the patient and the doctor, each for numerous reasons, contribute to the problem. Many senior golfers just don't like to talk about their emotional problems. Worse still, they find it even more difficult to seek medical attention for themselves. It's a lot easier to rationalize their dark moods by saying, "Feeling down and out is all part of getting old, and there's nothing that can be done about it."

True, one can do little about aging, but many things can be done about depression.

The first step in treatment is providing a careful history and getting a complete physical examination. Several medical disorders can lead to a depressed mood, and these should be ruled out. For example, correction of electrolyte disturbance or hypothyroidism can be a most effective and economical way of controlling depressive systems that arise from these sources.

Also, a number of drug-induced disorders, including depression, can afflict senior golfers. In some of these disorders, such as the dementias, medication toxicity can be readily recognized. Therefore, attention to what medications you are taking and mixing can afford some significant control over your mood disorder. For now, there are two highly touted approaches to treating depression in seniors: (1) drugs and (2) psychotherapy.

Antidepressant medication, the mainstay treatment, has come a long way during the past twenty years. The most widely used medications are tricyclic antidepressants (Tofranil and Elavil), monoamine oxidase (MAO) inhibitors (Marplan and Nardil), and serotonin-reuptake inhibitors (Prozac). All of these drugs take 10–30 days to work. Under your doctor's supervision, they are about 65 percent effective. The bad news is that a large number of people cannot or will not take the drugs because of side effects. Also, if you take a medication for awhile and then want to get off it, the risks for a relapse or recurrence are considerable. More bad news for seniors is that little information exists about the effects of such medications on this age group. I know that Sol will attest to the fact that the literature is very limited when it comes to studies demonstrating drug effectiveness for seniors. For that reason, there are knowledge gaps about the side effects of these drugs in treating seniors who are depressed, but some known side effects involve the cardiovascular system, including increased conduction time and increased heart rate.

Earlier concerns that tricyclic antidepressants might induce arrhythmias, however, were not the case. In fact, studies show that these medications can even reduce arrhythmias. Side effects include dry mouth, blurred vision, and urinary retention, a problem for some aging golfers. Constipation and delirium are other problems that could result in poor compliance.

Overdosage is a concern with any medicine taken by seniors. Difficulty in getting the drug out of the system is the major hurdle. It's easy to see why someone who is depressed might stop using medication.

Because my orientation is psychological and not medical, my approach to treating depression is with the use of psychotherapy. It is not only as effective as pharmacological therapy in less severe depression, but it is also safer because the troublesome side effects of medication are avoided.

Cognitive behavioral therapy is considered, by far, to be more effective in treating depression than any other psychotherapy. If you look closely through the sections of this chapter about the mental side of golfing, you will note that this approach is used to work through a number of other issues. The underlying etiology that embraces cognitive behavioral therapy is that changing how you think will change how you feel. Just getting up and doing something will also bring about a change of mood (see the answers in the sections on Anger in this chapter).

No doubt, depression can torment and plague a person's every waking moment, but the great news is that much can be done to prevent and treat it. Depression can be prevented by self-monitoring, that is, looking for early and subtle signs of the disorder. One of the earliest signs is a tendency to stop doing those little daily chores that everyone has to do. For example, you don't do your physical activities for a week. Perhaps you stop meeting friends for breakfast. You don't play golf as often as you used to or practice the way you once did. Of course, a change in a single item of your routine might have nothing to do with depression. If you notice that several routine chores are no longer getting done, however, I suggest that you look more closely at your mood, especially if these omissions continue for several weeks.

Tip: One way to determine if you are depressed is to ask yourself honestly, "Am I tired, heavy, bored, empty, indifferent?" Stay away from such comments as "Am I sad?" "Am I happy?" Instead, get in touch with the specific mood. Remember, depression rarely just happens. Its course is gradual and often goes unnoticed until it reaches a full-blown feeling of emptiness.

One of the easiest and most effective ways of stopping emptiness from creeping into your life is by just doing something. I have had clients merely get out of bed and walk to a chair. The act of performing a menial task is miraculously effective in lifting one's mood. The secret is to choose to do something that is extremely easy to accomplish. Sometimes, I have a depressed client get up once an hour, walk to the kitchen, and pour milk or water into a glass. Just the act of doing that, in a scheduled way, can help to combat emptiness. The rationale behind this approach is that depression cannot coexist with constructive behavior or performing some activity. So, forcing yourself to do at least one small activity, perhaps one of the chores you have been avoiding, might be all that is necessary to elevate your spirits. I have one client who deals with depression by cleaning her golf clubs. Another client, when he starts to feel insipid and doesn't want to play, will go to the course and look for lost balls. The point is to do something. A good motto:

Don't worry; plan an activity, one that you can easily do, and then do it.

DEPRESSION AND SENIOR GOLFERS ■

Question: "What is the relationship between getting older and becoming more depressed?"

Answer: Of all the possibilities for improving the quality of life as one grows older, none yields greater returns in a retiree's or aging golfer's zest for living than acknowledgment of and appropriate intervention for depression. Recent advances in the fields of medicine and psychology have made this disabling mental disorder treatable. Yet, only a minority of depressed senior golfers receive appropriate treatment, in large part because of a lack of understanding of depression. As depression is seriously overlooked and often untreated, it becomes an affliction that can affect the outlook of senior golfers and their joy in playing the game.

Time passes. Things change. Friends move on or die. Children grow up. People retire. Perhaps they feel more aches and pains. Golf takes on a different meaning when they no longer play with the strict purpose of beating their partners. When they do play, maybe the conditions at the course are more crowded and the joy of playing is not the same as what they remember from earlier years. Getting to the course on Saturday or Sunday after a hard workweek was something to look forward to. Suddenly, retirees can go to the golf course whenever they want, but they might feel that the pleasure of playing will not be as intense as it once was.

Often, these players golf by themselves. Members of the venerable old foursome have either moved away or don't play anymore. After awhile, depression with a big D sets in and lingers longer. There's no question that moving on in years can affect their mood, and their handicaps seem to jump five or six strokes overnight.

That alone can diminish the joy of playing or looking forward to playing.

Many senior golfers sell their memberships and give up the game, not because of physical limitations but because the game no longer does anything for them. A client who came to see me recently had not played golf for nearly twenty years despite efforts by his buddies to get him back to the course. He wouldn't even ride in a cart. When I asked why, he said he just woke up one day and realized he'd lost interest. I believe he was suffering from depression.

Until recently, depression in seniors had been neglected in research. Assessing depression is a difficult task for clinicians because of its various definitions. The term *depression* can refer to a mood, a symptom, or a psychiatric disorder. Although moods and symptoms can unfavorably influence the quality of life, they are treatable. Treatment can make a tremendous difference in how one spends his or her senior years.

I want to dispel the myth that aging causes depression. Many people mistakenly believe that they will inevitably become depressed as they grow older. Granted, there is the likelihood that spouses, friends, and relatives will die; that income will be less as the cost of goods and services increases; that grown children will perhaps move hundreds or thousands of miles away; and that the only thing to look forward to is death. Therefore the relevant question would appear to be: Should depression be seen as a predictable, normal part of aging? My answer is an emphatic "No." Considering all the things that can cause depression, why isn't every senior depressed?

If anything is true about depression in seniors, it is that they are probably more often exposed to situations that cause depression than are younger folks. Yet the fact remains that most of senior golfers, for example, rarely suffer severe depression. In addition, most forms of depression can be treated if they are properly diagnosed.

Finally, let me dispel another myth: The fear of death causes depression. Closer to the truth is that the fear of ending up helpless or the terror of becoming useless is what prompts the affliction.

The evidence regarding the mental health of senior golfers is a bit of an anomaly. Among physically healthy golfers, the rate of depression is much lower than among those who are physically ill. This suggests the importance of maintaining a healthy lifestyle by focusing on diet and exercise.

DEPRESSION FROM NOT PLAYING ■

Question: "I recently injured myself, and my doctor told me not to play golf. It's been a month now and I'm pretty down as a result. Anything I can do to lift my spirits?"

Answer: The question I immediately ask my patients to assess if they are depressed is, "Have you lost enthusiasm for things that you usually enjoy doing?" Other signs of depression are feelings of sadness and downheartedness, feelings that you are no longer useful or needed, weight loss, difficulty sleeping or sleeping longer than you usually do, restlessness, fatigue, hopelessness about the future, and—most serious of all—the feeling that others would be better off if you were dead.

The fact that you are aware of your depression is a good first step. Most people who could benefit from treatment don't recognize that they are depressed. If they do, they often will underestimate what you are telling them about their symptoms. You can help your doctor tremendously in evaluating your depression if you understand what the symptoms are. But that's just the first step. See the section, "Depression (General)," in this chapter.

Tip: Stay in touch with your game. Go out to the course, and go through the routine without playing. Enjoy the course's ambience. Walk or ride with your playing partners. A good friend who suffered a stroke missed playing, but he went to the course and hung out with his buddies. Also, he kept up his practice routine. His wife drove him to the driving range, and he hit ten to fifteen balls. He remarked that most of the fun of going to the driving range was to talk with the employees and look over the latest equipment, have a cup of coffee, and talk about the game. Keep in mind that golf is more than just playing. It's a way of life, and you don't have to throw it away because you can't go out and play. Remind yourself that you enjoy golf for the camaraderie. You can still be with your golfing buddies, even if you're not playing with them.

I also recommend that you catch up on your reading. You will be amazed at the number of golf books on the market today (see Bibliography). Choose a book or rent an instructional video to get some tips. As I mentioned before, a good part of the game of golf is mental. You can still play a round of golf in your head, which will help keep you mentally fit.

Finally, consider my response to the question in the section, "Depression (General)," in this chapter.

■ DRIVING RANGE PRACTICE VERSUS ACTUAL PLAY

Question: "I can hit near-perfect shots at the driving range, but when I get into a competitive round, I lose it. Somehow I can't seem to carry that experience over. What's the problem?"

Answer: In psychology, particularly behavioral therapy, a goal is to get our clients to generalize what they learn in therapy to situations in their lives. Often, this generalizing does not take place and the benefit of therapy is lost. In golf, what you learn while practicing will often apply only to the driving range. What you haven't learned is how to transfer the driving range experience to real playing conditions.

The technique for transferring what you learn while you practice is to visualize that you are on the course.

Tip: Try this. While practicing at the range, pretend you're at the course. In other words, remove yourself from the reality of being at a driving range. This might take a little practice, but, after a few shots, your imagination will transport you, say, to the first tee at your club. For example, if you're practicing your driving, rather than hitting ball after ball, imagine that you're at a certain hole that has given you problems. Say to yourself, "OK, my buddies are watching me tee it up. I can feel the pressure and the sun baking on my back. The wind is blowing. I look down the fairway and see that dog leg to the left. . . ." Then strike the ball. By visualizing this way, crucial situational cues will develop. (A situational cue is part of the muscle memory that you take with you to the course.) The result is a driving range swing that becomes more transferable to real play. In other words, to hit great shots when you play, develop situational cues while you practice and pretend that you're at the course.

Another approach is to practice playing a round of golf. That's correct. First pull out your driver and imagine being on the first tee. Strike the ball and watch it land. Then decide what your next shot will be. Say it's a 5-iron. You take out a 5-iron and pretend you're hitting to an elevated green. Then strike the practice ball— on and on.

When I work with low handicappers, I have them listen to a tape that guides them through a round of golf. That way, they can practice while they drive to work. First, they imagine playing a round or two while they practice hitting balls. Second, they take those same mental cues used during practice and apply them on the way to work. Give it a try.

FEAR OF WINNING ■

Question: "I've got a ten handicap and can pretty much hold my own until I'm competing. Then things seem to happen. I miss

3-foot putts for the win, or I might be shooting a subpar round until the last hole, when I knock it out of bounds. Why do these quirks happen?"

Answer: You probably won't like my answer, but you need to look at your attitude toward winning. You may have an irrational fear of winning. Most pros whose games backfire on them often have the same problem. If I could get into the heads of players who falter or "choke," I'm certain I'd find that they carry around an unacknowledged belief that winning will cause something terrible to happen. For example, a pro who blows a chance to win might have an ongoing fear that springs up at just the right moment, say, when a 3-footer is needed.

The choke could be the result of an irrational fear of all the publicity and attention that would take place. Or, the pro could feel that the extra money might mean that he or she would enter a new social stratum, and that would become scary for someone who had always felt uncomfortable in such a setting.

It's also possible that some pros unknowingly set themselves up to fall short because of an intense irrational fear of generating resentment and jealousy among friends, family, and other players. They could be afraid of losing these relationships if their success made these people feel uncomfortable with them. Of course, they can avoid this by not winning.

The truth is that you could win as many tournaments as Jack Nicklaus and you would still be the same person. The trick is to get that fearful part of you to understand that winning is just that. Life goes on, and most people forget.

Tip: I recommend that you ask yourself what is the worst, most ridiculous, and most terrifying thing that would happen to you if you did make all those putts to win in competitive situations, and/ or if you did end up shooting a subpar round? Then, write down your two best answers and see what you get. If you discover that your fear has to do with possible loss of family and friends, try disputing that fear by asking yourself if your relationships are simply based on whether or not you win at golf? If you find that you're fearful because you would enter a new social stratum as the result of your newly acquired success, challenge that belief by objectively looking at what it would really take to enter a new social world. The point is, whatever answer you come up with, dispute it so that you can see it for what it really is—just a fear, something based on nothing. Rather than hating yourself, which does no good at all, improve your mental game the healthy way. See the missed 3-footer as an opportunity for discovery.

FIRST-TIME GOLFER ■

Question: "I'm retired. Many of my friends play golf daily, and I feel left out. I'd love to learn the game, but I'm afraid I'm too old. What do you think?"

Answer: Hogwash. You're never too old. Sure, you won't be a scratch golfer, but you will be able to learn enough about the game to keep up with your buddies and enjoy the incredible richness of the game. So, please, get going.

First thing you want to do is take lessons. It might be a good idea to get them from a pro so that you can learn solid fundamentals. At the same time, make sure to pick up on golf course etiquette and golf rules. They're easy to understand. In no time, you'll have them down pat. Nothing upsets an experienced golfer more than playing with a beginner who does not follow etiquette. Most seasoned players have no trouble with errant shots by a beginner, but they get flustered when you leave your shadow in the line of a player trying to putt and/or you leave your bag in front of the green and then go back to get it after you putt out. If you don't know what I'm talking about, it's best to accompany your buddies for a couple of rounds and watch how they conduct themselves.

Tip: I have a friend who is just learning the game. He refused to play until he had several lessons and a chance to practice for awhile. Then he went to a par-three course late in the afternoon and played. He told me that when he felt he was holding up a twosome behind him, he simply picked up his ball and went to the next hole. That's what I recommend. The only problem you are facing as a new golfer is holding up other players. It's no crime to pick up your ball if someone is waiting or to let a group play through. Also, like my friend, pick your playing times when the course is less crowded; that's usually in the late afternoon. After awhile, you won't feel the pressure of people waiting and you'll be able to concentrate on improving your game.

■ FRUSTRATING ROUNDS

Question: "I'm about ready to toss my clubs and give up the game. I have been so frustrated by my poor play. I've seen my pro and practiced endlessly, and I still end up with lousy scores. I once was a very good golfer, and now I'm ashamed to show up at my club."

Answer: Even the best pro golfers play poorly and have their fair share of low periods when they want to quit the game. Many do because of the disappointments and heartache that the game can cause. The difference between the player who quits and the one who doesn't quit, however, isn't that one plays more poorly than the other, but rather what they say to themselves about their poor play and what they do about it.

Let me suggest what you might want to do with your frustration. Most folks who get into slumps and want to quit the game do things that make matters worse. When they get into a slump, they become obsessed with trying to understand and solve the problem they're having. They take more lessons and practice more in the hope that these things will take care of the problem.

Instead of trying to fix what's wrong, I suggest that you accept it and enjoy the game for other reasons (see the section, "Why We Play Golf," in this chapter). The secret in handling these low periods in your golfing career is to tell yourself that it's your turn to bear the cross of being smitten by the golf gods. In other words, rather than fight against the inevitable, surrender to it because you know that there is nothing you can do for the time being and it will surely pass. Taking this approach will allow you to develop a more positive mental state that is more conducive to problem solving. In other words, enjoy your bad play. See the joke of it. Know that it is temporary and will pass, and you don't have to do a thing.

Tip: I recommend that you take the attitude, "It's no big deal," when your game reaches an all-time low. Ask yourself, "What's the worst thing that will happen if my game stays that way?" Chances are that the worst doesn't happen. Instead of panicking and throwing away this wonderful part of your life, you can still be grateful for all the other gifts that the game provides. In no time, whatever is keeping you from playing well will fade and your old game will return.

GETTING WORSE ■

Question: "I had a series of lessons that didn't work for me. When I tried to go back to my old swing, however, I couldn't. Now my game is even worse than it was. What happened, and what can I do about it?"

Answer: In psychology, we call what you experienced retroactive inhibition. This is the simplest explanation: your first swing (A) is, as you describe, pretty much grooved; however, when you learn a new swing (B), it interferes with the retention of your old swing (A). If the two swings are quite similar, which in most instances they are, there is likely to be more interference. This interference then causes the difficulty that you are experiencing as you try to go back to your old swing. In a way, you can't because the new swing has blocked you from using the old one.

It's not easy, but you can get back to your old swing. The only way, however, is to start practicing your old swing to the point where the new stuff that you learned is now being interfered with by what you are using from your old swing. In other words, you must transfer your old swing into your muscle memory to interfere with the information you have learned about your new swing. As this negative transfer takes place, you will eventually get back to where you were.

Tip: The only way to bring back your old swing is with a lot of practice and mental rehearsing (see the section, "Mental Rehearsal [Visualization]" in this chapter). The repeated practice of the old swing will help you to unlearn the new swing, but it is going to take some time. Also, when you are in that middle zone between unlearning the new and beginning to relearn the old, you will probably have problems with your score. Don't fret. If you keep practicing, the negative stuff from the new swing will be unlearned and you will be left with what you had before.

■ GIFTS FROM A TERRIBLE ROUND

Question: "I had the worst round of golf in my career. I feel like quitting. I could do nothing right. Any advice on what I can do to keep from giving up the game? I mean, that is how bad it was."

Answer: I believe that every serious golfer has reached the level of frustration that you describe. The amount of frustration that you are experiencing, however, has more to do with what you're saying about your game than the game itself. In a way, most of us unknowingly make our bad play worse by what we think about it. To complicate matters, the more we want to resolve our bad play, the harder we try and the worse it gets.

The next time you're facing a bad round, think of your putting problems or hooked drives as potential teachers. This will immediately take you out of the mind-set of feeding the problem with negative thoughts that will make matters only worse. Negative thinking does not lead to solutions. By thinking that your bad play is really a gift in disguise, it will help you to accept the fact that bad play is a necessary evil now and then. This kind of thinking will help you to stop struggling to get at the bottom of your problems, which fuels even more frustration and stress.

By seeing a problem as a gift, a teacher that you are going to embrace, you become ready actually to figure out what might have gone wrong.

Tip: A lot of my clients complain that they don't solve a problem right away. That is why I tell them not to expect an overnight solution. What you need to do when you have a bad game is to keep on reminding yourself that you can learn something from the experience. It won't happen right away, but if you are patient, the lesson will pop up when you least expect it.

GOALS ■

Question: "My pro always tells me to set goals during play. Why is that? What's so important about goal setting in golf?"

Answer: One premental technique that most golfers overlook is goal setting. The term simply refers to making a deliberate plan to accomplish something specific during a particular round of golf. My golfing clients have set goals that range from the extreme, such as consistently scoring in the low 70s, to the more reasonable, such as playing bogey golf.

Tip: I tell all my golfing clients that the fundamental goal should be to achieve the zone of play. See the sections, "The Zone (Part 1)" and "The Zone (Part 2)," in this chapter.

Imagine your three most memorable moments while playing golf. Chances are that they were less about winning a match and more about, for instance, the scenery, the weather, camaraderie, or the sense of accomplishing a swing mechanic. The pleasurable memories are similar to those that people might remember from participating in youth sports. With few exceptions, they don't remember having won or lost specific Little League games, but they have fond memories of playing—hearing the crack of the bat, catching the fly ball, feeling the sweet spot at impact. Golfers past age forty should begin to place winning into a different context. It should mean something apart from and more than scoring, even though score is important. Winning typically means joy and a feeling of accomplishment, which can be fleeting sensations. The purpose of playing needs to be changed to recognition, acknowledgment, and endorsement of the zone. Senior golfers need to practice seizing the moment (carpe diem), in which they can find profound joy, wonder, connectedness, and oneness. Perhaps there was a time when they thought that golf meant banging balls—the longer and harder, the better. As they grow older, they can get more out of the game by playing golf at a higher level.

■ GOLF IS ONLY A GAME

Question: "I have a friend who plays golf like it's a life-and-death matter. If you give yourself a putt, he takes it personally and starts in on how the rules are not there to be broken. I think he plays golf to live and lives to play golf. Everything about him is golf. Any advice or insight into what's going on with my friend?"

Answer: Once people retire, they lose some of their identity that had been packaged with their roles at work. To get a new sense of who they are, some folks, such as your friend, get a sense of who they are by what they do, rather than just accepting that they are worthy even if they become bumps on a log. Those who are golfers believe that they must take their golf seriously in order to feel worthy. In other words, golf becomes the new yardstick as to how worthy they are as human beings.

No question, golf, like anything else you want to do well, ought to be taken seriously but not to the point where it is a life-or-death matter. In my opinion, the best way to play the game during your senior years is to see it as a series of challenges that you face as golden opportunities to learn new things about yourself. Golf is always a great gift to give yourself in terms of learning how to surrender to it. You can take the bad breaks on the course as challenges. If you see them as indictments of your self-worth, however, you're probably not going to get close very often to the wonder of the game. The only time that golf will be enjoyable is when everything falls into place. And all golfers know that rarely happens.

Tip: I suggest that you don't try to point out your friend's shortcomings to him. Instead, observe his behavior as an opportunity to remind yourself why you play. Tell yourself that you are going to approach each golf outing with the goals of learning what you can from the experience and trying to get plugged into the zone of playing. Achieving the great joy of the game rarely involves shooting a low round. That can bring some satisfaction for a bit, but the real stuff to cling to is learning how to accept and surrender to the ups and downs of play. In other words, see each round as a challenge that is waiting for you with wonderful instructional gifts. Say to yourself, "Now, let's see what I can learn about life from this round that I'm going to play."

GOLF LESSON BLUES (SEE APPENDIX C ON ELEVEN TIPS FOR TAKING A LESSON) ■

Question: "I finally got a golf lesson to take the kinks out of my swing; however, I'm playing worse than I did prior to the lesson. What went wrong?"

Answer: After learning something new about your golf swing, it takes at least several hours to store the information permanently in your brain. If you interrupt that period of storing the new information by trying something new, however, you can easily destroy what you have learned. That's one reason why I advise my pro to teach me one thing, and one thing only, in trying to tackle any of my swing flaws.

It is not enough just to practice your new swing. Once you get the idea of it, it will take five to six hours for the memory of that swing to move from the temporary storage site you have in the front of your brain to the permanent storage site at the back. During that time, you can easily erase the new swing information from your memory if you attempt to do something else. How many times have you played with a swing thought at the practice tee, only to keep it for fifteen or twenty minutes and then replace it with another swing thought? By the time you had finished your practice session, you had not learned anything new to help your swing, even though you feel like you had practiced it.

Tip: Once you learn a new swing thought that seems to work, follow it faithfully, even during those times when it backfires and causes your game to get worse. These occurrences should be temporary. Once you finish practicing, stay away from the how-to lessons in your golf magazines or playing with other swing thoughts while you golf. The lesson here is not to learn anything new. If you do, you will decode the new information and the golf lesson information will be lost.

■ GOLF TIP TOXICITY

Question: "I finally grooved a swing where I was shooting in the 80s. I had developed a shorter backswing. Nonetheless, during a round, my buddy suggested that I take a bigger backswing to get more leverage. I didn't take his advice, and yet I ended up playing poorly. What happened?"

Answer: Golfers are all ears when it comes to ways of improving their games. Perhaps that's one reason you purchased this book. It's also the reason for tons of books and videos and folks taking lessons and watching the pros and doing anything under the sun to play better golf. I suspect the reason for this willingness to take a tip and try it is that, during any one golf swing, twenty-three thousand things can go wrong. I kid you not. As a result, one small move this way or that way can impact the outcome of your shot. Unfortunately, the game is so elusive that the tip is at best short-lived. It works for a round or a few holes, and then it's some other problem. No wonder that golfers are forever searching for anything that will help them to hit that ball.

If a friend offers you advice or a tip and you find that it affects your round, consider telling him the next time out that you would prefer not getting any advice during your round. That way, what you are working on will not be influenced by what your friend recommends. If you have a swing that's working, stay with it until you feel the need to make a swing change.

Tip: The best advice, in my opinion, is what you can get from your pro, especially one who knows your swing. I would not go from pro to pro and try to change my swing each time. If anything, I would not try to implement a tip or swing thought while playing. The best way to deal with swing changes is on the practice tee. In fact, you need to hit a number of balls with the new swing thought and then compare the results by hitting just as many balls with your old swing thought to get a more useful assessment of which one is better.

Again, in a friendly way, tell your playing partners to avoid helping you with your swing during a round unless you ask them. I suggest, however, that you not ask them. Get through your round, and then head either to the practice tee or to your pro to figure out what you are doing wrong.

■ IMPROVEMENT: FACTS AND FALLACIES

Question: "I don't get better. I practice, take lessons, and my handicap stays put. Is it true in life and in golf that you can't teach an old dog new tricks?"

Answer: Research supports my belief that golfers aren't significantly improving despite the millions of bucks spent on equipment and lessons. A study conducted by the United States Golf Association demonstrates that, during the past ten years, the median handicap of U.S. golfers has gone from 17.0 to 16.2. Does this statistic challenge my thesis? Hardly. That 0.8 improvement is the result of the use of the slope system that generates indexes a bit below the home course handicaps. The sad fact remains that the 20 million plus golfers in the United States are going to finish where they began, with little change in their handicaps. Is it golfers' wiring that keeps them fixated with a game that doesn't improve? Not at all. It's how they practice. That is, everyone wants to tell you how to practice, but no one shows you how.

Your practice style can keep you from improving unless you learn the correct way to practice. No question, practice is the most boring and difficult endeavor for most senior golfers. You have to get out of your routine of spectator and drive all the way to the range. Once there, you start striking balls and occasionally get some positive reinforcement. Most of the time, you have no clue as to why you can hit one ball 250 yards, whereas the next one goes maybe 180 yards—and hooked at that. You probably tell yourself, "Why should I figure out why since I'm too old to really improve anyway?" Or, take a positive approach. Say that you hit a 230-yard drive with a sweet draw. Everything felt right. The inclination is to tee up another ball and do it again. I say, don't. To get the most out of your practice sessions, it's better to sit down and let the mind process what the body just did. The processing should not be forced. Just let your mind wander; when it's ready, it will come back to that drive and try to internalize the mechanics that led to the shot. Beating a ton of balls is okay to groove a swing. It is not okay when you are trying to find the keys to a swing flaw by trial and error. You end up grooving your swing flaw instead of your proper shot. Again, the method here is to pause, sit down, enjoy the ambience of the moment, and relish the shot without thinking about how it was done. Just let your mind wander. As you will see, the subconscious mind is hard at work.

While you are relaxing, your brain chemistry is lining up with your recent miracle shot and helping your muscle groups to internalize the new information. By doing this, your practice session becomes an enjoyable and positive reinforcing experience, not just a painful "swing until you get it" ordeal.

Another common misuse of practice sessions at a driving range has to do with how the time is spent. A senior client of mine couldn't understand why his efforts at practicing were so futile. I asked him how he organized his practice time. He was surprised when he recognized that, most of the time, he just banged balls. He devoted hardly any time to putting, chipping, and sand trap practice. Yet, when we looked at his problems on the course, most of his bogeys—and triple bogeys—were the result of three-putt greens, missed chips, and sand trap trouble. Remember: Driving makes up only 40 percent or so of your strokes.

Another driving range lament I often hear is: "Gee, I hit the ball so well at the range, and I can't do a thing on the course." (See the section, "Driving Range Practice versus Actual Play," in this chapter that focuses on this concern.) Practicing at a driving range, at best, is useful, but the transfer of learning to the real situation is not going to happen. The physical cues at the driving range don't prepare you for the physical cues on a golf course. The psychological cues are also different. If you mis-hit a drive on the driving range, you know you can tee up another ball and try again. As a result, you are prone to being less tense. On the course, you have one swing and what happens is recorded; there are no second chances unless you have a mulligan coming (and in formal play there are, of course, no mulligans). As a result, the psychological and physical cues on the course get in the way of hitting balls in the same way as you did at the driving range.

Tip: I strongly recommend that you do some practicing on the course. I make it a point to play an occasional round early in the morning or just before dark, when I can hit a few balls with all the psychological and physical cues in place. This helps to reduce the chance of getting stuck with the myth that I have often heard golfers state about certain holes that they can't master. I have them play a hole over and over during off-peak hours to dispel that myth. Note that many American golfers routinely fly to England weeks before the British Open to dispel some of the myths about playing on foreign soil. Repeatedly playing what once was regarded as a troubling hole can do wonders to help you lower your handicap. It gives you this message: If you used to freak out at the hole and now have it well managed, if not mastered, then there really shouldn't be another hole anywhere that can pose insurmountable problems for you.

■ IMPROVEMENT: LACK OF

Question: "I'm on the verge of quitting. I've tried everything, including new clubs, lessons, video tapes, and books, and now I'm really hitting an all-time low. But I can't improve my game. I shoot in the low to mid-80s. I play two to three times a week and take lessons constantly. What can I do?"

Answer: One of the most powerful strategies in psychotherapy is learning how to accept. You've worked very hard to improve your game. Now you need to learn how to accept where you are and to find ways of celebrating when you shoot an 85.

Tip: Rather than attacking your self-worth by putting yourself down for an 85, spend that time thinking about pleasurable par-saving putts or the birdie-making iron play. The paradox here is that this approach might be just what you need to go beyond the plateau that you've reached. Working on your patience could be more prudent than working on your backswing. Getting new equipment might trim a stroke here and there, but that's about it. So, relax, take your mid-80s score and savor it in the clubhouse. Chances are, you might find your next outing results in a score beyond your wildest expectations. The paradox here is that by not having inward pressure to achieve a lower score, you free yourself to shoot one.

JOURNAL KEEPING ■

Question: "I have a friend who keeps records of all his shots on the course. I think he enjoys that more than playing. Is there any advantage to doing this?"

Answer: No question, you can get an objective assessment of what could be causing your high scores by keeping a journal. For example, if you take forty putts per round, then you know you need to work on your putting to lower your score. I also use a journal to record the wonderful moments during play. Sitting down at the end of the day and composing a brief memoir of your round can help you to savor your experience, especially the good shots and the good times, and also get you closer to the larger reason for playing—to get lost in the present. See the sections, "The Zone (Part 1)," and "The Zone (Part 2)," in this chapter.

You will be surprised at how much joy a journal affords. As you make each entry, you'll probably feel like you're playing the round over again. No need to worry about spelling or punctuation or whether or not you're turning a phrase with poetic flair. Just do it. You can either write it or type it out. And here's the biggest kick. On a cold, snowy day when you can't play, sit by a fire, perhaps at the club, and read your journal. You will be amazed at how golf in your own kingdom will come to life through the journal and how it adds so much pleasure to the game. In fact, if you have the courage, read some of the entries to your golfing buddies. They will enjoy them, too.

Tip: I recommend any kind of journal writing for mental help with your game. Writing helps you to focus your attention on the real purpose of the game, which you will discover as you make journal keeping a regular part of your life. If you don't like to write, promise yourself to spend no more than five minutes to summarize the best moment of each round. After ten or eleven such entries, I suggest that you expand each summary to fifteen minutes. Before you know it, you will have a wonderful collection of golfing memoirs that you and your family and friends will treasure. A journal provides one more wonderful benefit that golfing brings to your life.

■ LEARNING TO LOSE

Question: "I notice that when a professional golfer loses a major tournament by missing a putt or mis-hitting a shot, he or she never seems to do well again. Is there something that can be done to overcome what looks like a jinx?"

Answer: Scott Hoch, Greg Norman, and, most recently, Swedish golfer Jesper Parnevik have lost major tournaments and have not been able to transcend themselves into the winning columns. They are not addressing the problem: They have learned how to lose. Unfortunately, little emphasis is given to helping golfers unlearn behavior that keeps them from winning. I believe that Tom Watson has suffered from this phenomenon for years, although he has tried dozens of putters and taken hours of lessons.

The approach to unlearn aversive behaviors is repeated practice of the missed shots. It is important that practicing be implemented immediately after losing a tournament. For example, Parnevik, who lost the British Open for a second time, would need to spend the following week or month practicing the putt that he missed over and over. In that way, he can overcome what he has learned about losing. If he waits too long, the loss will be ingrained. When he is in the same situation again, he will practice what he has learned—those subtle nuances of his shot that keep him from winning.

Tip: You must recreate the same situation, such as the putt in Parnevik's game, that led to your downfall. It is important to do it over and over while imagining that you are in that same situation with that same putt for the same stakes. For example, let's go back to Parnevik. He is on the seventeenth green and has a 4-footer for birdie that would put him into a tie for the lead. He must imagine that he still has a chance to win the tournament and practice that putt over and over. He must do it until he is bored by the practice lesson. This is the only way that he can extinguish what he has learned. He must overcome what his body has learned about missing the putt so that when he is in the same situation again, he has learned from practice how to make a similar putt under pressure. (See the section, "Choking," in this chapter.)

LISTENING ■

Question: "My game doesn't improve and I don't know why. I've taken a few lessons, and nothing has changed. What could be wrong?"

Answer: The same problem that you're having with golf instruction is similar to what often happens when I counsel clients. Many of them don't know how to listen to their spouses and children, so I spend quite a bit of time in teaching them how to listen. Listening correctly is an ability that most people have never mastered. They often distort what they hear and learn the distorted information.

One effective way of listening is to paraphrase your pro's instruction. For example, if your pro tells you to slow down your swing, you might say, "When you say slow down my swing, you mean that I must take the club back from the ball for the first foot or so very slowly. Is that correct?" Your pro might then point out that you should start the downswing slowly, too. When you repeat the instruction, your pro is able to determine if you understand it. Once the two of you are on the same wavelength, you will get a lot more out of your lessons.

Tip: One way of improving the quality of your friendships at the golf course is to become a better listener. I often eavesdrop on conversations when I'm in the clubhouse, and I'm amazed at how few people really listen to one another. One man was bemoaning his three-putt greens. When he finished, another friend just seemed to be waiting so he could talk about his game. It was like everyone was taking turns. When a friend tells his war story about a game, give him a little feedback by paraphrasing not only what he said but also the feeling that was behind it. For example, instead of telling your own story after your friend finishes his, create camaraderie by saying, "It sounds like you're pretty upset by those three-putt holes you had to endure today." This sort of thing works like magic in bringing friends closer together.

■ LIVING WITH IMPERFECTION

Question: "Sometimes I can't stand my golf game. I wish it were better, yet I don't have the time or motivation to do what it takes to get to where I want to be. Any suggestions on what I should do with the angst I sometimes feel about my game?"

Answer: Self-acceptance is tough for most people, especially in to-day's society where all the advertising implies that buying this or that will improve the quality of your life. People are constantly pro-grammed to believe that it is better to want more than to accept what they have. They are told that they need new cars, new wives, new faces, more hair, fewer wrinkles, new clubs, new friends, new desires; otherwise, their lives will be unfulfilled. Baloney! Getting what you want leads only to wanting something else.

Happiness isn't waiting at the end of the rainbow. It is in every molecule of the rainbow. You don't have to travel far to find what you want in life—enjoyment. Think about it. Will that new set of clubs really bring that much more joy to your game? I suggest that learn-ing how to enjoy and accept what we have right now is the best road to happiness. For example, instead of complaining about a so-called bad swing, celebrate your opportunity to swing at a ball, period. Cele-brate all those wonderful things that you do have and not just once a year at Thanksgiving. Imagine how much inner joy you can give yourself by making daily thanksgiving affirmations. Instead of dreaming of a week of golf in Hawaii, enjoy the game that you are able to play in your hometown. When you do that, you get closer to the true benefit that golf provides, a chance to seize the moment.

Tip: Take a few minutes after you finish reading this to make a list of all the wonderful things you have. You will be surprised at its length.

MENTAL CONDITIONING ■

Question: "Gary Player claims his mental game is his strongest suit. Tell me, isn't this mental stuff more hoopla than anything else? I mean, is there any hard evidence to support mental conditioning?"

Answer: Research demonstrates how mental practice turns on most of the brain's circuits when you swing at a ball. In turn, this activity strengthens the brain cell connections needed to smash a booming drive. When a golfer imagines a swing, all the brain areas dealing with the movement activate except that region associated with the final command, "Go." With this research, one can now have a data-based sense of why mental rehearsal helps.

There is no substitute for real practice. It's easy to get the idea that all you have to do is to think about your swing and you will improve significantly. Not so. Mental rehearsal *and* real practice are necessary to improve your game. When you've just started playing, you need more real practice than mental rehearsal because the brain circuitry isn't established yet. For a seasoned player, a good mixture of real play and imagined play is the "treatment of choice."

What the researchers did not suggest is that practicing a swing fault can wire you to perform poorly. That's why I constantly advise all my clients to get lesson tune-ups now and then.

The changes to come in golf technology will pale in comparison to the number of changes related to the mental side of the game that will take place. I say this to encourage you to consider seriously the old cliché that golf is mostly mental. Remember: It takes only one minute and thirteen seconds to play the game!

Tip: Model your play after Jack Nicklaus, who does a mental rehearsal before every shot. Jack plays a mental movie of his ball's flight before striking it. That's an excellent way to play and practice. Visualize what you expect to happen before every drive, swing, and putt.

■ MENTAL REHEARSAL (VISUALIZATION)

Question: "I heard a lot about how mental golf is. I'm interested in using some of that mental stuff to improve my game. What's the best mental rehearsal technique?"

Answer: Because most of the game of golf involves mental abilities, mental rehearsal, in my opinion, is the number one tool to help you improve your game. In making this statement, I'm assuming that you practice and play regularly and have sound swing fundamentals. Mental rehearsal is simply playing in your mind a movie of what you are going to do just before you swing or putt. Jack Nicklaus claims this is what he does prior to every shot and has been doing since he took up the game.

A study was done to help college basketball players sink more baskets from the foul line. The players practiced mental rehearsal every night just prior to going to bed by imagining that they were at the foul line. They watched themselves sink a hundred shots. At the end of the study, the team's overall foul shot percentage had significantly increased.

A few years ago, I made an instructional tape, *Golf before You Golf*, based on the principles of mental rehearsal. As you play the tape, it assists you in imagining the various components of executing a shot. See a sample under "Tip" below.

Before you swing at your ball or putt, you want to imagine that you are actually set up to do just that. Then you imagine swinging at the ball or putting it and watching it fly or roll toward the hole. Once that rehearsal is finished, you swing or putt. This procedure is followed for every shot. At first, you might not get any results, but after mental rehearsal becomes part of your playing routine, its benefits will astound you.

Tip: I recommend that you "golf before you golf" whenever you can. For example, by playing the tape described above, you can go through the rehearsal while you are quietly sitting in your room or driving your car. If you wish, record the following segment from the tape and play it to help you mentally rehearse your swing (note that this exercise is not designed for putting, but you can record another tape specifically focused on putting):

Imagine that you are getting ready to strike your ball. Observe the weather conditions, hear your friends off to the side, feel the wind blowing, the sun warming your skin. Feel the texture of the club in your hand and the tenseness in your muscles and set yourself up to the ball. Look at the ball while you feel your hands gently gripping your club. Now, with a slow deliberate movement, imagine taking the club away from the ball, feel the club in your hands as it moves away. Feel the tension in your muscles in your arms and shoulders as you complete your backswing. Now, feel yourself moving into your downswing, your hips and legs driving toward the ball as the club descends from an inside-out arc toward your ball. Feel the club striking the ball squarely and feel the follow-through. Now, look up at the ball against a deep blue sky as it ascends and heads toward the green. Watch it come down and hit the green and roll toward the flag.

As soon as you complete the rehearsal, do it again. The secret is to do it as many times as you can just prior to swinging at the ball. In other words, if you're driving in your car and you have the time, rehearse the same exercise over and over. The more you do it, the more you will benefit from the rehearsal. As the old saying goes, practice makes perfect. You'll be amazed at the results.

■ MOODS

Question: "I've noticed sometimes that when I'm on my way to the course I'm in a bad mood, and I turn back and call my buddies to tell them that something has come up. Any suggestions to help me deal with this?"

Answer: When you say that you're in a bad mood, I assume that you're not suffering from depression (see the section, "Depression [General]," in this chapter). I also assume that the mood usually goes away after a few hours. If that is the case, I suggest that you not be swayed to stay home because you're feeling down.

Often, your mood will lift just by playing golf. As I discuss in the section cited above, one effective approach that I use with patients is just to get them to do something. You'd be surprised how becoming busy can change your mood!

When you get struck by a down mood, you can jump into a lot of erroneous thinking that includes telling yourself that things are more terrible than they really are. Life might appear to be unbelievably gloomy and insurmountable. Your ability to see things clearly is gone, and you start taking everything personally. You might even get into an argument by misinterpreting a partner's attempt to joke with you. The point is, try to remind yourself that the gloomy disposition that you are feeling is temporary. It has nothing to do with who you are, although it's easy to believe that your life has been permanently changed when you're feeling down and that you are now a full-blown curmudgeon.

For whatever it's worth, realize that everyone is capable of having down moods at any time. Keep in mind that what you tell yourself during low periods is not part of your reality. It's just your mood trying to put you down. It's a subtle mystery how your mind seems to have this temporary need to suggest that everything about your life is wrong. Don't buy it. Feeling down is much like having a bad cold. Tell yourself that it will pass.

Tip: I suggest that you try the strategies used in rational emotive therapy (RET), as described in the section, "Anger: Five Steps to Control," in this chapter. They can help you to recognize that your life is not as bad as you think when you're feeling low. You can learn how to be your own defense attorney and argue that you are, in fact, just having a spell of moodiness that has nothing to do with who you are and who you will be. Instead of being stuck with the erroneous belief that you are getting nothing but bad breaks in your life, you can learn to see that all you're experiencing is a bad mood that feels negative but, at best, will be short-lived. Bad moods are as much a part of living as good moods. By saying that to yourself, you can learn to surrender to them and know that they will soon lift. The next time you are feeling low, don't make any rash decisions. Remind yourself that you can always make them when you get out of your funk. As the saying goes, "Funk happens, but funk also passes." All you need is a little patience (see the section, "Patience," in this chapter).

■ THE ONE-SHOT CATASTROPHE MYTH

Question: "I was playing the round of my life when I mis-hit a tee shot that ended up out of bounds. I hit another, and that too went out of bounds. To say the least, I blew up, lost the zone I was in, and ended up playing the worst golf in my life for the last five holes. What can I do about this in the future?"

Answer: The idea that one shot can ruin your game is a myth that most golfers actually believe. Many players, including pros, take the attitude that a bad shot is the beginning of a sensational, melodramatic moment in their round and must be perceived that way. In reality, a ball that rolls out of bounds is just that, and it has nothing to do with what will happen next. The only change that occurs is how you react to the ball out of bounds, but most golfers react as if it's a catastrophic event and start having all kinds of distorted thoughts.

Here's where you can get the edge and control how you react to bad shots. Remind yourself that your game doesn't have to feel like riding a roller coaster, regardless of how many bad shots you make. By saying that to yourself, you prepare for the inevitable, which is a powerful way of remaining focused and calm. The next time you feel like you're about to play out a melodrama after a bad shot, say to yourself, "Oh well, I'm getting ready to star in my own action-packed psychologic thriller." A little humor, applied at the right moment, can keep you from falling into the trap of believing that a catastrophe has occurred. Instead, you will see the situation for what it is—you just hit a bad shot.

Tip: I recommend telling yourself that there are no catastrophes in golf, period. As you approach a game, say this over and over. If you do hit a bad shot, you'll be able to react rationally and see the shot as simply one of the twenty-three thousand things that could have gone wrong during your swing. In that way, you won't make matters worse by thinking yourself into a quagmire of negative self-statements.

OUT-THE-DOOR, ONTO-THE-FIRST-TEE SYNDROME ■

Question: "I want to score better when I play and yet I can't seem to do that. My problem is that it usually takes me three to four holes to start playing to my handicap. Unfortunately, all the damage has been done. Any suggestions?"

Answer: No one, I argue, can step onto the first tee and have the ability to strike the ball consistently down the middle of the fairway. More times than not, you are going to waste strokes. Over the long haul, your handicap will be affected. Recall how Kenny Perry at the 1996 PGA Championship spent time in the announcer's booth instead of warming up for a play-off. I am convinced that he lost the tournament there. When he left the booth, he was not allowed to practice. Arriving cold at the first play-off tee, he proceeded to hit his ball into the rough and eventually lost the tournament. If even a great pro like Perry can't just go out and tee it up with success, how can you expect to do it?

"But I do warm up," I often hear from clients who still have trouble with the first few holes. On closer examination, the warm-up is not a proper one. To most golfers, warming up means swinging two clubs a few times or taking some practice swings, hitting a range ball or two, trying a few putts on the practice green, and that's it.

Warm-up, in the true sense of the term, means a routine that lasts up to forty-five minutes. It's a regimen that doesn't focus just on getting loose physically.

Tip: I have four recommendations for an effective warm-up:

1. Putt for fifteen minutes. Most golfers go to the driving range first and, after hitting ten or fifteen balls, they feel they are ready. Most scoring is achieved with the short game. Putting is often overlooked. Next time you go to your club compare the number of people at the driving range to those who are practicing their putting. This disparity is universal. I also want to point out, however, that practicing your putting does not mean stroking balls from 30 feet away. Spend most of your putting time in trying to make 3–5-foot putts.

2. Work on the short game for fifteen to twenty minutes. No, you can't go to the driving range yet. Practicing your short game helps you to focus on touch—your hand-and-eye coordination—which is still in a state of rigor mortis if you've been out of bed for only half an hour. A five-minute practice session of chipping just off the green and moving back 10 or 20 yards can do wonders for your final score. Also, don't forget to throw a half-dozen balls into a practice sand trap. One or two failed attempts to get out of a trap during play is all that you need to keep your handicap from improving.

3. Practice full shots with the remaining time. You have now filled the dendrites in your nerves with information for your tiny muscles, and your larger muscles are ready to be loosened up. Before swinging at a ball, do a few of the stretching exercises that Sol and I recommend in chapter 3. Once at the driving range, start with short irons and gradually move up to your driver. Remember to practice your preshot routine, too, to increase the transfer of learning to the real thing. This might seem like a lot of work, but if you want to reduce your handicap and minimize erratic and inconsistent play, this is what you must do. If you plan these pregolf fundamentals as part of the whole experience, you'll in-

crease your appreciation of the finer points of the game and be better prepared to play the first few holes. And your score will go down.

4. During the minutes before tee time, mentally practice your routine and all of its nuances. Then watch what happens. I doubt that your handicap will drop overnight and you might still have trouble getting out of bunkers, but, over the long haul, you will settle into the habit of being completely prepared. Your reward will be a reduced handicap.

PATIENCE (See Anger: Recovering from a bad shot) ■

Question: "The one thing I hate about golf is slow play. I get enraged when I have to wait at almost every hole. What can I do about my impatience?"

Answer: Patience has evaporated from our culture. With fast cars and fast-food restaurants, instant internet access and instant dinners, and tons of books suggesting that you can lower your golf score in thirty days, no wonder that you become upset when you have to wait for something. In reality, however, impatience only makes matters worse. No matter how impatient you become, the predicament that you're in will not change simply because of how you feel.

The best way to develop patience is to practice the art of being patient. Do this is by saying to yourself, "If the group in front of me takes too long to get off the green, I won't allow myself to be bothered by it. I'll spend this little additional time in savoring a shot that I made or rehearsing in my mind a swing thought that seems to be working. Or, I'll just enjoy the moment, the dazzling sunlight, and the azure blue sky." By doing this, you are not only practicing patience but conditioning yourself to be patient the next time you are put on hold.

Tip: Patience has a wonderful payoff in that it keeps you focused so that your emotions don't impact your game. In addition, by practicing patience, you can spend more time in the present. If you are upset, you are "should-ing" all over and wondering when you are going to play the hole. Your likelihood of getting into a golfing zone (see the sections, "The Zone [Part 1]" and "The Zone [Part 2]") is decreased considerably. Finally, patience allows you to keep in perspective the reasons why you're playing: enjoyment of the moment, the camaraderie, the fun of executing a shot here and there, and the health benefits of being active.

■ PRACTICE PRESSURE SITUATIONS

Question: "I came very close to winning my club championship. I had a 3-foot putt, and I missed it. That cost me the tournament. I felt so much pressure that I thought I would not be able even to putt my ball. Is there any way to deal with all the pressure that I felt and continue to feel when a shot or putt is on the line?"

Answer: Anxiety is a very common reaction to what your body perceives as life-threatening situations. Although putting to win a tournament is anything but life threatening, your body and mind react as if it is. That's one reason that you experience all of the physiological changes that create the sensation of being frozen. Surprisingly, to reduce this anxious body-tightening response is much easier than you might imagine.

Attention and practice are key to reducing the sense of pressure that you feel during a round. Do this by practicing, in your mind's eye, personal situations where you had putts or swings that were needed to win. The secret is to practice over and over. For example, visualize that you are putting to win that tournament again and putt. Do this again and again and then again. The more you try to simulate the actual situation, the more your mind will get used to the pressure. Repeated, simulated practice sessions of pressure situations will train your body and mind to relax when real situations occur.

Tip: To have some fun with this training approach, pretend that you are in the Masters and putting to win this major. Imagine the attention of all the folks and television cameras on what you need to do. Then putt the ball. If it goes in, fine. If it doesn't, do it again. The point is, the more you imagine and practice pressure-filled situations, the easier it will be to relax when you are actually in them.

RESISTANCE TO CHANGE ■

Question: "I'm too old to learn anything new is what I told my pro after a very frustrating lesson. Why can't I do what my pro tells me?"

Answer: Your angst is all too familiar. My interviews with golf instructors bring home this sad fact. Teachers are well aware of how difficult it is to get students to change their swings. One golfing instructor said, "Sure, they'll do it to their best advantage during the lesson and then go right out on the course and revert back to the comfort of their old swing—despite the disastrous results."

More so, many golfers have a tendency to resist change because of the age-old belief that it is too late to do anything about their games. "Why bother?" is a refrain that I often hear. "The swing is grooved and programmed as surely as the way I shave in the morning, and it would take too much time to change it."

Off the course, golfers, as well as other people, constantly resist change because old habits create levels of comfort that help them to get through the day with a minimum of effort. They put most of their behaviors into automatic mode because they are bombarded with a hundred thousand stimuli every minute. If you apply this technique to golf, you have to develop golfing habits, despite how ineffective they are, that provide the means to cope with all those stimuli. Therefore, you end up compulsively repeating erroneous swing mannerisms that you have programmed your mind to perform. You are in what I call the comfort zone, which keeps you from moving into new territory. You drive to the course the "same way"; practice the "same way"; and swing at the ball the "same way," even after your pro instructs you not to do it that way. The sad reality is that you have done it for so long that it has become the "right" way, even though it works against you.

When you take a lesson and step out of your comfort zone, you grow tense and anxious. Quickly and unknowingly, you do something that sweeps you back into a familiar place. Three pars in a row, which logically might be exhilarating, can be utterly terrifying if you have never experienced such a "trifecta." After such a feat, your mind might tell your body to tense up some muscles, which, in turn, can become one of the twenty-three thousand things that can go wrong as you swing and mis-hit the ball. If you have a mis-hit, you will be upset, but deep down you will feel a release from the tension and anxiety related to the prospect of going into territory that you have never experienced.

Watch out now—I'm going to get personal. Only five emotions can keep you resistant to change:

1. Guilt. Players who reach a new level by achieving strings of pars or birdies can feel guilty because they might not have a clue as to what happened or why. If you ask golfers why they were able to get into that zone and move to a new level of scoring, the usual answer is something like, "It just happened." To overcome guilt, accept the fact that you will probably feel guilty. Anticipate it, and then surrender to it by saying, "Oh well, I just got seven pars in a row and I've never done that before. Pretty soon I'll probably feel guilty about it. Ah, well. It's an imperfect world. Such is life."

2. Self-hatred. It's easy to hate yourself for doing well. (You don't believe that last statement?) If you get in touch with that little voice inside, it might not say, "Wonderful guy, I love you," after

you birdie a difficult hole. Instead, it will be most likely a broken record spewing out, "Now why can't you do that all the time?" In fact, observe how a playing partner responds to your compliment the next time he or she birdies a hole. A typical response is "Yeah, I can birdie a difficult hole, but watch me with this next one." Remember what I am suggesting here. That internal voice is practicing aloud to keep you from repeating an excellent performance. The solution is to anticipate the self–put-downs when you enter a new level of play.

3. Unworthiness. If you string two, maybe three birdies together, a sense of unworthiness sets in with self-statements such as: "I don't deserve this. My swing is bad and yet here I am with a string of birdies." Or: "I have no idea why this is happening and I should." (See the section, "Anger" in this chapter.) Again, the cure is to recognize the feeling and observe it intently because it will inevitably occur.

4. Anxiety. Whether you like it or not, playing above your comfort zone creates physiological and biochemical changes throughout your body. Adrenaline pumps through your veins and large and small muscles. You become physically tense. Your breathing is affected, and your mind, in reaction to this altered physical state, begins to think erroneously. A little voice inside starts preaching: "Something is wrong and it shouldn't be. I've got to do something to bring back the normal state. So, on the next shot, I'll get your muscles to tense so that you can mis-hit the ball and send it out of bounds. That will bring you back to normal and that will help reduce all this crazy stuff going on all over your body." Again, the remedy is to anticipate and welcome the tension. Many pros who win on the tour do this. Those near the top of the leader board going into Sunday spend Saturday night (and perhaps much of the wee hours Sunday morning) visualizing what it's going to feel like if they are in contention as they approach the eighteenth hole.

5. Fear. This emotion is the most common and probably has more to do with a return to "normal" by bogeying you back toward a better semblance of your handicap. There are two kinds of fears: fear of success and fear of failure. Both are fueled by that little voice discussed in the section, "Anger: Five Steps to Control" in this chapter.

- Fear of success: When you go to that new level, the voice within begins to speak a bunch of myths. It might tell you any of the following: "If you stay too long at this level, you will play better golf and lose all your playing partners." "Make some mistakes because if you continue playing well, you will have to deal with resentment and jealousy from your buddies." "If you continue to play well, you will have to practice more and change your lifestyle to stay at this new level of play."
- Fear of failure: The same inner voice continues but with a negative refrain. Keep in mind the irony of this fear. If you have a fear of failing, then why not continue birdieing holes? This voice is saying: "You'd better birdie the next hole or I will jump all over you." In other words, you are under increased pressure to continue to play well. You start thinking about playing at this new level, and it scares you because you might not know how to continue. So you start searching for what you're doing at this level. That, in turn, makes you tense, and the tension leads to failure.

The only way to prepare for fear is by asking yourself, over and over, what's the worst thing that will happen if you succeed and what's the worst thing that will happen if you fail. Of course, the answer is nothing. Your friends might kid with you, but they don't base their friendship on your level of play. If you do well and reach another level, so what? The purpose of playing is to enjoy all levels: the bogey-free rounds and the rounds where bogeys are the norm. As for failing, go ahead. If you do, what terrible consequence will there be if you follow a birdie with a triple bogey? (Tiger Woods had triple and quadruple bogeys in full view of a nationwide audience.)

Granted, a bogey stings. It can raise your handicap, and might keep you out of the money, but will it destroy your life? Of course not. The secret, then, to combat these fears is to have the question ready (i.e., reminding yourself to ask it after you reach the zone) when you start playing at a different level: "Now, what's the worst thing that will happen if I stay in it or fall out of it?" Ask yourself this question the next time that you feel a rush of fear jump into your hands and arms. Dispute it. When you dispute the erroneous thinking, it is less likely to affect you.

On a psychological level, remind yourself that you are keeping yourself from changing because you are wired to mourn loss of any kind. As people grow older, they lose friends, family members, physical agility, income, and, in many cases, hair, at least where they want it (Mel Brooks noted that about the only question his young relatives had for him was: "How come you have hair growing out of your ears?") No wonder they don't want change. When golfers change to a different level, they have to go through the emotional trauma of playing golf from a different perspective. They no longer have their familiar old habits, and with that realization, comes the fear that the game will lose its mystique. Also, they fear that a change for the better will not leave them shouting for joy but will keep them in a state of grief and mourning. The "old flame" will be gone, and they will never be the same. Again, note how that little voice gets in the way.

Tip: The trick for overcoming this is to see the new and uncharted territory—the unfamiliar and the scary—as little blessings waiting to help you grow. Rather than raging against the new and unfamiliar, embrace it. Staying with the unknown for a while will lift you to that new level. Those who are terrified of being away from home are most effectively cured of their agoraphobia by staying outside the house until the anxiety is reduced. When you start to think that acquiring a new technique means that you have lost the old familiar one, think again. Don't abandon it so quickly. Remind yourself that losing your old swing and assimilating the new one takes time. Moreover, compensating for a slice, perhaps by aiming more to the left in order to keep the old swing from dying, is just a postponement. It will not move you any closer to an improvement in your game.

The biggest myth in therapy is that people merely need to understand why they are doing something and then they will change. Why that myth has survived is beyond the scope of this book, but the fact is that nothing can be further from the truth. Insight does not lead to change. Just the opposite is true; most often, change precedes insight.

For example, I know about the flaws in my downswing. I've seen them on film. I've heard about them from playing partners and teachers, and I can even feel them when I'm playing. Jim Murray, the gifted sports columnist, was playing a round with Jack Nicklaus when the Golden Bear pointed out the "right" way to do something. "I *know* the right way to do it," Murray protested. "I just can't do it the right way." For my part, with so much empirical information at my disposal, you would expect that I could simply correct myself. Like Murray to some extent, I can't—not immediately, anyway. The course of change, both during therapy and on the golf course, is to develop a step-by-step behavioral game plan. That means breaking the swing down into small parts, accompanied by trial-and-error practice rounds, or it means developing a process of reeducating old habits. Insight is therefore useful in diagnosing the problem, that is, why you might do something and what it will do to your shots, but you still have to apply the knowledge by using a program to overcome the problem. That is how one accomplishes change, on and off the golf course.

Therefore, I start by breaking my problem into its component parts. For example, just as I finish my backswing, my fingers become tense. This makes my clubface move right across the plane.

But now I must break down that assessment further. So I notice that I'm talking about the fingers on my right hand feeling pressure, which loosens the club in my left hand and might cause the club to loop a little to the right. At that point, with the help of my pro and with some creative thinking by both of us, we develop strategies to prevent my gripping the club tighter during the backswing. I might think about loosening my fingers on my right hand that is holding the club, or I might tighten my fingers on my right hand, or I might tighten my fingers on my left hand, or I could practice strengthening my left hand by squeezing a rubber ball. Whatever I do, note how I have developed specific strategies to eliminate the swing flaw. Instead of saying to myself, "Don't tense up," I now have a more specific behavioral strategy that defines what I mean when I say, "Don't tense up."

SHANKING: THE PSYCHOLOGICAL EFFECT ■

Question: "I'm a pretty good player, but the other day I had a wedge to the green and I shanked my shot. The next time I had a short pitch to the green, I noticed that my body got real tense and a fear that I would shank the ball disrupted my confidence. What can I do about my fear of shanking?"

Answer: As you probably know, shanking is caused by your downswing striking the ball outside in, usually with the hosel of the club. As a result, the ball squirts to the right if you're right-handed. Shanking is also caused by moving your head and/or shoulders too soon during the downswing, standing too close to the ball, and/or excessive wrist action.

The psychological fear that you might have learned is quite common in golfers. Johnny Miller had this problem for a bit when he shanked a crucial shot during a round. He confessed that he developed this phobia about shanking, and it took some time to go away.

The best way to get over the fear of shanking is through

intense practice sessions of hitting tons of balls from 60 yards out. I'm talking about hitting more practice shots than you ever have in your life. Once you are aware of the causes of a ball being shanked, you need to practice hitting shots until this routine becomes almost second nature. By doing this, you're unlearning the fear that you created by shanking. In behavioral therapy, it's called extinction. That is, you are getting feedback from your practice, which signals your brain that the fear it wants to produce is unfounded. There's simply no evidence anymore to support the fear, and it slowly diminishes.

Tip: Unfortunately, as a number of other golf psychologists suggest, mental rehearsal and affirmations don't help much to reduce the fear of shanking. The best thing to do is to extinguish the fear; however, I recommend seeing your pro for a lesson to get an explanation for what is causing your particular kind of shanking. As mentioned above, several factors can cause shanking. Once you understand what you are doing, then it's time to practice until you're bored to tears. It's very important for you get to that stage of boredom in order to immunize yourself from the fear. Doing something over and over long enough will eradicate almost any debilitating emotions.

■ SIDE EFFECTS FROM NOT PLAYING (See Mental Rehearsal)

Question: "When the cold weather arrives, I go indoors, put away my clubs, and hibernate. Is this having any impact on my game when I start playing again in the spring?"

Answer: Yes. Not only are you losing the benefits of exercise, you are unlearning all that valuable stuff you picked up while you played. The harsh reality of this common habit is that you are setting yourself up for a mind-set that will keep you from improving the following spring. It can cause more damage to your game than you think.

When you do return to your game, perhaps five months later, you will, in a way, be starting from scratch. All of your groundbreaking lessons and swing thoughts will be lost. Perhaps you'll play a round, as all golfers have experienced, and strike the ball with perfection only to discover that the great shots and the swing thoughts that worked during that round are short-lived. Worse yet, the same seemingly everlasting problems of your golfing past will return to haunt your game and devastate your handicap.

My advice to counter this dangerous habit is to do some practicing during the off-season. Now, I'm not suggesting that you fly to Hawaii and spend your retirement money on golf. Something cheaper will work. You might even find that a less expensive solution can be quite enjoyable. I have had clients who confessed that they used the following technique before going to sleep at night. What you do is pretend.

Visualize being on the course and playing a round of golf. My advice is to sit in a quiet room or at the steering wheel while driving and pretend that you are playing golf. But I don't mean merely visualizing the shots of the game, but the whole golf experience. That is, imagine that you're driving up to your clubhouse, greeting your friends, sitting in the coffee shop, putting on your spikes, addressing your ball at the first tee, feeling the anxiety, observing the dogleg to the left, feeling the tension in your small muscles, noticing your breathing as it becomes heavier—the whole works. Then swing at the ball and capture one or two swing thoughts that you developed during your summer of golf.

Tip: Let me describe how I practice visualization. My one big breakthrough this past summer was to finish my backswing. So my thought involves finishing the backswing. I imagine myself arriving at the first tee and drinking in the ambience of the moment: gently sloping fairways, the electric orange of the morning sun, a green prison wall of trees, hills of shiny gold buttercups, distant foothills cloaked in velvet, deep blue sky, the warm sun on my body, and my partners joking and jostling for strokes. Then I see myself setting up to the ball and hear myself chanting: "Finish the backswing, finish the backswing." I swing and watch the ball, visualize it doing what I want, ascending and moving right to left slightly, dropping onto the Bermuda grass and bouncing to a resting place 200-plus yards away. The trick is to repeat this one scene over and over. You will be amazed at how this mental rehearsal will do wonders for you when you're getting ready to tee off the next time.

■ SILENCING THE MIND

Question: "Sometimes, I feel like I'm a schizophrenic when I play golf. I hear all these voices in my head telling me to do this and make sure I don't do that. I wonder if there are any tips you can offer on what I can do to quiet my mind so I can play my game without all these distractions?"

Answer: Silence has gotten a bum rap in modern society. Somehow, if silence sneaks into a conversation or grabs at people while they are relaxing, the immediate response is that something must be wrong. As a result, many people have lost the ability to keep their mouths closed and their minds quiet. The irony is that the effort to say something or to keep the mind active is an attempt to reach a goal of inner peace, but inner peace can be achieved only by learning how to quiet the mind.

Numerous strategies are used for reaching an inner state of tranquility. (See the sections, "The Zone [Part 1]" and "The Zone [Part 2]," in this chapter.) One that I use while I play golf is to make an extra effort to reflect on my surroundings. While walking to my ball, I try to look at the texture of the fairway grass, the color and shape of trees, the flowers in bloom, and the puffy cloud designs in the sky. Doing this helps me to empty my mind of negative thinking, which can lead to emotional paralysis and physical tension. Also, I concentrate on my breathing as I walk and attend to how I breathe in and out. I try to take slow, deep breaths while I enjoy the ambience of the course. If a negative thought comes rushing in, I ride it rather than try to get rid of it. Now, that doesn't mean I react to it; I simply observe that my mind is trying to tell me something negative. By doing that, the thought usually is short-lived. Over time, you will be amazed at how peaceful you can be while playing your round.

Tip: Please note that turning off the mind is not an easy task. It will demand a lot of failures before you are finally able to quiet things upstairs. If you say to yourself, "I must quiet my mind," you will end up keeping it quite active. In other words, don't insist that you keep your mind still. If it doesn't want to be, surrender to it. Before long, the resistance will lessen and you'll be in a better position to quiet your mind.

SLUMPS ■

Question: "Last weekend, I played in a best ball tournament. I played well for about five or six holes and then the wheels came off. Like clockwork, I began duck-hooking all my drives. Then on the greens, I three-putted three holes in a row. How can I break out of a slump?"

Answer: The Roman statesman Marcus Tullius Cicero once said, "Any man can make mistakes, but only an idiot persists in his error." Unfortunately, good old Cicero never played golf to realize that persistently making mistakes during a round is often the rule. I'm sure, however, that the last thing on your mind during a tournament is the repeated duck-hooking of your drives.

To help golfers break out of this curse, I use a technique that's been extremely effective with some forms of depression. I simply get clients to do something different. When you get burnout at work, a weekend away or a week off can do wonders to recharge the batteries. The same holds for slumps during play, but it takes a radical and risky approach. If you have the courage to do what I suggest below, your on-course slumping can be considerably reduced.

Tip: Instead of hitting off the tee with a driver, regardless of the distance to the hole, use a 4-iron. "A 4-iron?" friends will say. Yes, a 4-iron. Or, if you're missing mid-iron shots and the mechanical checkup that you do doesn't help, try hitting a 9-iron where you would normally hit, say, a 5-iron. Because you can't stop the round and head to the practice tee, the only approach left is to do something radically different.

Here's an example of the psychological mechanism that kicks in. Your mind is processing 5-iron, 160 yards or so, and it is also processing something that creates the hook. But when you set up with a 9-iron, the mind will become confused. For example, if your mind could talk, it might say, "He's got to hit a shot 160 yards or so. I'll tell him to take a 5-iron, and then I'll zap him with information that will cause a duck hook. Ha ha!" But by choosing a 9-iron, you end up tricking yourself. So your mind might go on, "OK, buddy, choose a 5-iron. Ha ha! Wait! No, not a 9-iron, a 5-iron! No! No! Don't strike that 9-iron." Then, when you swing the 9-iron the duck hook pattern that has been temporarily grooved is broken. The confusion you create for yourself (your mind) is all that's necessary to pull you out of the slump.

If this sounds too risky, then prepare for competitive slumping on the practice tee. While hitting balls, pretend that you've been hooking. For example, say to yourself, "OK, I've got a 5-iron to the green. So I'll practice hitting a 9-iron, just once or twice." By playing this mind game during practice, you're preparing yourself for the real slump during play.

Finally, if you're slumping with your putter, a radical approach can work wonders there, too. Because you don't want to putt with an iron, change the grip to break the routine. For example, you might want to putt cross-handed. Again, create confusing data so they can short-circuit the information that the brain has been processing to cause the missed putts.

There is one contraindication, as we say in the profession. You won't get results the first couple of times you do this. But practicing, over time, on and off the course, will help you to cut down slumping while you play. Sure, you'll lose distance on a few shots, but, more important, you'll break the temporary habit that's causing your sky-high scores.

STRESS REDUCTION ■

Question: "During a tournament, I feel a lot of stress. My wife tells me that I'm always fully stressed out. Any tips on what I can do to reduce the stress?"

Answer: Much stress is the result of the fight-or-flee phenomenon that you have when confronting life-threatening or seemingly life-threatening situations. Your adrenal glands release epinephrine (adrenaline), a hormone that activates your body's defense mechanisms, which causes your heart to pound, your blood pressure to rise, your muscles to tense, and the pupils of your eyes to open wide. These reactions prepare your body either to resist or to avoid the triggering event.

Continued stress can cause chronic fatigue; loss of appetite or overeating; a diminished ability to cope with situations; and, in some instances, depression. The body's immune system is also affected, and your vulnerability to illness and disease increases. Stress often results when you just can't seem to balance the demands of life and your ability to cope with them. Keep in mind that even positive events, such as marriage, a job promotion, or winning the club championship, can also cause stress. Other causes can be illness, loneliness, pain, and emotional conflict. The signs of excessive stress can include headache, upset stomach, and personality change.

Stress is diagnosed through recognition of the symptoms, both physical and psychological. I often use a questionnaire that identifies potentially stressful events. For example, a new job, a new home, or the birth of a child can cause quite a bit of stress in one's life. (Most psychologists can provide you with one of the many questionnaires available for this purpose.)

If you don't want to deal with stress by seeing a therapist, you can choose one or more of these ten approaches:

1. A simple way to reduce stress is by staying away from the situation that causes it when that is possible. If a playing partner gets on your nerves, for example, play less golf with that partner. If you can't tolerate long waits on the first tee, try making tee times earlier in the morning or later in the afternoon. Try to avoid playing golf on weekends if the course is usually overcrowded.

2. In an approach called the calming response, you take a deep breath and hold it (deep breathing slows down your heart rate). Tell yourself, "My body is calm," then release your breath and say, "My body is quiet." This simple exercise can be done on the course if you start getting stressed from slow play or pressure of the competition.

3. My favorite approach, as you can tell throughout this chapter, is to change the way you think about the situation that you're perceiving as stressful. Ask yourself what's the worst thing that will happen if you don't get stressed out over the situation. This helps you to realize that the situation is insignificant and not worth worrying about.

4. Exercise can help you to get into a more relaxed state. An aerobic workout will not only help to reduce stress, but it can be the first step toward improved health.

5. If you have chronic stress, a change in lifestyle can be very effective. Try getting involved with an activity, such as acting, playing a musi-

cal instrument, painting, or cooking, that will soothe you. Singing is my way of reducing stress, especially when I'm in the car and driving away from a rather humiliating golfing experience. Some songs are tailor-made for expressing the very emotions that I'm feeling at such times. If you want to hear me break into a few bars of "Nobody Knows the Trouble I've Seen," let me know.

6. Helping others can reduce stress by making you feel that you're doing something positive. Volunteering can give you a quick sense of accomplishment. If lack of time is one of the reasons why you get stressed, however, don't go overboard here.

7. Laughter is Sol's way of dealing with stress. Need a joke, he's got one up his sleeve. Laughter is cathartic because it changes some of your brain chemistry that can physiologically reduce your stress. Some studies suggest that laughter can also positively affect the immune system, heart, and lungs. Laughter relieves tension by relaxing the body and mind. (No wonder one hears so many golf jokes and one-liners during play.) I'm not suggesting that you spend all your time watching comedy movies. Just develop a playful attitude toward life to see the joke of it all.

8. Rosa, my significant other, reduces muscle tension caused by stress with a massage. Massage temporarily reduces tension as it warms and relaxes muscles. Look for a qualified massage therapist, or check with your local YMCA and health clubs.

9. Communication is a good stress reducer. Maybe that's why bartenders are sought out when someone wants to bend an ear. (Of course, it could also be the attraction of alcohol.) Playing poker, hanging around, and just talking after eighteen holes can give you opportunities to commiserate about your game or whatever is bothering you. These opportunities can help you to eliminate the feeling that you're the only one who is going through a stressful time.

10. Just trying to play golf better can also relieve stress. I'm not suggesting that you make it a way of life—you could create

more stress if your goal is to lower your handicap by seven strokes—but immerse yourself in the game. Read about the history of golf, practice for the fun of it, try a new putting stroke, or take golf vacations.

Tip: In addition to these treatment approaches, I recommend that you get more sleep and exercise. Take quiet breaks to enjoy your aloneness. Eat a balanced diet with plenty of fruits and vegetables. Most of all, don't fight stress by taking a stiff drink. If you are unsuccessful in relieving the stress, see your therapist.

■ UNEXPECTED CHANGES

Question: "I often get flustered when a buddy calls and cancels golf. I also hate it when I am told by my pro that I need to make some swing changes. And the biggest problem I have with change is all the things that are happening to me as I get older. I hate my stiff body in the morning and how much more difficult it is for me to walk eighteen holes. How can I ever learn to deal with all these changes without getting down?"

Answer: No question, the comfortable routines that people settle into are often difficult to let go because they abhor the uncertainty and mental effort involved in doing something different. Change also affects the comfort that comes from being on automatic pilot. If you resist the changes that life demands on and off the course, however, you will only create a whole set of problems that can leave you irritable and stressful. The reality of life is that things change, period. There is nothing to do but face that fact.

You must learn to expect the unexpected at all times. Plans change, people change, your game changes, your health changes, playing conditions change—everything changes. To deal with the unexpected changes in your golf game and in your life, you might want to look at what really matters to you.

It's easy to think that when things change your natural reaction should be frustration and anger. But are they natural? Think about what would happen the next time you have to face a change and you meet it head-on by saying to yourself, "Oh well, that's life. So be it." Chances are that you'll have more energy to face the change, especially because you're apt to feel less frustrated. When you think about and practice surrendering to possible changes, you gain inner peace because you grab onto what matters in life and don't get upset over what you can't control.

Tip: Remind yourself daily that the challenge awaiting you is not to fight change head-on but to learn how to be flexible by expecting change and practicing peace of mind. This technique works wonders when you are suddenly penalized with a bad lie. Expecting a few bad lies per round will help you to maintain your inner calm as you prepare to make a more focused swing. By doing that you thus eliminate the possibility of sacrificing the concentration needed to make the shot. The best part of adopting this approach is that your playing partners will see a changed person, on the course and off, who seizes life's hazards as opportunities. (I bet they applaud you.)

THE UNFAIRNESS OF GOLF ■

Question: "I had a 5-iron to the green to win my match. I struck the ball perfectly, and it landed just where I wanted it to. But someone left a rake in front of the green. My ball hit it and bounced into the sand trap. I lost the match. To say the least, I was ready to track down the golfer that did it. Any advice for these crazy things that happen during a round?"

Answer: Just ask Tom Lehman. He had a chance to win both the 1996 and the 1997 U.S. Opens. In 1996, his ball was caught by the wind and landed in deep rough on the eighteenth tee. In 1997, his perfectly struck 7-iron ball hit an abnormally hard green and found the water on the crucial seventeenth hole. Had he played earlier in the day in 1996, the ball would have ended up 10 feet from the hole. The moral? Golf is truly a metaphor for life when it comes to fairness. Both life and golf are unfair. We all get our turns. There is no cure.

Recognize and anticipate that you will get your share of bad lies and bad breaks during a round, and you will get less upset when they happen. Ben Hogan had a way of saying this differently. He figured that every time he played, he would, at best, be able to strike the ball squarely no more than eight times during a round. The rest of the shots would be pretty much off and could easily result in difficult outcomes. He used that thinking process to stay focused; when he did mis-hit a shot that ended up in a tough spot, he didn't go to pieces. He simply accepted what he anticipated and made the best of the bad lie.

The big mistake is to feel bad about what happens and to think that you don't get the breaks that you deserve. The fact is that you're just having your turn at bad breaks, which has nothing to do with who you are and what you do. By accepting bad lies, spiked greens, and so forth, you can still enjoy the good and not-so-good situations when you play. In other words, you can have fun. The secret is to see the joke of it all and enjoy the game despite the fact that a bad break could mean losing a match. If you do lose, what's the worst thing that will happen? Ask yourself, and I bet the answer won't be as bad as you thought.

Tip: I often look at bad breaks during play as opportunities to improve my game. For example, the other day my ball landed in a divot and I hit the shot poorly. After the round, I spoke with my pro about hitting out of divots and practiced what he advised. I'm no longer uncomfortable about hitting out of bad lies. I could have taken my torch to the bar and bent the bartender's ear and wallowed in my self-pity. Instead, the bad break turned out to be a valuable learning experience. Give it a try.

WHEN TO CHANGE YOUR SWING ■

Question: "I just got a great lesson from my pro, and it helped me hit the ball more consistently. The problem is the swing feels awkward, yet it seems to work. I've got a tournament soon, and I'm wondering if I should use my new swing or rely on my old?"

Answer: There is a right time and a wrong time to start committing to swing changes. If your pro has been working on your tempo and you read an article about ball positioning, don't take on the new information just yet. Stay with the specific mechanics that you're learning. If you add something new to what you're trying to learn, you'll only inhibit learning the initial stuff. That is, you will improve only if you practice one thing at a time. When I say practice, I mean staying with the new swing mechanics but understanding that practice, per se, doesn't help you to get better. It helps you to get better, then worse, then better, then worse, then a little better, and perhaps eventually even a lot better.

Let me explain. I often tell patients that psychological growth is not a steady upward path. When they try something different and get results, the fear and other emotions mentioned in an earlier section, "Resistance to Change," of this chapter kick into high gear and they usually resort to the old and familiar. Many folks in therapy actually get worse for a little while, but this is simply a test of the mind and body to determine if the old safe place is still there, even though it was abandoned. So approach change more realistically by reminding yourself that, as you take one step forward toward a new swing, expect to take two or three steps backward during the transition stage. That is, things might get worse for a bit but not for long.

Improving your swing takes practice, regular practice, boring practice—hundreds of repetitions—before the new swing becomes part of your muscle memory. If you don't believe this and yet really want to fix a swing flaw, keep in mind what Nick Faldo recently confessed. He said that hitting more than six million practice balls over the years was his secret to getting his game where it is today. (Nothing was said about all the mental time spent on it and all the hours probably consumed by cursing his teaching pros.)

Tip: Obviously, I'm not suggesting that you resort to the commitment that Faldo made to improve his game. I recommend that you just remind yourself how Nick reached his level of play the next time you find yourself wanting so badly to shoot lower scores. More to the point, take heed of my assertion that change is not essential to your enjoyment of the game. If you don't mind being inconsistent, play for the pleasure awaiting every round. That way, when your game becomes erratic, say, a birdie followed by a triple bogey or seven consecutive pars followed by five consecutive triple bogeys, remind yourself that golf is elusive and unpredictable—but one of the biggest kicks waiting to be enjoyed.

■ THE YIPS

Question: "The other day, I couldn't start my putter back. It took me longer than it usually does, and when I did so I was aware of my inability to pull the club back. At that point my hands began to shake. My concentration was shot, and I mis-hit the ball. The whole day was like that. Any suggestions?"

Answer: It sounds like you had a good case of the yips (defined by *Webster's* as "a state of nervous tension affecting . . . a golfer . . . in the performance of a crucial action"). The yips are the reason for so many putting styles and for more putters—long and short—on the market than any other club in a golfer's bag. In the past, Tommy Armour, Harry

Vardon, Charlie Owens, Sam Snead, and Ben Hogan all suffered from the yips. Today, chances are that any professional golfer using an extra long putter is probably trying to control the yips.

Before doing anything else, rule out the possibility that the cause is physiological. If you are on medication or have some physical health problem, either of these could have something to do with your putting problem. For someone in top physical shape, perhaps the following will help. Your inability to move the club back could result from fearing the consequences of hitting either a good or a bad putt. That's right, I'm back to my comments about the fear of success and the fear of failure (see the section, "Resistance to Change," in this chapter). It could be you are telling yourself that if you hit the ball well, some penalty will result. Perhaps your golfing friends would be envious; if you don't play well, you can keep their friendship. Or, it could be that you are "shoulding" to yourself. You might be saying that you should strike the ball well. By saying that, you could be creating a fear that if you don't, you'll have to deal with all the self-disgust that results. Again, these are just possible reasons.

Tip: If a long putter doesn't help in reducing the yips, you might want to consult a sports psychologist (see Appendix D), who can do a careful behavioral assessment to pinpoint specific variables that could be fueling some of the possible causes mentioned above. Once that's done, a relearning program can be set up to help extinguish fears and/or self-disgust. Give it a try. You can also call your local psychological association and/or college to get the names of practicing sports therapists.

WHY WE PLAY GOLF ■

Question: "Why do we put up with three-putt rounds and go back and play after spending thousands of lessons only to find our handicap pretty much the same?"

Answer: Let me add to your questions. Why do you wait in long lines to tee off at each hole? What fun is there in hitting balls out of bounds? In other words, have you ever thought of how much money you've spent on a game that can create so much heartache, anger, and frustration? I estimate that I have spent more than fifty thousand dollars on golf since I took up the game in my teens. Since then, I have probably gone through two thousand golf balls, seven sets of clubs, played more than a hundred thousand holes, and hit a million practice balls. In terms of time, I have probably totaled five years of play. And I'm just an average player. Given your commitment to the game, you might have spent more time playing than I have. Yet, "why" questions keep popping up from my non-golfing friends: "Why play golf?" "Why chase a white ball around acres of land that can be used for housing the poor or kept as wilderness so that wildlife can live?" "Why spoil a good walk?" I used to think that the answers were to get as close to par as I could; to hit drives that went beyond 250 yards; to put a string of birdies together; to eagle; to ace holes; and of course, to beat my playing partners. But the more I examined my reasons for playing, the more I gained insight into seven more significant explanations for the hold that this magical game has on its players:

1. You might play to see how you can practice a certain swing thought and keep at it until you achieve the desired results. The joy that you obtain from playing a round might relate to how much success you have with that swing thought. This learning process itself is extremely rewarding.

2. It's a wonderful challenge to the old adage, "To thine own self be true." In other words, what better way is there to see how honest you are than to play golf? How many times have you been tempted, after hitting a ball astray and being alone in the rough with no one observing you, to kick the ball just a bit to get a better lie (see the section, "Cheating," in this chapter). If you do kick it, you learn something important about your char-

acter (or lack thereof). But what if you don't kick it? Do you share this information with your friends or just keep it to yourself? There is no greater feeling than to know that you conquered temptation.

3. A top corporate executive, whom I counseled recently, confided that he loves to play golf with prospective customers so that he can learn all about them. By watching how they play, he can predict how they will react when there's a business crisis. How do they deal with adversity on the course? Chances are that if they throw their clubs when they get bad breaks, they'll opt for that type of behavior when life gives them a turn of bad fortune. If golfers can surrender to the reality that life is a pretty even playing field, on and off the course, and that they all have their share of good and bad breaks, they are apt to have developed a pretty solid moral fiber by the time they reach their senior years. I often like to imagine what a golfing partner is like on and off the course by observing the way that person plays. Most of the time, I'm delighted to see a rather strong correlation.

4. Another reason, recently noted in the literature, for men and women to tee up is bonding. This is a way for both men and women to share intimacy. They play golf not only to be with friends but to talk about their problems as they walk from hole to hole, thus creating their bonding. That's why I urge golfers to make their golfing commitments with care and stick to them. When a golfing date is broken, it is not taken lightly. Broken dates result in time away from that sacred space created during a round. One playing partner likened it to his being in a foxhole during the war and his feeling of kinship, closeness, and connection to the other men in the foxhole.

5. You might play golf because of your sense of physical well-being after walking six miles or more on a hot, humid day. Despite a horrendous score, collapsing in a chair at the nineteenth hole with a wonderful feeling of exhaustion might be a reason in

itself. You can hardly walk, talk, or lift yourself off the chair, but you love it and can't wait to get into that state of paralysis again.

6. Then, there are the long-term health benefits that you gain from playing a quick eighteen.

7. Of all the reasons for playing, however, the one I enjoy the most is the recognition, whether I'm playing in a foursome or by myself, that *I "am" the world or one with the world.* Nature can do that. Golf then becomes an opportunity to experience the setting sun, the smell of freshly cut wet grass, the sound of a crisp hit, the beauty of the splash of assorted colors of green, the wind and cold and heat and frost and sun and moon, and the feel of my shoes as they punch through the rough or dig into the sand in a trap.

My fondest golfing memory was my last night in Denver before moving to California. Sol, his brother-in-law, and I were playing the far side of a public course when we ran out of light. But the moon was full, and a car dealership across the way had illuminated just enough of the tee so that I could see the ball. We all played by feel and sound.

The most marvelous thing happened at the last hole, one that I had never birdied during all my attempts over the years. But, on this particular night, given the camaraderie and the joy of being lost in the moment, I hit my drive straight down the center of the fairway and then hit my second shot crisply. After looking everywhere for the ball, I discovered that it had rolled 5 feet from the pin—some 176 yards. That would have been more than enough, but if I made the putt, I would birdie the hole. I got down on my hands and knees, inhaled the damp grass, felt the path to the hole, figured there was a slight break, and stroked the ball in. It reminded me of the eagle that another friend had made in the dark—just playing by feel and with the use of flashlights.

So when things aren't going right, I grab these memories and replay them, savor my experiences, provide myself a bit of a retreat from the often ugly anxiety of day-to-day business.

So why do you play? Why do you spend so much money? Even though you cannot perfect your score that much, why do you continue to run out to the course and try? I say, look at the reasons that I've given you. See if they don't add up to the real explanations for making those 6 A.M. tee-off times "come hell or high water."

THE ZONE (PART 1) ■

Question: "I hear a lot about winning golfers who claim that they get into the "zone." Do you think this automatically happens, or is there something you can do to enter one?"

Answer: A zone may be loosely defined as a state of focused concentration that amounts to absolute absorption in your game. Every golfer experiences zones from time to time, and my hunch is that some top players are born with the ability to get into it without much effort. I suspect it's one more variable that made Jack Nicklaus great for so many years. Specifically, you're in the zone during a round when you feel strong, alert, in effortless control, unself-conscious, and at the peak of your ability. In addition, your sense of time and emotional problems seem to disappear while you play.

Tip: Can you do anything to control a zone and not just leave it to chance? Hold on to your 9-iron. You can. Beware, the editors might censor my comments to keep my credibility from going off a cliff. If what I suggest here sounds weird, it is. But please don't lock me up.

The object during a round is to become whatever it is that is occurring. Stay with me. Use this example: You hit a 5-iron to the green, and your ball lands in a trap. You become angry. Rather than reacting to the anger, to get into the zone you *become* the anger. You focus on the feeling and simply observe it. The object here is once you become the emotion, you cannot be affected by it. Why not? Because you have figuratively disappeared and have become the anger. Weird? Yes.

Try another example: You just finished three-putting a very important hole and you want to get into the zone, so you concentrate intensely on the present. As you walk away from the green, the present for you then would be observing the path, listening to a bird chirping, admiring the color of the grass, and so forth. By total absorption in the present, the three-putt green—a past experience—does not linger to inhibit your performance. It's over. It doesn't exist. Unfortunately, most golfers keep the past going during their rounds by thinking about such things as mis-hits, and three-putt greens. Over time, this sort of thinking eats away at their ability to flow—to concentrate on the present in order to maximize performance.

To control a zone, right now as you are reading, try to stay in the present by concentrating on everything I'm suggesting. If something comes up from the past, go with it. That is, rather than blocking it out, just become it. If you suddenly think of a bill you have to pay, don't block it out. Focus on the bill. If you get upset by it, observe the upset; don't react to it. Of course, that is easier said than done. If this still is not clicking for you, read the comments in the next section, "The Zone (Part 2)."

■ THE ZONE (PART 2)

Question: "OK, I buy your argument that playing golf to enter the zone is important. Now, can you tell me what I can do to achieve that zone while I play?"

Answer: Among the many books about the mental aspects of golf, few accomplish what they set out to do. That is, most of the literature fails to get you to plug into a zone where you play golf without thinking about what you're doing. Achievement of such a reality, where time seems to slow down, is elusive at best. Zoning must happen naturally. But to ask the golfer to analyze at once what must be done—which means thinking—while entering a state of nonthinking is to pose an obvious contradiction. It's like offering the instruction: "Don't read this sentence!" You can't help but read it. Similarly, you can't help but analyze it. In other words, what you're reading now might be useful as it applies to your understanding of what I'm suggesting but it becomes useless while you're on the golf course.

The first step toward entering the zone is to learn how to reach the "here and now" while playing; to depart from the vicissitudes of daily living; and to savor the grand experience of the gestalt of golfing, such as the joy of the walk, the camaraderie, the weather, the sights and smells, the wonder of making an occasional great golf shot (the fade that perfectly follows the fairway dogleg), the ecstasy of being alone with yourself tuned into the present, the presence of fragrances, the tacky feel of your grips, the sight of the ball in flight, the inimitable rattle of the ball catching the bottom of the cup. To play golf with a mind to these ultimate sensory goals will alone offer ageless benefits. Suddenly your reason for playing needn't be confined to scoring in the 70s. You can lose numerically to an opponent but still win the kick of having the experience. In doing so, you can play golf for a higher purpose.

As people grow older, golf becomes akin to other parts of their lives in that they need to find other ways, means, and reasons for doing things. Such aspects of golf as winning scores, new equipment, wardrobe, tournaments, variety of courses, and competition are mere means to an end, not the end itself. By adapting the goal of a zone-oriented approach, golfers allow themselves the luxury of reaching a more profound level of understanding why they love the game in its totality.

Tip: Paradoxical as it might seem, I'm asking you to read this section, understand it, and then forget it. Allow the subconscious part of your mind to go to work on this. You can't go to the golf course and consciously force yourself to do this. If you do, then you will be aware of what I'm suggesting and that will keep it from working. As I noted before, paralysis will be the result.

Here are three steps for achieving "zones" during play:

Step 1. To reach a higher level of play, the goal is to avoid striving for it. Comfort zones are directly related to what I asserted earlier—looking for the larger purpose of golf. Accordingly, as you approach the game each time, use it as a way of plugging into the moment and getting away from thinking about the past or worrying about the future. While driving to the course, say to yourself: "Ah, great! I can't wait to get out there today and just throw my fate to the wind and enjoy the wonderful experience of being caught up in the moment. I can't wait to feel the sun on my face, the joy of walking, the gift of those marvelously landscaped holes, the promise of an occasional great putt or shot, the fun of walking in the moment. . . ." By reaffirming the ultimate goal of playing golf, you can increase your chance of extending the comfort zone.

Step 2. Once on the course, make your wagers and practice your swing thoughts, but remind yourself over and over that you are not there to win or to shoot a low score. These things would be nice, but you are at the golf course to seize the moment and fully plug into the experience. Say that you are about to leave your comfort zone after having made six pars in a row. Rather than being paralyzed by the thought, "I've never done this before," say to yourself, "So what? It would be nice to break my record and get another par, but heck, I'm here to reach the goal of enjoying the moment. If I get a par, great. If I don't, it doesn't matter. What matters is that I enjoy it all, the good and the bad."

Step 3. Practice this away from the course. Think about your comfort zone as time goes on. Ask yourself: "What is the worst thing that will happen to me if I shoot a round of golf like I never have before?" Yes, what is the *worst* thing? Give yourself two answers to the question.

The following example can show you how step 3 works:

One of my senior clients wanted desperately to break eighty. He shot even 80s a few times but could never get lower than that. Something always seemed to happen. (All golfers can identify with that.) So I asked him to answer the question in step 3, and here's what he came up with: "If I shoot below 80 and accomplish what I've always wanted, I'll have to work harder on my game and figure out how to do it again. I'll want to do it again. And I don't want to be a slave to the game."

The answer provides the epiphany that he fears the changes that he will have to make if he remains out of his comfort zone and accomplishes what he would like.

At this point I offered him the following, "What is the worst thing that would happen if you made these changes?"

"I would have to spend more time playing golf," he said.

I asked him, "What terrible thing would happen if you spent more time playing golf?"

"I would ignore my wife," he answered, then hesitated, "but she wants me to play more. She tells me that I'm at home bugging her in the mornings when she likes working in the garden. So I guess that the worst just never happens."

See what I mean? My point is that by challenging your irrational belief that something terrible will happen, you begin to see that, in fact, nothing will. As a result, you allow yourself to go beyond your comfort zone.

Please note, of course, that these examples and suggestions take time. The larger point is that you don't even need to practice these techniques. They aren't like golf thoughts that involve setup or take-away or keeping the head still. Read these suggestions, and then forget about them. When you come close to leaving your comfort zone the next time you play, however, note how they come back to remind you of what you can do to push beyond your comfort zone. Don't get alarmed. Take your triple bogey to the next hole and cure yourself by plugging into a few seconds of admiring the new foliage and the cloud formations, smelling the freshly cut Bermuda grass, and feeling the wind blowing the wonders of the present against your body. Keep the ultimate goal of playing close to the heart and seize upon its beauty. Then watch what happens. I submit that you'll find, in a sensory appreciation at first and then in eventual performance, that playing golf past the age of forty is a heightened experience unlike anything you recall—or think you recall—from your youth.

NUTRITION 5

"A good walk spoiled." In these sixteen letters, Mark Twain suggested the essence of golf's frustration. The phrase has become the familiar expression of many who have tried the game but who don't "get" it and never will.

Golfers, of course, understand that a bad day on the course can be better than a good day at other pursuits. Moreover, they might sense, as they get older, that they can prevent the spoiling of golf's good walk by maximizing nutrition.

To put it simply, seniors who want to play and enjoy quality golf need to consign to the past the practice of consuming three fatty hot dogs and munching salty chips and peanuts while chugging beer during an eighteen-hole cart ride. That's not the way to play golf under any circumstances, but the point is particularly important after age forty.

The research is in. The impact of nutrition on aging demands serious attention. Nutrition influences most medical problems, such as cardiovascular disease and some forms of cancer, associated with aging. Another finding, about which most seniors are probably unaware, is that food intake should decrease with age. Also, some seniors can eat less but still gain weight. Longitudinal studies on aging show that the optimal energy intake of 2,700 calories a day at age thirty declines linearly to 2,100 calories a day at age eighty.

One explanation for this decline in caloric needs is that physical activity decreases with age. Related to this fact is another cruel reality: The level of body fat increases up to about age sixty; conversely, protein—lean body mass—decreases at a rate of about six pounds per decade from early adulthood. Most of the lean tissue loss represents lost muscle mass. Consequently, a golfer strikes a ball at age seventy with twenty pounds less muscle mass, on average, than he or she did at age forty. On top of that, some muscle mass is replaced with fat and connective tissue, which means that driving balls as we did at a younger age is probably out of the question. Bone mass also is commonly lost. While all of the above information may seem depressing, it need not be if senior golfers realize that the inevitability of such tendencies can be slowed and delayed. As they go through this metamorphosis, they can benefit from paying more attention to their diets and to the amount of time devoted to exercise.

Of course, much has been made of the apparent contradictions about diet. This has caused much confusion and bemusement, and not just among lay people. Professionals contradict one another more or less daily: eat less salt, eat more salt; use butter, use margarine; beer and wine are good for you one day, bad for you the next; diets should restrict proteins one day or be limited to liquids the next and carbohydrates the next. It's obviously bewildering.

In this chapter, we try to take the mystery out of diets and give you a sense of nutrition needed to maintain your health and to keep your game sharp. Again, it's up to you to decide which nutritional approach will lead you to a healthier game of golf. Whatever you decide, bon appetit!

■ CARBOHYDRATES

Question: I was told by a golfing buddy that if I put more carbohydrates in my diet, I'll have more stamina to walk my round of golf.

Can you help shed some light on my ignorance about carbohydrates?

Answer: Your body gets most of its energy from carbohydrates which are metabolized to make glucose or sugar to fuel the body so it can get you around the course, especially if you're walking. Carbohydrates are found in fruits, vegetables, legumes, pasta, breads, grains, and cereals. There are two types of carbohydrates: simple and complex. Simple carbohydrates need little digestion and are found in sweet-tasting foods such as fruits, some vegetables, honey, syrups, and the refined sugars derived from them. Complex carbohydrates consist of the starches and fiber found in cereals, grains and vegetables. When carbohydrates are detected in the bloodstream, insulin is released from the pancreas. The insulin pushes the glucose and amino acids circulating in the blood into the cells where they are used to make energy or build cellular structures.

Since simple carbohydrates require little digestion, they enter the bloodstream rapidly, elevating the blood glucose levels. In some individuals this causes the body to secrete too much insulin. These high insulin levels then cause too much glucose to leave the bloodstream and blood sugar levels plummet, leaving little glucose free to fuel your brain. Low blood sugar levels cause the familiar mid-morning slump you get after a simple carbohydrate meal such as coffee and donuts. To prevent this slump, eat a meal rich in complex unprocessed carbohydrates with a protein-rich food and a small amount of fat. This combination will decrease the rate at which the sugar enters the bloodstream and will help to keep blood sugar levels more even.

Tip: To make your diet rich in carbohydrates follow the USDA's new Food Pyramid. Base your diet on whole grains, cereals, pasta, rice, and legumes and eat a minimum of five to seven servings of fruits and vegetables each day. These foods will provide not only complex carbohydrates and fiber but important vitamins, minerals, fiber, and other nutrients that you need to stay healthy.

Choose whole grains and cereals rather than refined types which contain considerably less fiber and fewer nutrients. When you do eat pasta, be careful not to top it with rich sauces heavy in saturated fats such butter or cheese.

■ DIET (TO MAINTAIN YOUTH)

Question: "I am thinking of getting into dieting again. Is there such a thing as an anti-aging diet, and what's the best thing to do when choosing a diet?"

Answer: Dieting will provide a number of health benefits, but it won't turn back the clock. The best thing to do is to choose a diet program that you can consistently practice. Eat tasty, healthful foods and avoid high-calorie, high-fat dishes.

We recommend looking through a number of cookbooks, especially those written by dietitians or gerontologists that target seniors, and select one that appeals to you. Many cookbooks end up in the drawer after a few weeks. Your public library offers a wonderful assortment of specialized cookbooks that you can borrow.

Tip: See the Bibliography at the end of this book for recommended books on nutrition.

■ DIET (BALANCED) (SEE NUTRITION)

Question: "Do I need to take vitamins and minerals if I'm eating a good, balanced diet? What constitutes a well-balanced diet? And suppose I eat a good, balanced diet. Should I still be taking supplements?"

Answer: No, you don't need supplements if you're eating a good, balanced diet. Unfortunately, most people don't know what a good, balanced diet is and/or don't have the time to keep one. A good balanced diet is eating foods from the Food Pyramid published by the USDA. (See Nutrition in this chapter). If you assume that a healthy diet means eating eggs for breakfast, a steak for lunch and dinner, and a few vegetables thrown in here and there, you might have been told you were right forty years ago. Not today. Now, in order to meet the requirements for a good, balanced diet, it's essential to consume more than forty different nutrients, and no single food group can do the job. That's why it's crucial to eat a variety of foods to meet the daily nutrient requirements. (We suggest that you read the other sections of this chapter.)

If you follow three guidelines, you won't need to worry about taking supplements:

1. Eat foods daily that are low in fat, saturated fat, and cholesterol. They help to protect your body against heart disease, excessive weight, and cancer. To do that, you need to eat foods from the Food Pyramid, which includes grains, vegetables, fruits, dairy products, lean meats, poultry, fish, dried beans, eggs, and nuts.

2. Eat sugar in moderation. It adds calories but has no nutritional value.

3. Get into the habit of eating less salt and sodium (assuming that you eat more than you need, as many people do). Most of the salt that you need is already in the food that you are consuming. Foods high in sodium include frozen entrees, pizzas, cured meats and luncheon meats, hot dogs, canned fish, canned soups, canned vegetables and juices, salted nuts, chips, popcorn, baked goods, catsup, olives, pickle relish, mayonnaise, salad dressing—ah, you're getting the picture, right? In other words, most of the foods available at the snack bar are not much help in maintaining a balanced diet.

Tip: Prepare for your round of golf by putting together a plastic bag of fruits and crackers and perhaps a piece of sourdough bread. You will be surprised how much energy you can get from nibbling away on your goodies while you play. The temptation to eat those toxic hot dogs will be significantly diminished.

■ DIET AND WEIGHT

Question: "Sometimes I skip meals, and sometimes I eat a lot of fried foods. My doctor tells me that my health is excellent. Yet, I'd still like to lose a few pounds. Any advice that can help me without having to sacrifice my love for fried foods?"

Answer: It's important to remember the best diets are sometimes the ones that have been used for hundreds of years. Perhaps this is due to nature and tradition. For example, people in Japan used to have fewer heart attacks, strokes, cancer, diabetes, and other terminal diseases than folks here in the United States, but that changed after World War II when the Japanese people began to import our lifestyles and to mimic our fatty diets.

Assuming that you have begun an exercise program to become more fit, we suggest focusing your diet on nutrition and healthy eating, not just on losing a few pounds. Our thesis is this: It's more important to focus on staying healthy by eating sensibly. Get rid of the myth that you can develop a body that clones Gary Player. Gary has spent thousands of hours in exercising and conditioning his body and religiously adhering to a spartan diet. In addition, his genes have a major role in helping him to keep trim.

If you want to eat some fried foods now and then, that's fine. The point is, don't make an eating decision simply to lose a few pounds. Whatever you decide to eat, it should be because that food will help to maintain your health. In other words, if you are starving yourself for the sake of losing five or six pounds, you could be doing more harm than if you are eating healthy.

The best way to establish a healthy diet is to buy nutritional foods. Look at it this way, if you don't have lots of fats in the kitchen, you're more likely to eat healthy when you get hungry. In other words, the more you skip the foods that are not good for your health, the better off you'll be.

Tip: One reason that people eat what they do has a strong basis in family and cultural traditions. Chances are that your love of fried foods has something to do with your childhood and the nostalgia that results when you eat them. You can get the same nostalgia fix, however, by thinking about other childhood foods that are considered healthful today. When you shop, keep that in mind. For example, almost everyone relates turkey to Thanksgiving. Having some turkey around for a snack will be a lot healthier than having some leftover fried chicken. Remember, reducing the amount of fatty fried foods you eat will lower your risk of developing heart disease, hypertension, and stroke. Increasing foods with lots of fiber will reduce the likelihood of cancer, high blood sugar levels, arteriosclerosis, and many other chronic health conditions.

EATING HAZARDS AT TOURNAMENTS ■

Question: "When we have a golf outing, my friends and I usually have breakfast. The problem is I throw caution to the wind and feel pressure to eat a lot of bad food. That happens, too, when we have golf banquets. Any suggestions as to what I can do?"

Answer: What you put into your stomach the morning of your game will influence your performance for the rest of the day. Never skip breakfast. Remember by morning your body has been without food for ten to twelve hours. Both your brain and muscles desperately need to refuel. This fuel should come in the form of complex carbohydrates. Foods rich in starch are a time-release form of energy that will keep your brain supplied with glucose and your muscles supplied with glycogen all morning. Good sources of complex carbohydrate include cold and hot cereals, whole grain breads and bagels, and raw fruits such as unpeeled apples and pears, oranges and grapefruit with the white coat intact, and bananas.

In addition to this you must also include a protein source. Protein in the morning helps to prevent the mid-morning slump caused by low blood sugar levels. Protein also has an effect on your brain chemistry. Tyrosine and phenylalanine are amino acids necessary for the manufacture of epinephrine and norepinephrine, the neurotransmitters in the brain responsible for alertness. A high protein meal before a game will increase the amount of these amino acids reaching the brain and thereby increase your ability to concentrate. Good sources of protein include low-fat or skim dairy or soy products such as yogurt, cottage cheese, milk, eggs prepared without butter or other fats, and lean meats such as Canadian bacon.

Avoid high-fat foods such as donuts, croissants, muffins, fried eggs, and the traditional high-fat breakfast meats. These high-fat foods will make you feel sluggish. Do not stuff yourself. Even too much of a good thing can slow you down.

Avoid eating simple or processed carbohydrates on an empty stomach. This includes fruit juices and processed cereals. These foods will increase insulin levels in the blood and eventually lower blood sugar. Worse, these foods promote the secretion of serotonin in the brain cells. Serotonin is the neurotransmitter that helps you to relax and sleep. To play your best game of golf you need the secretion of the alertness neurotransmitters which protein promotes.

If you want to avoid developing the habit of eating poorly, stay away from eating out regularly or eating the food served at golf tournaments. Most of the foods are unhealthful and make it difficult for you to manage your weight.

If you are attending a banquet, eat a small low-fat meal before you leave the house. This will reduce your appetite so that you can make more healthy decisions about food. Or call ahead and ask the caterers to prepare you a special vegetarian meal or one that is low in calories and fat. If you have to eat what they serve you, eat less. If you participate in a lot of conferences and tournaments, ask the caterer to prepare a heart-healthy menu. You'd be surprised how many will go out of their way to put together a healthy dish even though it's not what's being served to everyone else. Avoid alcohol. Not only does it contain empty calories but it is dehydrating to the body and will muddle your mental faculties.

Breakfast is the most important meal of the day for golfers. What you eat before your game will have a direct effect on how well you play so make each calorie count when choosing breakfast foods.

Tip: If you are forced to choose what you are going to eat at a function, look for foods that are steamed, poached, broiled, or grilled. Again, the secret is to eat smaller portions of meats and soups and especially desserts. Have a few pieces of unbuttered bread before the meal is served to blunt your appetite and have salad dressings served on the side. Also, sip water throughout the meal and stop eating when you are full.

I often carry a plastic bag of crackers and fruit in my golf bag even though I know there will be catered food at a tournament. It's amazing how much control you will get over your weight and eating healthy just by doing this.

EATING HEALTHY TIPS ■

Question: "OK, I'm motivated to eat healthy and not be so concerned about losing weight. What's the game plan?"

Answer: The game plan is simple. Build a diet filled with nutritious and enjoyable foods. Remember, the goal is not to stay away from tasty snacks and delicious meals. Consider the following guidelines for replacing unhealthy foods with healthy ones.

Avoid whole milk; replace it with skim milk, 1 percent milk, or powdered milk. Use a nondairy product instead of cream in your coffee. Butter and margarine are both no-nos. A recent study suggests that ordinary stick margarine is even worse for the heart than butter. (Note: This does not apply to the newer low-fat spreads). What to use? Consider flavored olive oil or jelly. In place of ice cream, try ice milk; sherbets; and low-fat, low-calorie desserts, such as yogurt. Instead of eating potato chips, put popcorn or unsalted pretzels in a plastic bag and carry it with you. If you have a sweet tooth, buy sugar-free candies. Replace cookies with fruits.

When you eat bread, avoid white bread and rolls and substitute whole wheat. Choose high-fiber cereals and, when possible, substitute poultry for red meats. If you are an egg-a-day person, use a noncholesterol egg substitute. After a few days, you won't be able to tell the difference.

Remember, you're less likely to have problems following a healthy diet if you have a lot of good, nutritional foods around you. When you get that craving to snack, you'll be prepared.

■ EATING RIGHT (COMMONSENSE APPROACH)

Question: "OK. I know you won't endorse any one of the three hundred-plus "what to eat" programs for good health that exist. But generally speaking, what should I do in order to eat sensibly?"

Answer: You're right. I have no way of tailoring a specific healthy eating menu for each reader (some of you may have chronic medical conditions or other mitigating circumstances). One thing for sure, if you stuff yourself with a large meal and then head for the first tee box, you'll not only feel sluggish while contemplating the golf game, you'll also find it more difficult than usual to make a full turn. My advice is to eat an hour or two before the round.

Generally, however, I recommend that the aging golfer who is in good health avoid too many fatty foods and too much sugar. Eat the foods that provide the most nutritional benefits, such as high-fiber sources: whole-grain breads, cereals, and fruits. Also choose poultry (with skin off) and fish (with skin on) over red meat; salads with light, limited dressing; raw or lightly steamed fresh vegetables; and baked potatoes, which can become entire meals when prepared properly. And drink as much water as you can.

Tip: The foods that should be reduced in quantity are the fried and/ or fatty ones: bacon, red meat, cream and sour cream, butter, re- fined sugars, pastries, ice cream, and most desserts and sweets. A candy bar may harmlessly provide a little energy and a pleasant sensory diversion during a round. But six of them a day will get you into dietary trouble.

As for sodium: It isn't generally understood that we don't have to salt food. Those who gradually reduce the amount of added salt in their diets come to appreciate how great food tastes without extra saltiness. Food, of course, comes with its own flavoring and season- ing, sometimes more subtle than others. Some will accurately find it too bland to consider having a plain baked potato. But we needn't go to the other extreme: heaping on fat and salt in the form of but- ter, sour cream, and bacon bits. Try using low-fat milk and black pepper, or steamed, chopped broccoli and herb vinegar; or a light grating of cheese.

But keep in mind the importance of avoiding being so obsessive-compulsive about your diet that you forget to enjoy life. If you spend too much time agonizing about what not to eat and forcing yourself to consume foods you detest, then it's only a matter of time before you'll give up and abandon the whole idea of preserv- ing your health. My advice: Indulge yourself now and then, but with moderation. Every now and then, remind your taste buds about the sensation of bacon and eggs. Try a dab of butter on a baked potato once in a while. Eat a little chocolate. What you'll dis- cover is that the forbidden foods will lose their mystique. They won't seem nearly so tasty and tempting when the palate has learned to enjoy other flavors from healthier food selections.

■ FATS (GOOD AND BAD)

Question: "I hear so much about fats that are good and not good. Can you give me a few pointers?"

Answer: The first myth to dispel is that eating even a little fat is detrimental to your health. In fact, we need some fat to retain heat for survival purposes when faced with cold water or frigid weather. It also helps us to produce hormones that are necessary for life and reproduction.

There are also fat-soluble vitamins, body oils, enzymes, digestive fluids, and brain and central nervous system tissues that need fats in order to function. Fat allows us to float when in water and helps us maintain healthy skin and hair. In oil form, it protects our skin from the damaging effects of the air and water, sun, heat, and cold. Fat provides protection to our vital organs.

Finally, some fat can help to make us healthier. Oils rich in monounsaturated fatty acids such as olive and canola oils and the oils found in nuts and seeds can help raise our good cholesterol HDL (high density lipoprotein) which protects us from harmful cholesterol LDL (low density lipoprotein). In other words, HDL protects us against myocardial infarction, stroke, and several types of cancers.

Another type of healthful fat are the omega-3 fatty acids found in fish. These fatty acids protect the heart and reduce your risk of developing cancer or having a stroke. Unlike poultry where you should remove the skin, you should eat fish with the skin intact. This will increase your consumption of these healthful oils.

An average golfer requires about fifteen calories per day to maintain each pound of body weight. So a 170-pound golfer requires 170 times fifteen calories, or 2,550 calories per day to maintain the same weight. According to the American Heart Association, a golfer needs only one third or less of those calories from fats. Some researchers have argued that 10 percent of your daily calories from fats should be the goal. And those fats should be either monounsaturated which lower LDL and raise HDL or polyunsaturated which include the essential fatty acids and heart-healthy omega-3 fatty acids. Saturated fats are the ones we want to get you to remove from your diet. Butter, coconut oil, and palm oil should be avoided. They usually become hard at room temperature and tend to raise cholesterol levels in the blood. Although palm and coconut oil are vegetable fats and contain no cholesterol, their levels of saturated fats are so elevated that they are unhealthy as part of your diet. How do you know? Here's my point: Read the ingredient labels on food packages to get the saturated fats out of your diet, even though they boast no cholesterol. The other point is to limit your ingestion of good fats, because as I mentioned before, the body needs only about two or three teaspoons of fat per day.

Tip: Keep in mind that fat does not necessarily cause bad health. It is a symptom of those factors that can cause untimely death. In other words, overweight people lead lives without exercise, ride in carts, etc. These kinds of habits increase the chance for an early death. If you have some excess fat but you are active physically, that is, participate in aerobic activities, you will have a healthier body and live a longer life.

FIBER ■

Question: "I hear a lot about how important fiber is in your diet, especially as you get on in years. Can you offer some advice on what I can do to put more fiber into my diet?"

Answer: Along with all the essential nutrients we discussed in this chapter, we also need fiber in our diets. Fiber comes only from plant foods and, unlike cows and horses, we lack the enzymes to digest these complex carbohydrates. When fiber reaches our large intestines it is in basically the same form as when it was eaten.

However, undigested fiber is helpful in preventing and treating constipation, helps to protect against heart disease, lowers "bad" cholesterol, controls blood sugar for diabetics, and can reduce the risk of some forms of cancer. Sources of fiber include whole grains such as oat bran, oatmeal, brown rice, whole-wheat bread, fruit such as pears, apricots, apples, bananas, and grapefruit, vegetables such as peas, broccoli, carrots, and potatoes with their skin, and legumes such as kidney beans, pinto beans, split peas, lentils, and black-eyed peas.

There are two types of fiber to consider: insoluble fiber, which absorbs many times its weight in water and swells when it gets into the intestines, and soluble fiber, which appears to lower LDL blood cholesterol and partially inhibits glucose from entering the bloodstream. Although it has not been determined how much fiber we should have in our daily diets, several associations suggest between 20–35 grams. Translated, that means eating a minimum of five servings of fruits, and/or the vegetables plus eight to ten servings of the whole-grain products mentioned above.

Tip: If you're going to make a concerted effort to eat more fiber, make sure you drink plenty of fluids and do it gradually to reduce the likelihood of gas. I also recommend that you eat a variety of foods like fruits and vegetables which will also provide some of your daily essential nutrients. I would make it a point to select those foods that are unrefined and/or unprocessed because refining and processing can remove quite a bit of fiber from foods. Also make sure you eat all your fruits and vegetables with their skins.

■ MINERALS

Question: "What are minerals, and what is the correct mineral intake for someone like me who is past forty?"

Answer: Minerals are the inorganic elements found in the natural world. Of all the known elements, twenty-five are in our bodies. Minerals are not metabolized but help form part of the body structure and help regulate body processes. Macrominerals are the minerals needed in large amounts. These include calcium, magnesium, phosphorous, sodium, potassium, and chloride. Trace minerals are needed in much smaller amounts. The major trace minerals include zinc, iron, copper, chromium, manganese, cobalt, iodine, molybdenum, and selenium.

After age fifty, we need minerals more than ever, although it's not understood what amounts are needed. One thing is clear, a number of mineral deficiencies occur in folks past fifty where there is an increased need for calcium and zinc.

Tip: As you get older your body does not absorb nutrients as easily as it did when you were young. In order to meet the RDA (Recommended Dietary Allowance) if you're over fifty, we recommend that you take a comprehensive multivitamin, multimineral tablet. Avoid taking large amounts of any one mineral because this will interfere with the absorption of other needed minerals. Balance is the key.

NUTRITION (SEE DIETS-BALANCED) ■

Question: "Can you give a beginner like me some advice of what is considered good nutrition?"

Answer: The United States Department of Agriculture's (USDA) Food Guide Pyramid was put together to help you obtain a balanced diet from five major food groups: (1) meat, poultry, fish, dried beans, eggs, and nuts; (2) milk, yogurt, and cheese; (3) fruit; (4) vegetables; and (5) fats, oils, and sweets.

Although opinions differ about the proper ratios of essential nutrients in the foods that we eat, it is universally agreed that the present percentage of fat consumption is overwhelmingly high.

The average American diet is approximately 40 percent carbohydrate, 15 percent protein, and 45 percent fat. The consensus for an appropriate balance is 60 percent carbohydrate, 15 percent protein, and 25 percent fat. Some nutritionists advocate that as much as 75 percent of the diet should be carbohydrates and only 10 percent fat. Even if that were advisable, it would be difficult to achieve unless you are a vegetarian, which isn't necessarily a bad idea. Vegetarians stay thinner, live longer, and seem to have more energy.

Carbohydrates exist in all edible substances, but they are found in greatest proportion in grains, fruits, and vegetables. The simplest carbohydrate is glucose. Whether eaten as it is or converted by the body, glucose is the form that the body best uses to create energy. The most complex carbohydrate is cellulose, which is indigestible but necessary as fiber. Among its other functions, fiber keeps the fluid content of the bowel high, which is an obvious benefit.

Between glucose and fiber in complexity is the complex carbohydrate, which makes up the bulk of grains, fruits, and vegetables. It makes a very efficient fuel. It uses the full functioning of the digestive system, which allows the digestive system to run smoothly. Complex carbohydrates are converted into an easily retrievable substance called glycogen, which "burns" slowly so that you don't get energy peaks and valleys. And (more so than an advertising phrase used in a different context) it is less filling and tastes great. When complex carbohydrates are insufficient to maintain the glycogen stores, protein and fat are used for the body's fuel. A rule of thumb for the person trying to lose weight is that it takes about a half hour to deplete the glycogen stores; then fat stores are consumed.

There is very little fat in fruits, vegetables, and grains, with some notable exceptions. Avocados, hands-down, are the fattiest of vegetables, a medium-sized one (four ounces) containing twenty-seven grams of fat. You have to deep-fry the potato to get close to the avocado. Other big exceptions related to fat content in this food

group are nuts, which are essentially solid oil. Peanuts and pista-
chios have relatively less fat, at fourteen grams per ounce of nuts,
than macadamias, at twenty-one grams per ounce. Nuts, then, are
not the snack of choice for the discriminating consumer. Corn, in
its more natural state, has a modicum of fat, but it is a common
source of oil when it is refined.

Dairy products are an even greater source of fat. Butter is all
fat. Cheese is about nine grams of fat per ounce, but it is a reason-
ably good food source if used sparingly. My general feeling about
dairy fat, especially milk, is that it is an exceptionally good source
of nutrition—for baby cows. That dairy products continue to be
used today is more about what people are accustomed to eating
than it is about good nutrition.

Protein is essential for the diet, less as nutrition than for use
as the constituent of bones, muscles, and enzymes. Although you
can get the proper amount of protein in a well-balanced, purely
vegetarian diet, it is more commonly obtained from eggs, dairy
products, and meat, all of which also have fats and cholesterol. The
most beneficial type of meat is fish, and pork is the least beneficial.
Fowl, beef, and lamb are in between. Actually, wild meats, such as
venison, are better than domestic meats because wild animals usually eat only natural foods. As a general rule, restricting your meat
consumption is a healthful dietary choice. At the bottom of the list
of healthy meat selections, of course, is the hot dog offered at the
golf course.

Tip: If you occasionally suffer leg cramps when walking modest
distances, such as three to five miles on a golf course, you might
find calcium supplements to be helpful. Select a supplement that
has half as much magnesium as calcium, as well as some zinc.
Another cause of cramping is relative dehydration. Be sure that you
are taking enough fluids. Your average daily intake should be two
quarts. If you are active or if it is hot, the daily need could increase
twofold or more.

■ NUTRITIONAL SUPPLEMENTS

Question: "I have a golfing friend who takes tons of herbs and vitamins every morning. He vows that his energy level and health are the direct result of the more than twenty pills he pops a day. Can you tell me if he's right?"

Answer: If you want to make a lot of money, get into the business of nutritional supplements. People in this country alone spend billions of dollars each year on nonprescription nutritional supplements. In medical practice, nutritional supplements are used only for patients with weight problems and for those who have nutrient deficiencies. If you are in good health and eat a balanced diet with all of the daily required nutrients, there is really no need for supplements.

Supplements come in three forms: (1) vitamins and minerals, (2) caloric or energy supplements, and (3) ergogenic aids.

There are some studies that suggest that vitamin and mineral supplements, such as vitamin E, vitamin C, and beta-carotene (vitamin A), can reduce the risk of cancer and heart disease. Perhaps at some time in the future, such supplements will be proved effective in preventing disease, but, for now, it's a coin toss. Most important, vitamin supplements should not be used as a substitute for poor eating habits.

Fortified liquids sold in cans and candy bars with added protein and vitamins are examples of caloric supplements. They were designed for folks recovering from illness or surgery to help them gain weight. These days, the manufacturers direct their advertising to seniors and suggest that the products can put more zest into their lives. Although they do offer calories, they are high in fat and low in fiber. Most of all, they are very expensive.

The term *ergogenic* relates to so-called life-enhancing claims. Lecithin, ginseng, and chromium are examples of such products.

Some of them might be helpful, but no conclusive studies demonstrate that they offer any benefits to your health. In large doses, they can even be dangerous.

Tip: Your body needs about forty different nutrients daily for good health. So you have to eat a variety of foods to meet the daily nutrient requirements established by the U.S. Department of Agriculture. If you want to ensure that you are getting all the nutrients you need while getting a boost in energy, I recommend carbohydrates as the main source of your diet. Also, eat apples, bananas, and low-fat yogurt. They cost less and taste better than supplements and help to keep down the hunger pangs that often lead to "junk food" bingeing. There is no substitute for good eating habits and a diet that includes a variety of foods low in fat, saturated fat, and cholesterol, such as whole-grain cereals, fruits, and vegetables. Use sugar in moderation, limit your use of salt and sodium, and drink plenty of water.

OVERWEIGHT AND GOLFING ■

Question: "I'm overweight but seem to be able to play a round with little difficulty. Why all the hoopla about losing weight? Is it going to affect my golfing?"

Answer: The following is a very rough rule for measuring your ideal weight. A man starts with 105 pounds, adds 6 pounds per inch of his height over 5 feet, then adds 10 percent of the total as a fudge factor. That would make 155 pounds the ideal weight for a five-foot-six man. A woman starts with 100 pounds, adds 5 pounds per inch over five feet, then adds 5 percent. A five-foot-four woman would then ideally weight 126 pounds.

For every extra pound that you carry beyond normal weight, you add 10 pounds of pressure on your back. Consequently, if your waistline has expanded, you increase the chances of hurting your back. If you do, you could unknowingly adopt a posture that compromises the proper address of the golf ball—all because of being overweight.

Instead of standing correctly with your back straight and your arms hanging from the shoulders, you're likely to stand too erect, with your hands too far from your body. Or, perhaps you have to reach for the ball. Being overweight then, especially around the waistline, can seriously affect your ability to find proper balance in the golf swing. Without balance, your legs don't work properly during the swing and you can't perform a proper weight shift. In this situation, you have diminished power when striking—or, more likely, mis-hitting—the ball.

Obviously, you should consider what we say about weight control and diet programs in this chapter. Also, have your pro take a look at your posture as you address the ball. If you have begun to stand more erect, which affects your balance throughout the swing, have your pro recommend posture and stance adjustments to maximize the balance that is so crucial to striking the ball consistently.

Tip: We strongly recommend that you videotape your swing today and keep a video history of it as you lose weight so that you can see how your posture changes. Also, spend some time strengthening your back with exercises (see chapter 3) if you have difficulty in losing weight. Our goal, of course, is to help you remain physically active with the least amount of physical discomfort.

PROTEIN ■

Question: "I'm always confused when I read that I should have protein in my diet. So I start eating a lot of meats to get that protein.

Then I read that I should restrict the amount of protein in my diet. What's the story?"

Answer: Protein is an essential element in our diets. The amino acids that our bodies need come from dietary protein. Amino acids are the building blocks that help our bodies manufacture their own source of protein. Proteins are essential to repair or support the growth of new body tissue including bones, muscles, blood vessels, skin, hair, and nails.

Protein needs vary widely. A large man with an active lifestyle usually consumes all the protein he needs and then some. A small woman, on the other hand, is forced to consume far fewer calories in order to maintain her fitness level. If she eats less than 1000 calories a day, her protein needs may not be met. If your caloric intake is limited, we recommend you see a qualified nutritionist to be sure you are getting enough protein for your needs.

If you are following the recommendations found in the US-DA's Food Pyramid, you are probably getting all the protein you need. Remember, protein is not found just in meat. Nonfat milk, eggs, whole grains and legumes are also good sources.

A word of caution. Although animal sources of protein are often touted as the best way to get all your amino acids in one meal, you're also getting a lot of fat and cholesterol that may be harmful to you in the long run. Limit your intake of meat and dairy foods and increase your legume and grain sources of protein. Although high-protein diets (greater than 20 percent of calories) are all the rage at the moment, there is little evidence that they will make you any healthier or improve your performance on the golf course.

Tip: On a daily basis, I would try to eat no more than sixty grams of protein if you are male, and fifty grams if you are female. Most of us over fifty can meet our needs by having our daily caloric intake of protein at about 15 to 20 percent. Just one 3.5 ounce serving of meat (about the size of a deck of cards) contains about thirty grams of protein, half of what you need for the day!

■ VITAMINS

Question: "I've read a lot about vitamin supplements. What are they and isn't it foolish to take them if you're eating properly?"

Answer: Vitamins help our bodies perform metabolic functions to restore body tissue, especially bone, hair, skin, nerves, and brain. The good news is we need only small amounts. Since our bodies don't produce vitamins, the only source is either from foods or supplements. Vitamins are categorized by their solubility. For example, vitamins A, D, E, and K are called fat-soluble vitamins because they are soluble in fat but not in water. Water-soluble vitamins are soluble in water and include ascorbic acid (vitamin C), thiamin (B_1), riboflavin (B_2), pyridoxine (B_6), niacin, folate, pantothenic acid, and cobalamin (B_{12}). As we age it is very difficult to get all of the vitamins and minerals we need from food alone. The aging digestive tract has difficulty absorbing some vitamins such as B_{12} and vitamin D. Some medicines used to keep us healthy also interfere with vitamin synthesis and absorption.

Tip: To be sure you're getting all the vitamins you need, use a multivitamin and multimineral supplement containing balanced amounts of vitamins, minerals, and antioxidants. While vitamin supplements should not be used as a substitute for poor eating habits, they should be viewed as an important part of a healthy diet.

Those liquids sold in cans—and candy bars with protein and vitamins added—are examples of caloric supplements. They were used for folks recovering from illness or surgery to help them gain weight. These days, the manufacturers have been advertising them for older folks, suggesting that you can put more zest into your life.

Although they do offer calories, often they are high in fat and low on fiber. Most of all, they are very expensive.

Tip: Your body needs about forty different nutrients for good health. So you have to eat a variety of foods to meet the daily nutrient requirements established by the USDA. If you want to ensure that you are getting all the nutrients you need while getting a boost in energy, I recommend carbohydrates as the main source of your diet. Also, eat apples, bananas, and nonfat yogurt. They cost less, taste better, and help to keep the hunger pangs down which often leads to "junk food" bingeing. There is no substitute for good eating habits. Good eating habits include a variety of foods like whole-grain cereals and fruits and vegetables, and foods that are low in fat, saturated fat, and cholesterol. Use sugar in moderation, limit your use of salt and sodium, and drink plenty of water.

WATER ■

Question: "I'm reluctant to drink a lot of water because it makes me go to the bathroom often. I'm seventy-two years old, and I'm told that at my age I should drink a lot. OK, how much should I drink and how much when I'm playing golf?"

Answer: We believe that the more water you drink, the better. Water is an essential nutrient, perhaps more important for life than food because you can't create your own water or store it in the body. Water makes up about 60 percent of your body weight. You can survive about seventy days without food but just ten days without water.

You need water for almost every function in the body. Water helps to digest food, absorb other nutrients, and transport these nutrients into the bloodstream. It aids in the removal of waste products from tissue, and it is instrumental in all of the chemical reactions that take place throughout the body. Your body might be telling you that you need water or are dehydrated when you develop cramps, have a loss of coordination, feel nauseated, and become constipated, but these symptoms also have other causes.

Drink all the water that you can and as much as you can. This is especially important as people get older because their desire to drink decreases considerably, whereas their need for water increases. Also, if you take diuretic medications, drink a lot of coffee and/or alcohol, or live in a hot, dry climate, an increase in your water intake is even more crucial.

Tip: Drink a minimum of eight cups of water daily unless you have medical problems, such as edema, congestive heart failure, or renal failure. Check with your doctor just to be sure. When you are exercising, your body might need even more water before you actually feel thirsty.

We recommend drinking lemonade or other fruit beverages or eating crushed ice as a way of adding variety to drinking plain water. Drink at regular intervals and during your meals to keep adequate hydration.

Remember, if you are playing golf in very hot weather, go out of your way to increase the amount of water you drink. Estimates indicate that more than half of golfers who experience heat stroke are age sixty or older.

■ WEIGHT (NORMAL)

Question: "I'm a little heavy around the waist. How do I know if I'm overweight?"

Answer: The 1997 edition of *Dietary Guidelines for Americans* offers a wide range of weights considered to be desirable. An athletic, well-muscled male golfer thirty pounds over the desired weight for his height and body structure, however, will be considered overweight and unfit, according to this book. On the other hand, a sedentary male golfer who falls within the guidelines of being the right weight will get the false impression from this book that he is fit, healthy, and right where he should be to live a long, healthy life.

Nothing could be further from the truth. The golfer who doesn't exercise will have less energy, less endurance, less strength, and less resistance to injury than the one who does. Further, he will probably have far worse cardiovascular and cardiopulmonary health, higher blood pressure, a much higher resting pulse rate, a higher level of low-density lipoprotein (bad cholesterol), and a lower level of high-density lipoprotein (good cholesterol) than the muscular golfer. The irony is that the so-called normal-weight golfer will probably have an easier time getting insurance than the so-called overweight golfer.

WEIGHT LOSS ■

Question: "OK, I've decided I want to go on a diet, but I was shocked by how many diets are being advertised. Which, if any, should I choose to help my game?"

Answer: Check with your physician to see if complications could result from dieting because of some existing medical condition. Having done that, consider the largely inalterable fact that weight gain is caused by overeating, lack of exercise, or a combination of both. Dieting, then, means eating less, concentrating on better nutrition, and exercising more. It is as simple as that.

We have observed that many golfers past age forty are genuinely unaware of the impact that diet and exercise have on their golf performance, to say nothing of their general health and well-being. As we grow older and our bodies change, a balanced diet and exercise become essential.

Disabuse yourself of the myth that weight gain is necessarily a part of the aging process. If this were the case, how would we account for all the trim seniors that we see? Also, be aware that when we mention eating too much and not exercising enough, we refer to overeating and underexercising for your age. Remember that as you get older, you need less food—period. That's why your adherence to eating the amount and, in some cases, the type of food that you consumed during your twenties will cause weight gain for you today. When you were younger, you were probably more active. An active lifestyle called for more carbohydrates, which you burned up faster. As you get older and become less active, the excess calories that you consume don't burn up, which results in excessive fat. In order to avoid such a fat buildup, you need to eat less.

Tip: Research shows that the optimal time to eat is prior to when you will be most active, rather than before resting periods. That means, contrary to most behavior, that eating heavily in the evening is worse for you than in the morning. Another myth to be challenged is that eating three meals a day is always desirable. Maybe it isn't. The three-a-day standard was important while you were growing up, but as you get older, maybe it's time to concentrate more on eating when you're hungry—perhaps a large meal at mid-morning; a healthful snack (and here, obviously, I mean something apart from hot dogs and chips at the golf course) or two during the day; and a light, nutritional dinner.

Another problem for many people is having to deal with the catered food served at such affairs as golf outings, meetings, conferences, business lunches, and parties. At night, for example, you might consume a glorious but caloric meal at a dinner party (or a not so glorious banquet meal). The next morning you have little appetite, but you feel that the clock is telling you that it's time for breakfast. Our advice: Skip the big breakfast; have some fruit juice and a good bagel or a piece of toast. Or, if you've spent a few days or a week eating heavy food during a conference, take a break for a day or two by fasting. Consume only fruit juices and water. Believe us, you won't die and your stomach will get a well-deserved rest. The moral here is to listen to what your body tells you. Eat when you're hungry, not when the clock indicates the traditional meal-time. If circumstances demand that you attend a meal when you aren't particularly hungry, eat lightly and leave food on your plate.

6 MISCELLANEOUS TIPS FOR HEALTHY GOLFING

■ BIFOCALS AND GOLFING

Question: "I'm having trouble with my glasses. I wear bifocals, which help me to read the scorecard but drive me crazy when I try to focus on looking at the ball. If I move my head a bit, everything gets fuzzy. What can I do?"

Answer: You're not alone. Bifocals are headaches for most people who play golf or any sport that requires looking through the lower part of the lens. That lower part of a bifocal pair of glasses is focused for reading and other kinds of close work. When you move your head or try to look at something that's more than sixteen inches away, you'll end up with distortion that definitely can impede your game.

Your best bet is to ask your optometrist for the sort of bifocal that doesn't have the sharp division between lenses. If you try them, as Syd did, and they still distract you, you might want to get single-vision glasses or contact lenses adjusted for distance vision when you play. Having two pairs of glasses, one for reading and one for playing golf, should solve your problem.

Tip: The same treatment applies for golfers who wear contact lenses using a monovision system that involves wearing different lenses for near and distant viewing. We also recommend that you consider wearing contact lenses because they allow for more natural vision, don't restrict side vision, and don't get wet and muddy in the rain. If you continue to wear eyeglasses, we recommend lenses made of polycarbonate. This is considered to be the most impact-resistant lens material on the market today.

Finally, always remember to have your eyes checked at least once a year because a slight change in your vision could have a significant impact on how well you see and how well you play.

DISABILITIES AND GOLFING ■

Question: "I lost my left arm in an automobile accident. I was a golf fanatic before the accident, but I haven't played since. My friends keep trying to get me to play despite my disability. What do you think?"

Answer: Syd met a player on a public course who had lost his left arm. He asked if he could play along. He teed up his ball and hit it almost 200 yards straight down the middle of the fairway. At first, Syd thought that it was a lucky hit, but he continued to demonstrate fine iron play with a short game that was flawless. Syd asked him what his secret was, and he said practice. He said that he just spent a lot of time learning how to keep his balance and timing, which made all the difference in hitting the ball. Another confession that Syd had to make concerns a little wager for drinks that they made. He ended up buying.

Dispel the myth that you can't play golf because of a disability. Blind people, amputees, stroke victims, and people with all kinds of disabilities play golf. In fact, you can contact the National Amputee Golf Association at (603) 673–1135 for literature that will probably convince you that you have no reason to stay off the course.

■ GOLF BALLS

Question: "I know this might sound silly, but my friend told me that the golf ball I use is causing the wrist problems that I am having. Can you tell me if there is any relationship between the golf ball that I hit and my injuries?"

Answer: A ball that is wound inside, called a three-piece ball, transmits force that differs from the force released by a two-piece ball. Your friend probably read somewhere that wound balls cause less stress. Wound balls have either a solid or a liquid center packed in rubber that is wound around it. The cover is made from a natural rubber that comes from a balata tree. Most wound balls, however, have a synthetic or surlyn cover that can be made with certain degrees of hardness, feel, spin, and so forth.

Two-piece balls have rubber centers. That's pretty much it. Surlyn covers are usually used to give the golfer a sensation of hitting a harder ball. The fact is, two-piece balls are harder than three-piece balls, but there is no research to support your friend's theory. All balls must weigh no more than 1.62 ounces. Also, the type of club shaft that you use has more to do with injury than the ball that it hits. Your friend might be trying to say that the shock of your club hitting the ground before it hits the ball could be doing the damage.

■ GOLF CLUBS AND HEALTH

Question: "My pro was trying to convince me that I should change to graphite shafts because I have chronic wrist and elbow problems. I thought he was trying to make a quick buck off me. Any truth to his claim?"

Answer: When we all started playing, the fourteen clubs in our bag were usually steel shafted with forged-iron heads. Not much variety and hoopla. Today, there are about a hundred variations on a theme of how to put together a shaft and a golf club head. We also have metal woods, oversized metal woods, perimeter-weighted irons, and cavity-backed irons that appear to help us increase the sweet spot for more effective shots. So a mis-hit can still have a successful outcome. In addition to graphite, shafts are also being made of titanium and boron and a bunch of other constituents. All of these choices can drive you to chapter 4 on psychology and related matters.

Your pro probably read the literature of one of the graphite shaft manufacturers who perhaps claimed that hitting its graphite shaft will help to reduce wrist and elbow injuries. The fact is, there are no facts to support this, but, in our opinion, there could be some truth to it. Graphite has a much softer feel, and we believe that, as a result, graphite shafts might generate less shock to your hands and elbows.

We also believe that a set of perimeter-weighted and cavity-backed irons could help. The rationale for this belief is that even if you mis-hit a shot, the head of your club will twist and turn less, thus causing less shock to your hands and elbows. All in all, using graphite shafts with perimeter-weighted or cavity-backed heads will hurt only your pocketbook. It's up to you.

GRIPS ■

Question: "My pro suggested that I change my grips to help me because of arthritis in my hands. When he told me about the different grips available, I became totally confused. Can you help me sort through all the grips and tell me if there is indeed a particular grip for someone like me with arthritis?"

Answer: Grips are made of all kinds of materials: leather, quasi-leather, rubber, cord, and so forth. Leather grips have a soft feel, and we all probably grew up using them until the sixties. Get a leather grip wet, however, and it becomes quite difficult to keep your hands from slipping during a swing. Rubber grips fare better, but they can also cause your hands to slip during hot weather. There are numerous variations on cord grips; although they hold up in hot and wet weather, they can be tough on your palms. If you want people to think that you are a tough guy or gal when shaking your hand, use cord grips. They will build up calluses on your palms. Grips also can be built up with a lot of tape so they feel bigger when you hold your club. This might be what your pro was recommending for your arthritis. There are also some grip makers who offer oversized grips to help reduce the shock resulting from a mis-hit shot.

Thin or undersized grips are a benefit only to those golfers who don't have wrist and elbow problems but have weak arms and forearms. Undersized grips can help you to move through the ball faster at impact, but whether or not this makes a difference in your game depends on many other factors. You might want to try a round with one club prepared undersized to see if it helps.

Finally, I learned the hard way, but please consider changing your grips at the first sign of wear and tear. You'd be surprised how a bad grip can lead to higher scores.

■ MIDLIFE CRISIS

Question: "I'm forty-five, and friends are telling me to look out for my midlife crisis. What is a midlife crisis? And if I am having one, how do I deal with it?"

Answer: In its essence, a midlife crisis is merely the realization that we've changed. At its worst, the crisis is accompanied by the sense that we didn't want to change. Examples of behavior resulting from a midlife crisis include abandoning loved ones, going overboard with supposedly youthful trappings (the Harley or the proverbial red sports car), and trying—often with patent futility—to turn back the clock regarding one's appearance. Dressing like kids is at one end of the midlife crisis extreme. Opting for penile enlargement surgery is at the other. Somewhere in between would be an attempt to perform athletically as though we were in our prime physical years.

Because certain changes are inevitable, the optimistic approach is to embrace the newness that a midlife crisis presents and use it as a point of departure for greater challenges. In some cases, midlife "craziness" might be worthy of encouragement, but not when it is manifested out of panic and certainly not when the downside is a broken home or bone. At its most healthy, the midlife crisis can be an experience during which we reiterate the possibility of changing our lives for the better. This is a sublime insight, but because of our inevitable physical changes, the insight must be accompanied by the awareness of those changes. Then, we can go forward with an understanding we didn't have when we set out on a path that middle age has beckoned us to change.

Moreover, a healthy response to personal growth and change can help to prevent us from slipping into Thoreau's "life of quiet desperation" once the fever has passed. The wise person desires that which inspires growth and balance, even though certain behavior along the way might seem crazy to family and friends.

Tip: Although this might sound like a paradox, the best approach to dealing with the anxieties that result from the pangs of a midlife crisis is to accept yourself each time you feel a sense of the crisis. For example, if you look at yourself in the mirror and say to yourself, "How did I get to be so old?" rather than going out to your nearest face-lift center and spending a couple of grand in an attempt to transcend the inevitable, the best reward is to surrender to that inevitable. You can do that by saying to yourself, "It's OK to look older." In other words, the key to dealing with a midlife crisis is to accept it and realize that it is only a part of the total life experience.

Appendix A

AGING, MEMORY, AND PERSONALITY CHANGE

Let me throw a contraindication at you. Or, using nontechnical jargon, what I'm about to discuss here is, at best, soft science. That is, none of the data about the mental aspects of aging can be easily measured or studied. I know that instruments to measure the flow of blood through the heart are readily available and quite accurate, but all the commotion that goes on between your ears is still controversial and is being refuted in the literature as I write. What was thought to be true about memory occurring in one specific area of the brain has been shown not to be so. Recent studies suggest that memory is all over the place, not only in your brain, but in your legs and toes, and—who knows—maybe somebody will find a way to transfer a little memory to your putter.

Just as no one is looking forward to the prospect of declining health during aging, no one will admit to being less than terrified about the possibility of losing mental faculties, a process that inevitably changes personality for the worse. The good news is: Most of us don't have to worry about this. In fact, more good news is that, as we get older, our minds and personalities actually get better in certain ways.

The "personality" that we are is physically represented in all of the dendrites and neurons in our brains. Yet, with all the technology that is available today, we are still incapable of explaining or describing how these nerve cells register personality.

What little we do know is that the brain of a male is a bit larger than that of a female. As both sexes age between the years of twenty and eighty, the brain loses about 10 percent of its weight. (Why can't that be the case with the rest of the body?) But brain weight has little to do with mental functioning. We know that brain cells die and the total number significantly decreases over time, but this loss does not lead to a deficit of any importance. This might have to do with the idea that even the greatest geniuses use only a fraction of their mental potential.

So the changes that do take place in our mental functions and our personalities over time (and the net impact on our lives and on our golfing) have less effect on us than does the way that we interpret and react to the changes. Again, it's that little voice in our heads, which we control.

■ MEMORY

Mental functioning tests have created tons of debate in the field of psychology. Much of the research here has compared college-age adults to institutionalized elderly folks, primarily because both populations are more readily accessible. Comparing extremes helps to pinpoint differences, but institutionalized seniors are usually uncharacteristic of their peers.

Other factors also confound things. The change in nerve conduction activity, for example, slows down reaction time; however, this does not necessarily affect memory or intelligence. A slower reaction time among elderly people suggests that mental functioning has declined, but it remains unclear whether this is a valid conclusion. For example, if a senior takes longer than a college student to complete a crossword puzzle, that fact might be totally unrelated to the senior's competence to use his or her intelligence socially and professionally.

So the notion that the mind, like the body, deteriorates with age is mere myth. Research offers ample evidence that declining mental functioning is of less magnitude and affects fewer functions than was once commonly believed.

What about forgetfulness? Is it the result of getting older? Not being able to remember the name of a movie star, someone's birthday, or the course where you scored your first ace and even losing track of what you were trying to say in midsentence are common occurrences at almost any age. Such occurrences are liable to cause anxiety now and then, but rest assured that they don't signal impending Alzheimer's disease. The fact is that people store myriad bits of information. It would be uncommon if they could retrieve every detail that they wanted without having to flex their memories a little.

One distinction that is often made in terms of how age can affect memory is between short-term and long-term recollections. Short-term memory refers to what you shot on the course yesterday or what you had for lunch at the course. Long-term memories relate to such things as who won the U.S. Open in 1952 or when you first took up the game of golf. Short-term memory changes refer to the immediate recall of things or stimuli. Once information leaves this very limited storage center, it travels to the secondary, or long-term, memory banks.

Short-term memory is the ability you have to retain information up to thirty seconds, but its capacity is limited to remembering up to seven items. It changes hardly at all with aging. Slight deficits might develop by age sixty but usually not before. Long-term memory is the ability to remember material for an hour or more. Problems with long-term memory, however, begin long before the middle years and are not the same for all individuals. The decline is marked more with memorizing long passages of text than with trying to remember somebody's phone number.

The question that I hear from so many golfers who want to know why they forget things is: "Can I do anything about it?" The solution is simple. The decay of stored information is due to lack of use. Research supports the notion that you lose it if you don't use it.

This very point is one reason why senior golfers sometimes have a hard time improving their scores. Reading an article or taking a lesson that addresses a swing flaw is the first step toward improving, but many senior golfers fail to remember the fine points of the lesson or article. To overcome this forgetfulness, I have my clients make notes on a little pad that they carry in their back pockets while they practice. Please note: Trying to summon from memory certain points about a swing tip has a negative effect as you play (see the sections, "The Zone [Part 1]" and "The Zone [Part 2]," in chapter 4). It's best to carry notes from your lesson or an idea from an article to the driving range, where you can assimilate the idea through repetitive practice. Unfortunately, unless you do this, all the tips in the world are lost somewhere in a dendrite that will refuse to cooperate.

The will to learn is crucial in keeping your learning curve moving along an upward slope. Learning depends not only on memory and other cognitive factors but also on your desire to learn. The myth that you stop growing and improving and/or learning is more often the result of being unmotivated than the effect of changes resulting from growing older. Taking longer to master complex swing thoughts and mechanics is easily compensated by knowing how and what to learn. In short, so-called old dogs can learn new tricks; it just might take a bit longer.

With a twenty-four–hour golf channel, dozens of golf publications, and nonstop network television coverage, information overload can lead to the feeling that you're falling behind. To keep up, seniors might abandon time-tested swing thoughts for new faddish, nondata-driven tips that inevitably lead to disappointment. More so, once you toss aside something that worked and replace it with something new, getting the new approach out of the system and getting back to the old one takes time. You might have to unlearn the new information and relearn the old. As a result, the feeling of getting worse, not better, is often attributed to aging and not to the true source, which is the nature of learning.

No matter what you hold true or what you experience regarding memory, the fact remains that the laws of memory are the same for everybody, regardless of age.

Such feelings as anger and worry can block, distort, displace, and rework memory in anyone at any age. Regardless of age, everyone will remember the pleasant and forget the unpleasant. It's easy to forget to do things that you don't like and to remember to do things that you do like. I have a photographic memory for certain golf events on TV, but when I go to the grocery store for my wife, I'm out in left field. Of course, she doesn't accept my lament that my age causes me to forget. (She's the editor of this chapter.)

So what can you do, given there is no physical evidence of memory loss? The trick is to understand the fuel that keeps your memory vibrant. That fuel consists of novelty and stimulation. What's even more important is to tie your emotions into the novelty as well.

Here are nine ways to keep your memory muscles flexed and active:

1. The next time you can't think of a name or words, rather than keeping everyone waiting, just say. "That golfer who used to look so relaxed when he played." (Note: As I tried to think of the golfer's name, I couldn't. I used this technique, however, to retrieve the name, which is Julius Boros.) When elusive names or words nag you, relax and allow your mind to free-associate toward the word or name you're trying to remember. Dozens of words will pop up. Focus on those words or names that are close to the one you want. Free-associate around the letters in that word. As memories and emotions surface, stay with them. Let your mind travel freely as you recall events. Sure you've gone astray from your original quest, but, as you will see, your mind will be free to drop the word or name out of a dendrite and into your recall.

2. Exercise your memory cells. Each day, look up a new word in the dictionary and try to remember it. Use the word in imaginative

ways to keep the idea fresh. Memory is activated by creating unusual combinations of what you already know and what you are trying to learn. For example, take the word *panache*. If you don't know what it means or haven't seen it before, you can remember it by exercising it into memory and breaking it down. What I did to memorize it for a later recall was to think the word *pan* and imagine someone hitting me with one over the head. The effect would be a headache; the word *ache*, of course, is the last four letters of the word. So, to recall the word, I picture a scene and think about it, which, in turn, triggers memory of the word. The technique here is to use what you know to learn something new by connecting old memories to new ones. The more you do this exercise, the easier it gets.

3. The meeting-new-people exercise. Once you are introduced to someone new, find some body part that is slightly flawed. Create a connection between that part to the name of the person. For example, a golfer joined me months ago. His name was Robert Locke, and I can still remember it. He wore thick-lens glasses. I imagined that I *robbed* him of his glasses to remember his first name, Robert, and, as a result, I was *locked* up for the crime. Just the folly of the act of robbing someone of his glasses and being locked up for it was enough to help me keep his name in my long-term memory.

4. An old trick that I learned while I was in college still helps me today to remember, say, a series of grocery store items or the number of topics I want to discuss during a lecture. The trick is to memorize the association between the numbers and words, such as those in the following list:

    1—glass
    2—Noah's ark
    3—Pick-Up Sticks
    4—door
    5—law

6—pack of beer
7—Seven-Eleven Store
8—ball
9—baseball
10—tee, the tenth.

Make the list as long as you like. I have words associated with thirty-five numbers. Once you memorize the words associated with the numbers, hook the idea or word you want to remember to the number. For example, I'm shopping and I want to remember four things: butter, paper towels, soup, and cheese. Rather than writing them down, I exercise my memory by attaching each item to a number. For no. 1, I imagine that I have placed a bar of butter into a glass; for no. 2, two people on Noah's ark holding a strip of a paper towel; for no. 3, Pick-Up sticks in my soup; and for no. 4, the door is made out of cheese. So when I think of no. 1, the image of a glass with butter comes to mind and I recall butter. Again, the idea is to use this technique not to overburden yourself but to exercise your memory.

5. Using the methods described above, I often recommend the most enjoyable memory exercise to my clients. After a round of golf and before going to sleep, replay the round. Think about each shot before and during, and savor the round afterward through your memory. If you have trouble remembering, work at it and see if you can free-associate to bring back a putt or drive or score on a particular hole. Obviously, the idea is not to recall perfectly the entire round but to enjoy replaying what you remember in order to exercise your mind.

6. There are hundreds of crossword puzzles and problem-solving books that can energize your memory. My adage is that doing a crossword puzzle a day keeps the shrink away (thank goodness!). You will be surprised how your mind will become energized by exercising it this way daily.

7. Probably the most enjoyable way of keeping your memory active is to collect jokes and practice telling them. Norman Cousins demonstrated that laughter and a sense of humor can help to boost the immune system. Note the way Sol sprinkles his chapters with humorous anecdotes. Sol has been collecting jokes for years, and that might be one reason why he has such a keen memory. I always wanted to compliment him about it, but I kept forgetting to do that. (That will be my turn on the old vaudeville exchange: Why do you drink? To forget? Forget what? I forgot.) In any case, Sol, good work.

8. Another great exercise, believe it or not, is "living" in the past. Contrary to the myth that it's not a good idea to do that, thinking about past years can do wonders to exercise your memory muscles. Studies show that people who think about the past are not emotionally harming themselves but rather are increasing their well-being. So enjoy the past, savor it, replay it as often as you like. That will lead to contentedness and, even more so, will help to exercise your long-term memory muscles.

9. Finally, an extremely effective treatment for keeping your sense of self alive and your memory genes active is to keep those old vinyl records dusted and on your turntable. Let a tune inspire you to break out into a song. I do this all the time and often recall tunes while I drive. Not only do you arouse past memories, but emotions can be triggered, which might be just the inspiration you need to lift yourself out of the blues. Ultimately, getting a sense of who you are by generating memories of the past and who you were can help you to face yourself as you grow older.

■ PERSONALITY

If age doesn't significantly affect memory, then what about personality? Well, the fact is that aging does, to a limited degree, affect your personality, which, in turn, can lead to how you perform on the course. For example, the way you look and how you think obviously will affect how others perceive you, but who you are—the whole person—remains the same. In other words, you might have less hair and shoot higher scores, but you're still you. Your friends are going to love you for who you are, not for how well you play. If they judge you for that, then they aren't really friends.

Who you have been is important to your sense of self and to others in that they can predict how you will react in situations. As you get older, physical and attitudinal changes can generate modifications in your personality and in the role that you are expected to play. When you tell your friends that you are going to walk only nine holes and not eighteen from now on, it's certainly not earth-shattering news, but your friends know that something has changed. A friend of mine who was highly competitive every time he played golf recently told me that he now plays just to get his money's worth. That was why his score has skyrocketed.

In the area of life span development, psychologist Erik Erikson never used the concept of middle age. Instead, he simply called this stage of life "adulthood." About this stage, he said that the goal should be helping the next generation, not necessarily just one's own offspring. It is also a time of life when one is charged with productivity and creativity. Erikson also said, however, that when this stage of growth fails, creativity regresses into stagnation, self-absorption, and personal impoverishment. Obviously, if this happens, it certainly does suggest that an individual's personality has changed. You probably have a friend who has become an expert curmudgeon, complaining about people who don't recognize his or her accomplishments and angry at all the young people who waste their time and deplete the value system. Also, you must know people who become enraged because courses aren't played anymore—they are trampled. Their rage is directed at the loss of their sense of freedom and escape from the bedlam of the morning rush hour and the injustices and catch-22s of work. They complain about electric cart requirements with high-tech equipment, restrictions about the length of short pants, and rules that don't permit carry-on bags. Some lose their composure at tee boxes, where the waiting lines are worse than those during the dinner hour at supermarket checkouts, and it adds to their angst when sand trap rakes are broken or missing.

Unfortunately, wanting things to be the way that they were (or the way that we think they were) will not help. Progress brings crowds of young stockbrokers with their three-hundred-dollar drivers. The game is not the same and never will be. Older golfers might feel that they're perceived as slow or in the way and that the game is being taken away from them, but only if they let it happen. My advice is to learn how to accept that there are many more golfers and it takes longer to play the game, but lamenting about how things used to be won't bring them back. It's time to move on.

Regardless of your stage in the life cycle, your personality is in a continually changing process. As other things change, you must learn to surrender to the changes. Who you are doesn't stop when you become a senior. Who you are is dependent upon what you have done to become who you are today, and you continue to grow, change, learn, understand, and adapt. Perhaps that is wisdom—learning how to surrender, practice restraint, share with others, and give. Ultimately, this wonderful sense of compassion can be felt, not only for others, but for yourself. Perhaps that is self-acceptance.

So personalities do change but perhaps more on a subjective level than anything else. For example, in what ways do you see yourself as different from your self-images of earlier times? More so, in what ways do you see yourself according to your projections of who you will be in, say, five years or ten or twenty?

Perhaps one factor that offers the illusion that personality changes is one's perception of time. During the first half of life, people often recall the past. At midlife, their attention turns to the future and to the time that is left. They become used to the growing awareness that time is ticking away and mortality is approaching.

As seniors, I believe that people tend to look more at what I call *inner truths* about themselves and spend less time comparing and evaluating external objects. They are less concerned with ways of trying to understand the chaos that bombards them on a daily basis and are more inclined to get in touch with their inner cores. The joy of golfing means not only shooting a low score but also taking a stroll in good weather with friends and sharing the moments, one by one. They learn to play for the sake of playing, for the joy of being there, and to relish the time spent.

As people head into their late fifties, they begin to experience a reduction in their interests and a gradual decline in the drive toward another accomplishment. They are being prepared for the more drastic shifts that will occur in the years to come. They don't play to win, to achieve par-golf, to outdrive their partners. Those goals might have been important once, but they lose their hold on people as they get on in life. Thank goodness. If that is what is meant by personality change, embrace it.

Another shift in personality that takes place has to do with the external world and the need to control it. Control is less important now. Thirty-year-olds hold on to the belief that controlling things out there will be rewarded, so their efforts are directed accordingly with bold and risky behavior. Sixty-year-olds do it a bit differently. They perceive the environment as difficult, uncertain, and resistant to whatever they do to try to change it. As a result, they learn to surrender to it gradually, but inevitably. As they do, they retreat further into their inner selves, their core values, and lock into their habits of living. In these ways, personality changes become discernible after age sixty. Trying new golf swings and different courses is not as appealing to aging golfers. There are exceptions, of course, and you might be one of them. There's certainly nothing wrong with that. Regardless, it's not a reflection that you have taken on a new persona, that you are no longer you.

Most people, however, realize that the clock is ticking and it's time to get to know one's inner self in order to sort out the ridiculous from the sublime. It's time to give up the notion that ambition, material possessions, and self-importance will lead to peace and happiness, and it's time to learn that only a handful of things are truly important. Perhaps the greatest lesson at this age is to learn how not to take life and oneself too seriously. It is a time to allow the wisdom genes to become activated. If you have spent your life looking for answers to the whys and hows, now, with wisdom, it's time to ask: "What for?" (Note, however, that this shift suggests only wisdom, not a shift in the core of your personality.)

Being older gives you good reason to think well of yourself. Sure, you might miss some aspects of being younger: shot length, stamina, and so forth, but there is little fear of getting older. You have developed this finely tuned instrument called *me,* full of wisdom, experience, and introspection.

You have learned how to adapt to and cope with the vagaries of life. No matter what you have accomplished, you will have to contend with loss, stress, and conflict. Everyone has war stories of sorrow and regret, but they have much to appreciate and stories of joy to share. Ultimately, life's journey has been uniquely designed to help you reach the pinnacle of coming to terms with yourself and others. You can define what is unacceptable to you and resist being affected by it. You have wisdom of what matters most to you, and this allows you to live fully and with purpose. Although time might be running out, you still have this wonderful willingness to grow, this curiosity of what the next moment will bring. You head to the course and get on the first tee and meet life head on. Golf is really a metaphor that affirms your being, your existence, and your essence.

Appendix B

GRIEF: TIME HEALS ALL, BUT IS THERE A QUICKER WAY?

Each year, more than 700,000 people age fifty or older lose their spouses. The side effects of death, grief, and mourning are known to produce significant physical changes in the bereaved, and yet people do little to prepare for this event. Some find security in denying that, one day, they will inevitably face the loss of someone close to them, either through death or the end of a relationship. Also, people can suffer other losses—loss of home, loss of money, moving away from neighborhoods where they were happy.

There is so much loss waiting for all of us and so few tools to deal with it because we live in a death-denying society. If we haven't been forced to deal with loss and someone brings up the subject, we grow tense and look for ways to change the subject. Our Western emphasis on youth, beauty, individuality, and control makes death an outrage, a tremendous affront to humans, rather than the logical and necessary process of old life making way for new. Unfortunately, most of us do not have adequate tools for coping with death and bereavement. In our secular society, there is little social help in coming to terms with grief and mourning. Losing a spouse or lifelong friend can be profound, particularly because it is hard to find any kind of substitute for our loved one.

The typical grief reaction has an almost predictable pattern of onset, regardless of one's age. The initial response is numbness and the inability to accept the loss, followed by the shock of reality as it begins to take hold. There are physical feelings of emptiness deep in the stomach, weak knees, perhaps a feeling of suffocation, shortness of breath, and a tendency toward deep sighing. Emotionally, people often experience great distress. They might feel a sense of unreality that includes delusions and obsessive preoccupation with the image of the lost person and acting as though the deceased were still present. Generally, feelings of guilt represent, as well as generate, an irritability, even toward friends and relatives. There is usually a disorganization of normal patterns of repose, with a sense of aimless wandering and the inability to work or to take social initiative. Anxiety and longing alternate with depression and despair. Insomnia, digestive disturbances, and anorexia are common.

With today's greater longevity, however, the loss of a spouse has been pushed into the later decades for many people. Currently, only one in twenty women between the ages of forty-five and fifty becomes a widow. The likelihood of a man in this age group becoming a widower is even smaller (one in one hundred), and most widowers of this age readily remarry. Widowhood is more common among women than is widowerhood among men because the great majority of women outlive their spouses, women tend to marry older men, and widows are less likely to remarry than are widowers. A middle-aged or older man who is widowed often faces a period of confusion. The death of his wife represents not only the loss of his primary caretaker, friend, and confidante, but also his main link to friends and relatives.

There is no question that the loss of a spouse is a major source of stress. One fifth of surviving spouses continue to show signs of depression a year after the death of a husband or wife. For a period of five years following the death of the spouse, the death rates of surviving partners are higher than predicted death rates for their age groups. Beyond that period, however, life expectancy for widows and widowers returns to average rates. With the passage of time, most people who have lost a spouse are psychologically reconstituted fully and show no significant differences from other people in mood, sense of self-worth, satisfaction with accomplishments, and sense of integrity.

A person's reactions to the loss of a good friend can be just as intense as the reactions to the loss of a spouse. When my best golfing buddy, Oscar Gamache, passed away a few years ago, I lost all interest in golfing. I had always looked forward to our get-togethers and the camaraderie that we shared while playing. Oscar was unique. He never walked toward his ball along a straight path but meandered into the woods and came out with five or six newly found balls. His hobby was to fill egg cartons with balls and give them away. That was his legacy. Once, we played forty-five holes on a hot humid day. I figured Oscar played equal to sixty holes because he did all that extra walking. At day's end, he boasted that he had found three dozen balls. What a man! After he died, I had all these memories of Oscar and expected him to come out of the bushes at any minute with a ball or two that he would toss at me. But there was no Oscar.

It took me a bit to get over the pain, but much like my clients who enter therapy to deal with all kinds of loss in life—family members, friends, financial—I used an experimental method that can help to accelerate the healing process. It has been very effective with my clients during therapy.

The old expression still holds: Time heals all. Recent research conducted by Dr. Ronald W. Ramsey, author of *Living With Loss,* however, offers people who are mourning the loss of someone close to them a quicker way to get on with the business of their lives. The technique is called *guided mourning,* which can accelerate the healing process for someone who wants to get beyond the emotional trauma resulting from the loss of a loved one.

Guided mourning is a therapeutic procedure in which patients are taught to face situations that trigger the grief response. Simply stated, patients are helped to expose themselves repeatedly to thoughts, feelings, and situations that are directly or indirectly related to the deceased. They are asked to ventilate negative feelings (e.g., anger, hostility) and to face distressing places, objects, and/or people. In short, anything related or painfully connected to the loss needs to be repeatedly faced. This could include cemeteries, photographs, books, relatives, restaurants, television shows, and music. The key word here is *repetition*.

It is believed that repeated exposure to situations and/or objects related to the deceased can lead to changes in the brain. Specifically, for reasons still being studied, repetition appears to reduce a number of receptor sites in the central nervous system. The very genetic structure of cells within the locus coeruleus might be altered during repeated exposures, thus reducing chronic hyperarousal. For example, looking at a picture of a loved one might trigger a strong, emotional grief reaction. After many exposures to the picture, the person who is mourning the loved one might still react emotionally to the picture but with less intensity. When I say that time heals all, I am suggesting that the number of receptor sites needed to trigger a strong grief reaction is reduced through repeated exposures to them over time. Thus, the grief is less. If one receives a great number of exposures during a short period of time, the grief may be even less for the same reason. An example can demonstrate how this works.

A golfing patient of mine, Robert, was vacationing in Yosemite. He was sleeping at a luxurious resort hotel when he woke up in the middle of the night and reached over to touch his wife. But Barbara was not next to him. At that realization, Robert broke down and cried. He still missed Barbara so much, even though it had been almost a year since her death. Bob wanted to get over the loss, but he didn't know how.

He came to the office deeply depressed. His wife's terminal illness had become manifest several months before Robert had scheduled a golf outing across town. Although his wife was ill, she insisted that he go. Barbara said she had lasted this long and she seemed to be in good spirits. So Robert left to play golf with his buddies. On his arrival at the club, the assistant pro told him that

Barbara's doctor had called. When Robert called the doctor, he learned that Barbara had passed away. Robert had no serious problems with the loss until some months later. Then, he found himself getting irritable with coworkers, he fought with family members, lost his appetite, and had no desire to play golf. His sleeping was interrupted almost like clockwork. At about three o'clock each morning, he would awaken and stay up. That made his day, to say the least, most difficult.

During therapy, Robert was very tearful and tense. He suffered from tremendous guilt because he felt that he hadn't done enough for Barbara. I showed Robert how he was avoiding thoughts and blocking resentment and suggested that he confront some of these thoughts and feelings during the following weeks. At one session, I asked Robert to imagine himself seated in an empty chair and cross-questioning himself about whether he could have changed anything if he hadn't gone on the golf outing. During later sessions, I instructed Robert to describe, in the past tense, the final encounter with his wife in order to identify how he would have wished it to be different (e.g., to have been there with her before she passed on) and then to describe the revised scene in the present tense. In this scene, Robert talked to the empty chair and imagined that he was by his wife's side before she died. He immediately broke down and cried.

I prescribed guided mourning tasks both within sessions and between sessions as homework. The key assignment was repeating the scene in which Robert imagined being by Barbara's bedside. Because that was causing a great deal of guilt, he was to set aside three times a day to repeat the scenario in detail. He was to visualize himself walking into the hospital room, smelling the aroma of the roses near the bed, and seeing nurses come and go and to imagine his wife's facial features over and over as he looked at her in the bed. The therapy was the result of continued exposure to that last scene. Other homework assignments included facing situations that he had avoided repeatedly, such as visiting the grave site, looking at photographs of Barbara, listing Barbara's positive and negative characteristics (this would address the anger that he was avoiding), writing a letter to Barbara, and spending a prescribed amount of time in rooms associated with strong memories of her.

After several weeks of numerous repeated exposures, Robert found himself feeling less depressed. He began to sleep more regularly and started contacting friends to pursue his golf. At the end of treatment, Robert reported feeling like his "good old" self. He still missed Barbara but not in a way that inhibited his day-to-day routine.

Guided mourning is most effective when the morbid grief persists to the point where the grieving person is unable to function in a normal way. Also, this approach is not suitable for everyone. Some mourners might not need to use any technique. With the passage of time and natural exposure to situations associated with the beloved, they will eventually get over the loss on their own. If you or someone you know can't seem to get on with the healing process, however, guided mourning, with the help of a psychologist, might be the treatment of choice.

What kind of therapist should you choose? Consider one trained in behavioral therapy because guided mourning relies on the behavioral technique of exposure with response prevention. Unfortunately, not all therapists are trained in this technique. With that in mind, it's crucial to ask three preliminary questions when seeking help:

1. Does the therapist have a cognitive-behavioral orientation? If the answer is yes, go to the next question.
2. Is the therapist familiar with the work by Dr. Ronald Ramsey for overcoming unresolved grief?
3. How many clients has the therapist treated with the use of guided mourning?

If you can't find help or get a referral, contact the Association for Advancement of Behavior Therapy in New York. The telephone number is (212) 279–7970.

Appendix C

ELEVEN WAYS TO GET THE MOST OUT OF A GOLF LESSON

Charlie, a twenty-plus handicapper, decides it's time to work on his game. He's been playing golf for several years and just can't seem to break 90. Pro after pro on TV suggests that lessons are the key to lowering golf scores, so Charlie takes a lesson. Thirty minutes later, he's hitting the ball worse than before. When he gets back to playing, he tells his buddies how he wasted thirty bucks learning how to screw up his game.

What Charlie and thousands of other golfers don't realize is that taking a lesson is more than just getting a quick magical cure. Ed Luethke, PGA Class A teaching pro at Peachwood Driving Range in Fresno, California, was kind enough to offer some tips on how to get the most out of a golf lesson. If you've been to your pro recently only to see your game get worse after the lesson, you might want to heed Ed's advice.

In fact, Ed vows that much can be done to prepare for getting the most out of a lesson if you are willing to take the time. If you're getting serious about your game, consider his eleven no-nonsense tips:

1. **"The Ken Griffey, Jr., theory."** Ed points out that golfers are gullible. The man in the moon could give a golfer a swing tip and right away the golfer tries to incorporate it into the game. That's dangerous. An analogy would be Ken Griffey, Jr., lis-

tening to a fan in center field who advised him how to play the next hitter. Ken would be out of his mind to take and implement that advice. Beware of friendly advice. Everyone wants to help, but few people really know how. "When the tip comes from your pro," Ed says, "stay with it until it has a chance to sink in."

2. **Honesty is the best policy.** If a swing thought that you worked on fails you on the course, let your pro know. "You'd be surprised how many of my students don't tell me this. The truth is, I want to know. I really like it when a student can come to a lesson with specific details about what worked and what didn't," Ed says. He emphasizes, "If the swing thought failed on the course, it may, in fact, have worked. The real problem might be something else might have gone wrong, like a closed setup. That's why I like it when my students level with me."

3. **The magic potion is practice.** Don't expect your pro to have magical powers that will transform your game. Your pro will definitely point out what you are doing wrong and what needs to be corrected, but that is the first step. The next step is crucial. "You gotta practice what you learned not only at the driving range, but on the course. And the key here is quality, not quantity practice," Ed suggests. "A thousand golf balls hit incorrectly will groove a swing flaw, not eliminate it. Watch the flight of the ball and try to figure out why it fades to the left or hooks to the right. Then try another shot."

4. **The shortcut is the short game.** If you really want to lower your score or handicap but you don't have time to work on reconstructing your overall swing, spend your time in practicing the short game, particularly putting. A 5-foot putt counts the same as a 250-yard drive.

5. **Avoid self-deception.** While you are taking a lesson, your pro might be enthusiastic about a swing thought which is second nature to him or her. Perhaps you intellectually understand

what your pro is saying, but that's not enough. Ed warns, "You need to have a trigger thought that will help you do the right thing, rather than simply knowing what to do. Insist that your pro tell you again in a different way. For example, if your pro is suggesting that you have to finish your shot, ask him to define operationally what that means. An operational definition might be the pro taking your hands and working them through the shot. Another operational definition might be the pro demonstrating how his or her hands work through the shot."

6. **The latent stage of learning.** "This is probably the most incredible phenomenon that occurs as a teacher," Ed says. He goes on to explain, "The lesson doesn't click right away. I'll be working hard with a student programming a swing thought. The student understands intellectually, and once or twice during the lesson, he or she will execute a good swing. But on the course, somehow, the thought just doesn't work. Then, some months later, the student will call telling me that the idea we worked on is now working. The moral here is to remember the payoff for your lessons might take place months later." Ed theorizes, "Maybe the mind's got to work on the new thoughts awhile before the body can do them and before the swing thought makes perfect sense."

7. **Beware of the natural tendency to resist.** Ed cautions, "Everyone can improve at the game, but the biggest stumbling block to learning is a student who comes to the lesson with the 'I don't buy it' attitude. I'll show a student what to do and he or she tries it once and then says 'I don't like it. My way is better.'" At that point, Ed believes the student may not be able to go beyond a certain amount of improvement. "If I'm going to give any advice, then it's to be open to swing suggestions that, at first glance, seem strange and awkward," Ed says. "I've yet to come across a pro who was misleading a student by giving faulty advice."

8. **Face the facts.** "There are some golfers like Ray Floyd who don't want to see what their swing looks like," Ed says. "But seeing yourself—a rude awakening, I can assure you—can get you motivated to do some necessary swing overhauling. That's why videotaping can be a valuable learning tool." Ed recommends that you get the swing from four different angles: the side, the back, in front, and behind. If your pro is willing, get each angle analyzed in slow motion.

9. **Get a second opinion.** Ed recommends and sometimes encourages his students to get a lesson from another pro. "One time, a student of mine took a lesson at a golf clinic in Minnesota and solved a long-standing problem we were working on. Essentially, the lesson was similar to ours. But, sometimes, you hear the same ideas from someone else and something clicks. So I'll suggest to serious students to take what they have learned from me and try getting another pro's point of view. It's amazing how that can sometimes unblock a swing problem."

10. **Driving range teaching pros are for real.** Get beyond the myth that you are getting less when you are being taught by a pro at a driving range. Ed points out that driving range teaching professionals are not inferior to club professionals. If anything, they might have a slight edge in that their number one priority is just that, giving lessons. Ed advises, "Always take a lesson from a PGA-certified pro because he or she has had schooling and a certain amount of experience."

11. **Continuing education.** Want the secret to being a better golfer? Ed's answer is to get "lessons for life." The pros get tune-ups constantly, and the avid golfer ought to get a tune-up at least once a year. Ed says, "You can learn the game on your own and read all the books on how to swing the club, but that can take you only so far. A good pro can diagnose your swing flaw in a matter of minutes and develop a program to help you get rid of

it. The irony of this game is that you develop swing flaws without knowing it. And that's where your pro can really help! I'll see some bad habit that may have crept in and point it out. That's where teaching becomes rewarding. Saving my student a lot of wear and tear and lowering his or her handicap, ah, that's what it's all about."

Appendix D

A DIRECTORY OF GOLF PSYCHOLOGISTS

Albaugh, G., Ph.D., 1672 W. Longview, Stockton, CA 95207.

Cave, P. A., Ed.D., 1439 Park Hill Lane, Escondido, CA 92025.

Cohn, P. J., Ph.D., 7380 Sand Lake Road, Suite 500, Orlando, FL 32819.

Cook, D., Ph.D., Mental Advantage, Inc., Fort Worth, TX (e-mail: david-e-cookc&notes.pw.com).

Coop, R., Ph.D., Department of Educational Psychology, University of North Carolina at Chapel Hill, CB #3500, Peabody Hall, Chapel Hill, NC 27599.

Dorsel, T. N., Ph.D., Psychology Department, Francis Marion University, Box F-7500, Florence, SC 29501.

Drake, C., Ph.D., P.O. Box 24306, Columbus, OH 43224.

Epstein-Shepherd, B., Ph.D., Box 221383, Carmel, CA 93922.

Fox, R., Ph.D., 11838 Bernardo Plaza Court, Suite 205, San Diego, CA 92128.

Frost, B., 1193 W. Desert Grains Way, Tucson, AZ 85737.

Graham, D., Ph.D., P.O. Box 1976, Boerne, TX 78006.

Grant, E., c/o Subconscious Golf, Inc., 9495 E. San Salvador Drive, Suite 100, Scottsdale, AZ 85258.

Harriet, S., Ph.D., Psy.D., P.O. Box 4956, Fresno, CA 93744–4956 (e-mail: shO62@csufresno.edu).

Hebron, M., PGA, c/o Smithtown Landing CC, 495 Landing Avenue, Smithtown, NY 11787.

Hogan, C., PGA, Sports Performance Corporation, 1700 Alta Vista Drive, Suite 210, Columbia, SC 29223.

Jensen, P., Ph.D., Performance Coaching Inc., P.O. Box 119, Rockwood, Ontario, Canada N0B 2K0.

Keefe, R., Ph.D., Duke University Medical Center, Box 3270 (express mail: Room 3525 Blue), Durham, NC 27710 (e-mail: rsekeefe@acpub.duke.edu).

Kubistant, T., Ed.D., CSP, P.O. Box 13309, Reno, NV 89507 (e-mail: Kubistant@aol.com).

Kurtz, R., Ph.D., and M. Hart., Ph.D., c/o The Golf Institute at Rolling Hills, 3501 W. Rolling Hills Circle, Fort Lauderdale, FL 33328.

Lauenstein, R., M.A., c/o Athlete's Advisor, 58 Village Way, Brookline, MA 02146.

Mackenzie, M. M., Ph.D., Professor of Education, Teachers College, Columbia University, 43 Helms Hill Road, Washingtonville, NY 10992.

Miller, L., PGA, 805 Canary Pine Court, Mandeville, LA 70471.

Mumford, C. G., PGA, 202 N. Main Street, Suite 110, Crossville, TN 38555 (e-mail: yoda@multipro.com).

Piparo, T., Ph.D., 1712 Aftonshire Drive, Greensboro, NC 27410.

Pirozzolo, F. J., Ph.D., Department of Neuropsychology Service, Baylor College of Medicine, 6501 Fannin, Houston, TX 77030.

Rotella, B., Ph.D., University of Virginia, Sports Psychology Department, University Hall, Charlottesville, VA 22903.

Saunders, T. C., M.D., 105 Sierra Morena Terrace, SW, Calgary, Alberta, Canada T3H 3A2.

Shapiro, A., Ph.D., Albany, NY.

Shaw, D., Ph.D., Psychology Department, Nova University, Jupiter Corporate Center, 825 South U.S. Highway 1, Suite 360, Jupiter, FL 33477.

Shoemaker, F., 27505 Via Sereno, Carmel, CA 93923.

Stewart, D., Ed.D., One Cerrado Court, Santa Fe, NM 87505 (e-mail: Stewart@rt66.com).

Vardy, D., Star Sports Technology & Research, Ltd., University Park, Nottingham NG7 2RD, England (e-mail: dv@psych.nott.ac.uk).

Vicory, J., Ph.D., P.O. Box 363, Aurora, IL 60507.

Appendix E

ORGANIZATIONS OF INTEREST TO SENIOR GOLFERS

Alcoholics Anonymous
P.O. Box 459
Grand Central Station
New York, NY 10163
(212) 870-3400

Alzheimers Association
919 N. Michigan Avenue, Suite 1000
Chicago, IL 60611
(800) 272-3900

American Academy of Allergy, Asthma & Immunology
611 E. Wells Street
Milwaukee, WI 53202
(800) 822-2762

American Academy of Dermatology
P.O. Box 4014
Schaumburg, IL 60168
(708) 330-0230

American Academy of Environmental Medicine
4510 W. 89th Street, Suite 110
Prairie Village, KS 66207
(913) 341-6912

American Academy of Ophthalmology
P.O. Box 7424
San Francisco, CA 94120
(415) 561-8500

American Academy of Otolaryngology—Head and Neck Surgery
1 Prince Street
Alexandria, VA 22314
(703) 836-4444

American Academy of Physical Medicine and Rehabilitation
1 IBM Plaza, Suite 2500
Chicago, IL 60611
(312) 464-9700

American Aging Association
University of Nebraska Medical Center
Omaha, NE 68105

American Association of Retired Persons (AARP)
1909 K Street N.W.
Washington, DC 20049
Check directory for local telephone listing.

American Board of Medical Specialties
1007 Church Street, Suite 404
Evanston, IL 60201
(800) 776-CERT
(To confirm if your physician is board certified.)

American Council on Exercise
5820 Oberlin Drive, Suite 102
San Diego, CA 92121
(619) 535-8227

American Dental Association
211 E. Chicago Avenue
Chicago, IL 60611

American Diabetes Foundation
1660 Duke Street
Alexandria, VA 22314
(800) 342-2383

American Dietetic Association
National Center for Nutrition and Dietetics
216 W. Jackson Boulevard, Suite 800
Chicago, IL 60606
(800) 366-1655

American Geriatric Society
10 Columbus Circle
New York, NY 10019
(Aging and health information)

American Heart Association
7272 Greenville Avenue
Dallas, TX 75231
(800) AHA-USA1

American Kidney Fund
(800) 638-8299

American Liver Foundation
1425 Pompton Avenue
Cedar Grove, NJ 07009
(201) 256-2550

American Lung Association
1740 Broadway
New York, NY 10019
(800) LUNG-USA

American Paralysis Association
Spinal Cord Injury Hotline
(800) 526-3456

American Psychiatric Association
Division of Public Affairs
1400 K Street N.W.
Washington, DC 20005
(202) 682-6220

American Psychological Association
750 First Street N.E.
Washington, DC 20002
(202) 336-5500

American Society on Aging
833 Market Street
San Francisco, CA 94103
Check directory for local telephone listing

American Speech-Language-Hearing Association Helpline
(800) 638-8255

American Tinnitus Association
(for ringing sounds in the ear)
P.O. Box 5
Portland, OR 97207
(503) 248-9985

Arthritis Foundation
P.O. Box 7669
Atlanta, GA 30357
(800) 283-7800

Association for Advancement of Behavior Therapy
(information for grief and mourning)
(212) 279-7920

Asthma and Allergies Foundation
(800) 7-ASTHMA

CancerCare
1180 Avenue of the Americas
New York, NY 10036
(800) 813-HOPE

Centers for Disease Control and Prevention
1600 Clifton Road, N.E.
Atlanta, GA 30333
(404) 639-3311

Depression & Related Affective Disorders Association (DRADA)
Meyer 3-181
600 North Wolfe Street
Baltimore, MD 21287
(410) 995-4647

Digestive Disease National Coalition (DDNC)
711 2nd Street N.E., Suite 200
Washington, DC 20002
(202) 544-7497

Elderhostel
(for those over age 55 who wish to travel)
100 Boylston Street, Suite 200
Boston, MA 02116
(617) 426-8056

Epilepsy Foundation of America
(800) 332-1000

The Gray Panthers
3635 Chestnut Street
Philadelphia, PA 19104

Hospicelink
(800) 331-1620

Impotence Information Center
(800) 843-4315

Narcotics Anonymous
World Service Office
P.O. Box 9999
Van Nuys, CA 91409
(818) 773-9999

National Coalition against the Misuse of Pesticides
701 E. Street S.E.
Washington, DC 20003
(202) 543-5450

National Council on the Aging
600 Maryland Avenue S.W.
Washington, DC 20024
(202) 470-1200

National Council on Alcoholism and Drug Dependence Hotline
(800) 475-HOPE (24 hours)

National Council of Senior Citizens
1511 K Street N.W.
Washington, DC 20005

National Digestive Diseases Information Clearinghouse
2 Information Way
Bethesda, MD 20892

National Headache Foundation
428 West St. James Place, 2nd Floor
Chicago, IL 60614
(800) 843-2256

National Head Injury Foundation
(800) 444-NHIF

National Heart, Lung, and Blood Institute
(301) 496-4236

National Hospice Organization
901 N. Fort Myer Drive, Suite 402
Arlington, VA 22209
(703) 243-5900

National Institute on Aging
P.O. Box 8057
Gaithersburg, MD 20898
(800) 222-5900

National Institute on Alcohol Abuse and Alcoholism
6000 Executive Boulevard, Willco Building
Bethesda, MD 20892
(301) 443-3860

National Institute of Mental Health
Information Resources and Inquiries
5600 Fishers Lane, Room 7C-02
Rockville, MD 20857

National Kidney Foundation, Inc.
303 E. 33rd Street, 11th Floor
New York, NY 10016
(212) 889-2210

National Library of Medicine
8600 Rockville Pike
Bethesda, MD 20894
(301) 496-6095

National Mental Health Association (NMHA)
Information Center, 30
1021 Prince Street
Alexandria, VA 22314
(703) 684-7722

National Organization for Rare Disorders
(800) 999-NORD

National Rehabilitation Information Center
(800) 34-NARIC

National Women's Health Network
514 10th Street N.W., Suite 400
Washington, DC 20004
(202) 628-7814

Nutrition for Optimal Health Association, Inc. (NOHA)
P.O. Box 380
Winnetka, IL 60093
(708) 786-5326

Older Women's League
1325 G Street N.W.
Lower Level B
Washington, DC 20005

Organ Donation Hotline
(800) 24-DONOR (24 hours)

Parkinson's Educational Program
(800) 344-7872 (24 hours)

Prostate Information Line
(800) 543-9632

Skin Cancer Foundation
P.O. Box 561
New York, NY 10156
(212) 725-5176

Smokenders
4555 East Camelback Road, Suite D-150
Phoenix, AZ 85018
(800) 828-4357

Widowed Persons Service
Department NB
AARP Programs Department
1909 K Street N.W.
Washington, DC 20049

Women for Sobriety
P.O. Box 618
Quakertown, PA 18951
(215) 536-8026

GLOSSARY

adrenaline—Also called epinephrine; a substance produced by the adrenal gland that causes general arousal.

aldosterone—A steroid hormone that regulates salt and water in the body.

allergen—An element that causes allergies.

allergies—Intense or pathological reactions, such as sneezing, itching, labored breathing, or rashes, to elements, circumstances, or physical states that don't affect the average person.

alzheimer's disease—A degenerative disease of the central nervous system identified by premature senility.

angina—A disease distinguished by erratic attacks of intense, suffocating pain.

angioplasty—The surgical repair of a blood vessel.

Antabuse—Drug that causes intense nausea if a person drinks alcohol while the chemical is in the bloodstream.

antibody—An element produced by body tissue as a reaction to the introduction of a foreign substance.

antigen—A foreign substance that produces antibodies when introduced into blood or tissue.

anti-inflammatory drug—A drug used to counteract inflammation or a nonsteroidal anti-inflammatory drug (NSAID). Examples include aspirin, ibuprofen, ketoprofen, and naproxen.

apnea—A temporary interruption of respiration.

approach-avoidance conflict—A conflict situation in which one is both attracted to and repelled by the same goal.

arrhythmia—A change in the rhythm of the heartbeat, either in time or in strength.

arthoscopic surgery—A surgery used to examine the interior of a joint with a special surgical instrument.

arthritis—An inflammation of the joints.

asthma—A chronic disorder of respiration identified by difficulty in breathing, attacks of coughing, or gasping.

atherosclerosis—A condition in which the walls of arteries thicken and lose elasticity; also known as "hardening of the arteries."

atrophy—Wasting away of any part, organ, tissue, or cell.

audiology—A science dealing with hearing.

auditory nerve—The nerve that connects the inner ear with the brain and is concerned with hearing and balance.

autonomic nervous system—The peripheral nervous system that controls the function of many glands and smooth-muscle groups. It is divided into the sympathetic and parasympathetic systems.

aversive therapy—Any stimulus that pairs unpleasant stimuli with inappropriate behavior.

bacteria—Simple microscopic organisms; some cause disease, whereas others are useful.

behavior therapy—The application of learning theory in treating behavioral disorders.

beta-blockers—A group of medications used to treat angina, hypertension, and cardiac arrhythmia.

biceps—The large muscles at the front of the upper arm.

bronchi—The tubes within the lungs.

bulli (blisters)—A raised spot on the skin filled with liquid.

butterfly bandage—A bandage in the shape of a butterfly that is used to close small cuts.

carotid—The artery or pair of arteries that passes up the neck and supplies blood to the head.

cell—The most basic structural unit of tissue.

cell division—The process by which cells multiply.

circadian rhythms—Patterns of change in physiological functions, such as hunger, sleep, and body temperature, that occur at approximately 24-hour intervals.

cochlea—The base of the inner ear; it is shaped like a snail shell.

cognitive psychology—An approach to therapy that focuses on how emotions are caused by irrational beliefs and/or distorted thoughts.

congenital—Acquired during development in the uterus and not through heredity.

conjunctivitis—Inflammation of the membrane that lines the inner surface of the eyelid.

connective tissue—The body's supportive tissue; it includes strands of collagen, or elastic fibers, between muscles and muscle groups.

contracture—The permanent shortening of muscle, tendon, or scar tissue, which results in deformity or distortion.

contraindication—A symptom or condition that makes a particular treatment inadvisable.

COPD (chronic obstructive pulmonary disease)—A disease resulting from any of several lung diseases that lead to increasing breathing difficulties.

coronary artery—Either of the two arteries that arises from the aorta (one on each side) and supplies the tissues of the heart.

corticosteroid—A steroid used as an anti-inflammatory medication.

CVA (cerebral vascular accident)—Better known as a stroke.

cystitis—The inflammation of the urinary bladder.

dehydration—The excessive deficiency of body fluids.

delirium—A mental disturbance identified by confusion, disordered speech, and hallucinations.

dementia—A condition of deteriorated mentality.

depression—A mental disorder characterized by sadness, inactivity, difficulty in thinking and concentration, and changes in appetite and sleeping.

diabetes—A metabolic disorder caused by excessive amounts of sugar in the blood.

diastolic pressure—The lower of two numbers recorded when a person's blood pressure is taken.

diuresis—An increased excretion of urine.

diuretics—Medications used to treat fluid retention; effective in the treatment of hypertension and heart failure.

dysplasia—The abnormal growth or development of organs or cells.

dysuria—The difficult or painful emission of urine.

edema—A swelling of parts of the body that is caused by fluid retention.

emphysema—The abnormal dilation of the air spaces in the lungs that is caused by the rupture and expansion of the alveoli.

environment—The circumstances, objects, or conditions that surround us.

enzyme—A type of protein that is produced by cells and acts as a catalyst in cell metabolism.

epilepsy—A disorder identified by disturbed electrical rhythms of the central nervous system.

epinephrine—See adrenaline.

ER—Emergency room.

estrogen—A hormone that stimulates the development of female sex characteristics.

exercise—Bodily activity done for the purpose of developing and maintaining physical fitness.

fainting—The loss of consciousness caused by the temporary decrease of blood to the brain.

fascia—A sheet of connective tissue.

fiber—An indigestible material in food that stimulates the intestine to contract.

flatulence—The state of being affected by gas produced in the intestine or stomach.

gastric—Of or relating to the stomach.

generalization—Relating to forming an idea or judgment that applies to an entire class of objects, people, or events.

genetic—Refers to the inherited characteristics of an organism, type, group, or condition.

gerontology—The study of aging and problems of the elderly.

glaucoma—A disease of the eye characterized by an increase in internal pressure of the eye that can result in gradual loss of vision.

gonioscopy—An examination of the initial chamber of the eye with an optical instrument.

HDL (high-density lipoprotein)—A protein that transports the so-called good cholesterol in the bloodstream and is responsible for carrying excess cholesterol away from the artery walls and into the liver where it is metabolized.

heatstroke—A condition characterized by high body temperature, inability to sweat, and collapse caused by prolonged exposure to high temperature.

hemorrhoids—A section of dilated veins in the tissue around the anus.

hernia—The protrusion of an organ through a hole in the abdominal wall.

hormones—Chemicals produced by various glands and tissues and released into the blood.

hyperemia—The excess of blood in a body part.

hyperglycemia—Abnormally high level of blood sugar.

hypertension—The condition of having abnormally high blood pressure.

hypoglycemia—Abnormally low level of sugar in the blood.

hypothyroidism—Reduced activity of the thyroid gland that is characterized by lowered metabolic rate and sluggishness.

immune system—An internal system of the body that protects it from foreign substances, cells, and tissues.

incontinence—An inability of the body to maintain voluntary control of bodily discharge.

indigestion—An inability or difficulty in digesting something.

inflammation—A response to an injury that is characterized by redness, heat, and pain.

influenza (flu)—An intense, highly contagious viral disease characterized by its sudden onset, fever, and severe aches and pains.

insulin—A hormone created in the pancreas that is necessary for the metabolism of carbohydrates and is used in the treatment and control of diabetes.

lactose—A sugar present in milk.

laxative—A drug used to loosen or relax the bowels.

LDL (low-density lipoprotein)—A protein that carries the so-called bad cholesterol in the bloodstream. High levels of LDL cholesterol are significant risk factors in the development of atherosclerosis.

learned helplessness—The acceptance of what appear to be the unalterable consequences of a situation on the basis of previous experiences, even if change still might be possible.

ligament—A tough band of tissue connecting the bones or supporting an organ in place.

ligation—Something that binds.

liniment—A liquid applied to the skin to soothe pain or irritation.

long-term memory—Memory for learned material over a long retention interval (i.e., an hour or more).

lumbar—Refers to the lower part of the back.

macula—An anatomic spot or blotch distinctive from surrounding tissues.

melanin—A dark brown or black pigment.

Ménière's disease—A disorder of the inner ear characterized by periodic attacks of dizziness and deafness.

menopause—The natural ending of menstruation in women, usually between the ages of forty-five and fifty.

metabolism—Refers to all the chemical reactions in the body that involve nutrition.

migraine—A condition identified by recurring, severe headaches and often including nausea and vomiting.

mole—A pigmented mark, spot, or bump on the human body.

MRI (magnetic resonance imaging)—A special radiologic study that allows visualization of damage to internal areas of the body.

mucosa—A mucous membrane that lines a body cavity or passage.

neuropathy—An abnormal and deteriorating state of the nervous system.

nocturia—The act of urinating at night.

NSAID (nonsteroidal anti-inflammatory drug)—A drug that reduces inflammation, fever, and pain. Examples include aspirin, ibuprofen, ketoprofen, and naproxen.

onychomycosis—Fungal infection under the nails that slowly progresses and is difficult to eradicate.

osteomyelitis—An inflammation or infection of the lining of a bone.

otology—The medical science of treating the ears.

otosclerosis—The growth of spongy bone in the inner ear that causes gradually increasing deafness.

pancreas—An organ in the abdomen that secretes hormones, such as insulin and digestive enzymes.

parasympathetic nervous system—A division of the autonomic nervous system that functions to maintain and conserve bodily resources.

paresthesia—An abnormal sudden sensation, such as burning or numbness.

PET (positron emission tomography)—A diagnostic technique that traces emissions from an injected radioactive substance to create images of specific brain receptors.

photosensitivity—Oversensitivity of the skin to sunlight or other radiant energy, or following exposure to sensitizing chemicals or drugs.

plaque—An abnormal patch of skin on a body part or surface.

presbycusis—A gradual loss of hearing as the result of aging.

prostate—An organ surrounding the beginning of the urethra in the male; it secretes a fluid that is the major constituent of ejaculatory fluid.

prostate hypertrophy—An increase in the size of the prostate gland. Although it can be caused by cancer, an enlarged prostate is more often benign in nature.

psoralen—A drug used in treating the loss of skin pigment.

pulmonary rehabilitation—A series of techniques, using exercises, medications, and machines, that helps to improve lung function.

quadriceps—The largest muscle group in the leg. Situated on the anterior of the thigh, it connects the pelvis to the knee.

reflux—A backward flow of fluids, for example, from the esophagus or veins.

REM sleep—A stage of sleep during which brain waves that are recorded look like those recorded when the person is awake and rapid eye movements (REM) occur; often called the dream state.

resuscitation—To restore to life after apparent death.

retina—A membrane inside the eyeball that receives an image from the lens and converts it into chemical and nerve signals to the brain.

retinopathy—A noninflammatory disorder of the retina. If not treated, it can eventually cause blindness.

retroactive inhibition—Difficulty in recalling learned information as a result of having learned additional information subsequent to the information that one is trying to recall.

rhinitis, allergic—A condition involving sneezing, watery eyes, and inflammation of the nose as a reaction to allergies.

rhinitis medicamentosa—An inflammation of the nose caused by an overuse of the medications that initially relieved the symptoms.

rorschach ink blot test—A projective personality test consisting of ten cards, each containing an ink blot. Subjects are instructed to tell what each blot represents in their lives.

sacroiliac—The joint that connects the lowest part of the spine, the sacrum, to the pelvic girdle at the ilium. It is a semirigid joint with many ligaments attached along its anterior and posterior surfaces.

saliva—A fluid secreted into the mouth that begins the process of food digestion.

sciatica—A painful condition in which the largest nerve coming from the spinal cord to the leg is compressed; it can also result in muscle weakness.

sclerosing agent—A factor contributing to the hardening of tissue.

short-term memory—Ability to store up to seven items of information for thirty seconds or less.

sodium—A silver-white, soft element of the alkali metal group.

sphincter—A circular ring of muscles that regulates the flow of matter through a passage. The cardiac sphincter lies between the esophagus and the stomach.

spondylolisthesis—The partial dislocation of one of the lower vertebrae.

streptococcus—Infectious bacteria that enter the blood system and cause inflammation.

stress fracture—A fracture that is the result of normal stress on the bone, such as walking.

stroke—The loss of sensation and voluntary motion caused by damage or blocking of an artery of the brain; also referred to as cerebrovascular accident (CVA).

sympathetic nervous system—The part of the autonomic nervous system that controls heart rate, size of blood vessels, and numerous bodily functions.

systolic pressure—The higher of two numbers recorded when a person's blood pressure is taken.

tendinitis—Inflammation of a tendon.

tendon—A connective tissue that joins a bone to a muscle.

tenosynovitis—Inflammation of a tendon and the sheath that surrounds it.

tension—An inner feeling of unrest or imbalance, often accompanied by physical indications of emotion.

tinnitus—The sensation of ringing or buzzing in the ears.

tonometer—An instrument to measure eye pressure.

tourniquet—A device, such as a bandage, that is tightened by twisting to stop temporarily or to slow bleeding.

tracheostomy—Surgical opening of the trachea through the neck to allow air to pass.

triceps—The main muscle on the posterior of the upper arm. Its function is extension of the arm.

trochanter—Part of the femur, the bone of the thigh. It is an anchor for a number of muscles on the lateral thigh.

ulcer—An erosion of tissue, most commonly in the stomach, duodenum, or skin.

ultrasound—A technique using high-frequency sound to view normal and abnormal internal structures of the body.

ultraviolet light—Light that is beyond the violet end of the visible spectrum.

vertigo—Dizziness; a feeling in which people feel that they or their surroundings are moving or spinning when they are actually motionless.

vestibular—Resembling or referring to the cavity at the entrance of the ear.

virus—An infective agent composed of DNA or RNA enclosed in protein molecules. There is no known drug to kill viruses (except herpesvirus) when they infect the body.

vitrectomy—Surgical removal of all or part of the transparent jelly that fills the eyeball behind the lens.

wheezing—Hard breathing with an audible sound, the result of a constriction of the bronchioles.

BIBLIOGRAPHY

BOOKS

GOLF—GENERAL

The following valuable sources are either golf books that have good chapters about the mental aspects of the game or books unrelated to golf that are classics in the psychology of human performance.

Bailey, C. W. *The Professor on the Golf Links*. London: Silas Birch, 1925.

Beach, D., and B. Ford. *Golf: The Body, the Mind, the Game*. New York: Villard, 1995.

Bernadoni, G. *Golf God's Way*. Carol Stream, Ill.: Creation House, 1978.

Bunker, L. K., and D. Owens. *Golf: Better Practice for Better Play*. Champaign, Ill.: Leisure Press, 1984.

Csikszentmihalyi, M. *Flow*. New York: Harper & Row, 1990.

Daro, A. F., with H. Graffis. *The Inside Swing: Key to Better Golf*. New York: Crowell, 1972.

Doak, T. *The Anatomy of a Golf Course*. New York: Lyons & Burford, 1992.

Flanagan, M. *Use the Head*. Kildare, Ireland: self-published, 1986.

Freeman, C., comp. and ed. *The Golfer's Book of Wisdom*. Nashville, Tenn.: Walnut Grove, 1995.

Gaivano, P. *Seagrams' Guide to Strategic Golf*. New York: Gemi Studio, 1960.

Gallwey, W. T. *The Inner Game of Tennis*. New York: Random House, 1974.

Gallwey, W. T., and B. Kriegel. *Inner Skiing*. New York: Random House, 1977.

Garfield, C. A., and H. J. Bennett. *Peak Performance*. Los Angeles: Jeremy P. Tarcher, 1981.

Gendlin, E. T. *Focusing*. New York: Everest House, 1978.

Golf Magazine's Your Long Game. New York: Harper & Row, 1959.

Hackbarth, J. C. *The Key to Better Golf: A Mental Plan*. Madison, Wis.: self-published, 1929.

Harris, D. V., and B. L. Harris. *The Athlete's Guide to Sports Psychology*. New York: Leisure Press, 1984.

Haley, Jay. *Ordeal Therapy*. New York: Jossey-Bass Publishers, 1984.

Herrigel, E. *Zen and the Art of Archery*. New York: Pantheon, 1953.

Hilton, H. H. *Modern Golf*. New York: Macmillan, 1926.

Horn, S. *Concentration!* Menlo Park, Calif.: Crisp Publications, 1991.

Huang, C. A., and J. Lynch. *Thinking Body, Dancing Mind*. New York: Bantam, 1992.

Jones, E. *Swing the Clubhead*. Trumbull, Conn.: Golf Digest for Tennis, 1952.

Jones, R. T., Jr. *Bobby Jones on Golf*. Trumbull, Conn.: Golf Digest for Tennis, 1966.

Jones, R. T., Jr. *Golf by Design*. Boston, Mass.: Little, Brown & Co., 1993.

Kirkaldy, A. *My 50 Years of Golf Memories*. London: T. Fisher, 1921.

Kite, T., and L. Dennis. *How to Play Consistent Golf*. New York: Golf Digest/Pocket Books, 1990.

Klavora, P., and J. Daniel, eds. *Coach, Athlete, and the Sport Psychologist*. Toronto: University of Toronto Press, 1979.

Knudson, G. *The Natural Golf Swing.* Bellevue, Wash.: Kirsh & Baum, 1988.

Kranzler, Gerald. *You Can Change How You Feel.* RET Press, 1974.

Kriegel, R., and M. Harris Kriegel. *The C Zone.* Garden City, N.Y.: Anchor/Doubleday, 1984.

Kubistant, T. M. *Performing Your Best.* Champaign, Ill.: Human Kinetics, 1986.

Kubistant, T. M. *Mind Pump: The Psychology of Bodybuilding.* Champaign, Ill.: Leisure Press, 1988.

Lardner, R. *Out of the Bunker and into the Trees.* Indianapolis: Bobbs-Merrill, 1960.

Leonard, G. *The Ultimate Athlete.* New York: Viking Press, 1975.

Links, B. *Follow the Wind.* New York: Simon & Schuster, 1995.

Locke, B. *Bobby Locke on Golf.* New York: Simon & Schuster, 1954.

Lohren, C., with A. Barkow. *Getting Set for Golf.* New York: Viking, 1995.

Maiorana, S., with D. Love. *Through the Green.* New York: St. Martin's Press, 1993.

Maltz, M. *Psychocybernetics.* New York: Pocket Books, 1969.

Mayer, D. *How to Think and Swing Like a Golf Champion.* New York: Thomas Y. Crowell, 1958.

McCluggage, D. *The Centered Skier.* New York: Warner Books, 1977.

Miller, J., with D. Shankland. *Pure Golf.* Garden City, N.Y.: Doubleday, 1976.

Miller, L. *Holographic Golf.* New York: HarperCollins, 1993.

Millman, D. *The Warrior Athlete.* Walpole, N.H.: Stillpoint, 1979.

Moone, T. *Golf From a New Angle.* London: Herbert Jenkins, 1934.

Morehouse, L. E., and L. Gross. *Maximum Performance.* New York: Simon & Schuster, 1977.

Murphy, M., and R. White. *The Psychic Side of Sports.* Reading, Mass.: Addison-Wesley, 1978.

Nash, B., and A. Zullo. *The Hole Truth: Inside the Ropes of the PGA Tour.* Kansas City: Andrews and McMeel, 1995.

Nelson, B. *The Little Black Book*. Arlington, Tex.: Summit, 1995.

Nicklaus, J. *Golf My Way*. New York: Simon & Schuster, 1974.

Nicklaus, J. *Jack Nicklaus: My Most Memorable Shots in the Majors*. London: Stanley Paul, 1988.

Nideffer, R. M. *The* Inner *Athlete*. New York: Crowell, 1976.

Orlick, T. *In Pursuit of Excellence*. Champaign, Ill.: Human Kinetics, 1980.

Pace, R. *Target Golf*. Tucson, Ariz.: Body Press, 1986.

Palmer, A. *Arnold Palmer: My Game and Yours*. New York: Simon & Schuster, 1963.

Palmer, A., and P. Dobereiner. *Arnold Palmer's Complete Book of Putting*. New York: Anteneu, 1986.

Pelz, D., with N. Mastroni. *Putt Like the Pros*. New York: Harper & Row, 1989.

Penick, H., with B. Shrake. *Harvey Penick's Little Red Book*. New York: Simon & Schuster, 1992.

Penick, H., with B. Shrake. *And If You Play Golf, You're My Friend*. New York: Simon & Schuster, 1993.

Penick, H., with B. Shrake. *For All Who Love the Game: Lessons and Teachings for Women*. New York: Simon & Schuster, 1995.

Penick, H., with B. Shrake. *The Game for a Lifetime*. New York: Simon & Schuster, 1996.

Piparo, T. *Mind Mastery for Golf: Getting Started Right*. Greensboro, N.C.: TPG Enterprises, 1994.

Porter, C. *Top Golf*. Sparks, Nev.: Life Enhancement Services, 1993.

Porter, K., and J. Foster. *The Mental Athlete*. New York: Ballantine, 1986.

Potter, S. *The Theory and Practice of Gamesmanship*. New York: Henry Holt, 1947.

Potter, S. *Golfmanship*. New York: McGraw-Hill, 1968.

Pressfield, S. *The Legend of Bagger Vance*. New York: William Morrow, 1995.

Ramsey, R. W. *Living with Loss*. New York: William Morrow, 1981.

Rees, D. *Dai Reese on Golf*. New York: A. S. Barnes, 1959.

Reinmuth, D. *Tension Free Golf.* Chicago: Triumph, 1995.

Saunders, V. *The Golf Handbook.* London: Pan, 1989.

Scarbrough, R. (Duffer Reed). *From Wishes to Wealth in Four Easy Steps: Golf Lovers' Edition.* Maryville, Tenn.: Gift Books of America, 1992.

Scott, T. *Secrets of the Golfing Greats.* South Brunswick, N.J.: A. S. Barnes, 1965.

Smith, D. W. *Winning at Golf.* Lancaster, Pa.: Starburst, 1995.

Stancliffe. *Quick Cuts to Good Golf.* London: Methuen, 1920.

Stobbs, J. *Tackle Golf This Way.* London: Stanley Paul, 1961.

Taylor, P. *Golf's Great Winner: Jack Nicklaus.* Mankato, Minn.: Creative Educational Society, 1977.

Tutko, T. *Sportspsyching.* Los Angeles: Jeremy P. Tarcher, 1976.

Vanek, M., and B. J. Cratty. *Psychology and the Superior Athlete.* London: Macmillan, 1979.

Van Kampen, K. *Visual Golf.* New York: Simon & Schuster, 1992.

Veigele, B. *Golf Is Like Love.* Santa Barbara, Calif.: Astral, 1994.

Von Hayes, B. *Golf Therapy* [humor]. Ketchum, Idaho: Randt, 1988.

Wade, D. *Swing Thoughts.* Chicago: Contemporary, 1993.

Wallach, J. *Beyond the Fairway.* New York: Bantam Books, 1995.

White, F. R. *Golf in the Seventies for Those in the Sixties.* Newport News, Va.: White Company, 1962.

MEDICINE, NUTRITION, AND FITNESS

The following books address the body and mind aspects of the game of golf. They are either books specifically directed to the subject or books in which the major emphasis is on injuries, illness, psychology, fitness, and/or nutrition and golf.

Anderson, B. *Quick Stretches for Better Golf.* Bolinas, Calif.: Shelter Publications, 1997.

Bucci, L. *Healing Arthritis the Natural Way: The Breakthrough Program for Reversing Arthritis Using Nutrition and Supplements.* Arlington, Tex.: Summit, 1997.

Burke, L. *The Complete Guide to Food for Sports Performance: A Guide to Peak Nutrition for Your Sport*. Atlanta: Allen & Unwin, 1996.

Carpenter, S. M., and F. P. Kendall. *Golfers Take Care of Your Back*. Vestal, N.Y.: Thistle Ridge Press, 1997.

Carrido, J. *The Fitness Approach to Power Golf*. New York: Perigee, 1997.

Charles, B., D. Pirie, and G. Player. *Golf for Seniors*. Gretna, La.: Pelican, 1995.

Clark, N. *Nancy Clark's Sports Nutrition Guidebook*. Champaign, Ill.: Human Kinetics, 1996.

Clayman, C. B., ed. *Exercise, Fitness, and Health*. The American Medical Association Home Medical Library. Brampton, Ont.: Readers Digest Association of Canada, 1991.

Clayton, L. *Everything You Need to Know About Sports Injuries*. Need to Know Library. New York: Rosen Publishing Group, 1995.

Comeaux, G., and L. Cano. *Stretch and Strengthen Your Way to Great Golf*. Grand Rapids, Mich.: Masters Press, 1996.

Devincenzi, P., and S. Curtis. *Foreplay: The Art of Stretching for Golf*. Napa, Calif.: Pica La Balle, 1992.

Duyff, R. L. *The American Dietetic Association's Complete Food & Nutrition Guide*. Minnetonka, Minn.: Chronimed, 1996.

Farnsworth, C. L. *See It & Sink It: Mastering Putting Through Peak Visual Performance*. New York: HarperCollins, 1997.

Flegel, M. J., *First Aid*. Champaign, Ill.: Human Kinetics, 1996.

Giam, G. C. *Health & Fitness Tips to Improve Your Game*. Los Angeles: Fit Golf & More, 1995.

Griffith, H. W. Illustrated by M. Pederson. *Complete Guide to Sports Injuries: How to Treat Fractures, Bruises, Sprains, Strains, Dislocations, Head Injuries*. New York: Perigee, 1997.

Grisogono, V. *Sports Injuries: A Self-Help Guide*. Freedom, Calif.: Crossing Press, 1994.

Guten, G. N. *Play Healthy, Stay Healthy*. Champaign, Ill.: Human Kinetics, 1991.

Jobe, F. W., et al. *Exercise Guide to Better Golf.* Champaign, Ill.: Human Kinetics, 1995.

Levy, A. M., and M. L. Fuerst. *Sports Injury Handbook: Professional Advice for Amateur Athletes.* New York: John Wiley & Sons, 1993.

Lillegard, W. A., and K. S. Rucker, eds. *Handbook of Sports Medicine: A Symptom-Oriented Approach.* Boston: Andover Medical Publishers, 1997.

MacHray, D. *Par Excellence: A Fitness Guide for Golfers.* Oak Brook, Ill.: Institute in Life Principles, 1986.

Mallon, B., and L. Dennis. *The Golf Doctor: How to Play a Better, Healthier Round of Golf.* New York: Macmillan, 1996.

Mueller, F. O., and A. J. Ryan, eds. *Prevention of Athletic Injuries: The Role of the Sports Medicine Team.* Cesm Series, vol. 4. Philadelphia: F. A. Davis, 1991.

Null, G., and H. Robins. *Ultimate Training: Gary Null's Complete Guide to Eating Right, Exercising, and Living Longer.* New York: St. Martin's Press, 1993.

Peterson, M. S. *Eat to Compete: A Guide to Sports Nutrition.* Saint Louis: Mosby-Year Book, 1996.

Pettrone, F. A., ed. *Athletic Injuries of the Shoulder.* New York: McGraw-Hill, 1994.

Pfeiffer, R. P., and B. C. Mangus. *Concepts of Athletic Training.* Sudbury, Ont.: Jones & Bartlett Publishers, 1998.

Player, G. *Fit for Golf.* New York: Fireside, 1995.

Player, G. *Golf Over 40.* New York: William Morrow, 1997.

Player, G., and D. Tolhurst. *Golf Begins at 50: Playing the Lifetime Game Better Than Ever.* New York: Fireside, 1989.

Potparic, O., and J. Gibson. *A Dictionary of Sports Injuries and Disorders.* New York: Parthenon, 1996.

Sallis, R. E., and F. Massamino, eds. *Essentials of Sports Medicine.* Saint Louis: Mosby-Year Book, 1996.

Tubesing, D. A. *Kicking Your Stress Habits: A Do-It-Yourself Guide for Coping With Stress.* Duluth: Whole Person Associates, 1981.

PSYCHOLOGY OF GOLF

Armour, T. *A Round of Golf with Tommy Armour.* New York: Simon & Schuster, 1959.

Bailey, C. W. *The Brain and Golf.* Chicago: Adams Press, 1924.

Blanchard, K. *Playing the Great Game of Golf.* New York: William Morrow, 1992.

Bolt, T., with W. C. Griffith. *How to Keep Your Temper on the Golf Course.* New York: David McKay Company, 1969.

Boomer, P. *On Learning Golf.* New York: Alfred A. Knopf, 1946.

Boy, A. V. *Psychological Dimensions of Golf.* Durham, N.C.: Evergreen, 1980.

Brown, R. A. *The Golfing Mind.* New York: Lyons & Burford, 1994.

Carpenter, E. *Subjective Golf Strategy.* Chicago: Adams Press, 1979.

Cisco, B. *The Ultimate Game of Golf.* Glendale, Calif.: Ultimate, 1993.

Cohn, P. *The Mental Game of Golf.* South Bend, Ind.: Diamond Communications, 1994.

Cohn, P. J., and R. K. Winters. *The Mental Side of Putting.* South Bend, Ind.: Diamond Communications, 1995.

Crail, M. *Golf: Its Roots in God and Nature.* Edinburgh: The Crail Press, 1893.

Cranford, P. G. *The Winning Touch in Golf.* Englewood Cliffs, N.J.: Prentice-Hall, 1961.

Dunlop, S. *The Golfing Bodymind.* London: Wildwood House, 1980.

Enhager, K. *Quantum Golf.* New York: Warner Books, 1991.

Epstein-Shepherd, B. *Mental Management for Great Golf.* Carmel, Calif.: Becoming Press, 1996.

Epstein-Shepherd, B. *Mental Management for Great Golf: How to Control Your Thoughts and Play Out of Your Mind.* Los Angeles: Lowell House, 1997.

Fasciana, G. S. *Golf's Mental Magic.* Holbrook, Mass.: Bob Adams, 1992.

Fine, A. *Mind Over Golf.* London: BBC Books, 1993.

Ford, D. *How I Play Golf*. Englewood Cliffs, N.J.: Prentice-Hall, 1960. British edition: *The Brainy Way to Better Golf*. London: Stanley Paul, 1961.

Foster, D. *Thinking Golf*. London: Pelham, 1979.

Gallwey, W. T. *The Inner Game of Golf*. New York: Random House, 1979.

Golf Mind vs. Business Mind. Chicago: Superior Services Press, 1924.

Graham, D. *Mental Toughness Training for Golf*. New York: Green-Pelham, 1990.

Hahn, P. *Links Logic*. Ormond Beach, Fla.: privately printed, 1951.

Handy, I. S. *It's the Damned Ball*. Houston: Anson Jones Press, 1951.

Haultain, A. *The Mystery of Golf*. Boston: Houghton Mifflin, 1908.

Hebron, M. *See and Feel the Inside, Move the Outside*. Smithtown, N.Y.: Rost Associates, 1984.

Hebron, M. *The Art and Zen of Learning Golf*. Smithtown, N.Y.: Rost Associates, 1990.

Hebron, M. *Building and Improving Your Golf Mind, Golf Body, and Golf Swing*. Smithtown, N.Y.: Rost Associates, 1993.

Heise, J. G. *How You Can Play Better Golf Using Self-Hypnosis*. North Hollywood, Calif.: Wilshire, 1961.

Heise, J. G *Super Golf with Self-Hypnosis*. London: Elliots, 1961.

Hogan, C. *Five Days to Golfing Excellence*. Sedona, Ariz.: T&C Publishing, 1986.

Hogan, C. *The Magic of Imagery*. Sedona, Ariz.: Sports Enhancement Associates, 1989.

Hogan, C. *Learning Golf*. Clifton, Colo.: Zediker Publishing, 1993.

Hovanesian, A. *Golf Is Mental*. New Britain, Conn.: HB & HC, 1960.

Huff, B. *Be the Target*. Chicago: Contemporary, 1996.

Hyslop, T. B. *Mental Handicaps in Golf*. Baltimore: Williams & Wilkins, 1927.

Kemp, C. F. *Smart Golf*. Fort Worth, Tex.: Branch-Smith, 1974.

Kemp, C. F. *The World of Golf and the Game of Life.* Saint Louis: Bethany Press, 1978.

Keogh, B. K., and C. E. Smith. *Personal Par.* Champaign, Ill.: Human Kinetics, 1985.

Kinsman Fisher, A. *The Masters of the Spirit.* New York: HarperCollins, 1997.

Kubistant, T. M. *Mind Links: The Psychology of Golf,* Reno, Nev.: Performance & Productivity Specialists, 1994.

Lewis, L. T. *The Tao of Golf.* Saratoga, Calif.: R&E Publishers, 1992.

MacKenzie, M. M. *Golf: The Mind Game.* New York: Dell, 1990.

MacMillan, R. *Masterminding Golf.* Privately printed, 1960.

Mapin, Major G. F. *The Golfing You.* London: Skeffington and Son, 1948.

McDougal, R., Jr. *A Positive Approach to Better Competitive Golf.* Chicago: self-published, 1956.

Miller, L. *Beyond Golf.* Walpole, N.H.: Stillpoint, 1996.

Moore, C. W. *The Mental Side of Golf.* New York: Horace Liverlight, 1929.

Morley, D. C. *The Missing Links.* New York: Atheneum, 1976.

Morrison, A. J. *Better Golf Without Practice.* New York: Simon & Schuster, 1940.

Mulvoy, M., and A. Spander. *Golf: The Passion and the Challenge.* Englewood Cliffs, N.J.: Prentice-Hall, 1977.

Mumford, C. G. *Golf's Best Kept Secret.* Titusville, Fla.: ProForm Associates, 1988.

Mumford, C. G. *The Double Connection II.* Crossville, Tenn.: ProForm Associates, 1992.

Murphy, M. *Golf in the Kingdom.* New York: Delta, 1972.

Murphy, M. *The Kingdom of Shivas Irons.* New York: Broadway Books, 1997.

Nelson, K. *The Golfer's Book of Daily Inspiration.* Chicago: Contemporary, 1996.

Nichols, B. *Never Say Never.* New York: Fleet, 1965.

Nieport, T., and D. Sauers. *Mind over Golf*. Garden City, N.Y.: Doubleday, 1968.

Ollstein, B. W. *Combat Golf*. New York: Irving, 1996.

Owens, D., and D. Kirschenbaum. *Smart Golf: How to Simplify and Score Your Mental Game*. The Jossey-Bass Psychology Series. San Francisco: Jossey-Bass Publishers, 1997.

Palmer, A. *Golf Tactics*. London: Kaye and Ward, 1970.

Palmer, A. *Go For Broke!* New York: Simon & Schuster, 1973.

Parsons, R. *Golfing Thinking*. Cheam, England: Entryown Patents, 1983.

Pendleton, A. *Better Golf with Brains*. Mount Morris, Ill.: Kable Brothers, 1941.

Pirozzolo, F. *Mental Training for Golf*. Miami, Fla.: Doral Golf Learning, 1992.

Pirozzolo, F., with R. Pate. *The Mental Pocket Companion for Golf*. New York: HarperPerennial, 1996.

Ramsey, L. W. *Secrets of Winning Golf Matches*. New York: Pilot, 1960.

Refran, D., and A. Burgoyne. *Golf-o-Genics*. Tampa, Fla.: Information Press Services, 1978.

Reinmuth, D. *Tension-Free Golf*. Chicago: Triumph, 1995.

Rose, W. C., and C. M. Newcomb. *Cut Down That Score*. Cleveland, Ohio: privately printed, 1925.

Rotella, R. J., and L. K. Bunker. *Mind Mastery for Winning Golf*. Englewood Cliffs, N.J.: Prentice-Hall, 1981.

Rotella, R. J., with B. Cullen. *Golf Is Not a Game of Perfect*. New York: Simon & Schuster, 1995.

Rotella, R. J., with B. Cullen. *Golf Is a Game of Confidence*. New York: Simon & Schuster, 1996.

Rubenstein, L. *Links*. Rocklin, Calif.: Prima Publishing, 1991.

Saunders, T. C. *Mind-Body Golf*. Calgary, Alberta: Mind-Body Golf, 1991. Includes audiocassettes.

Saunders, V. *The Golfing Mind*. New York: Atheneum, 1988.

Scharff, R., ed. *Golf Magazine's Handbook of Golf Strategy*. New York: Harper & Row, 1959.

Schon, L. *The Psychology of Golf.* Boston: Small, Maynard, and Company, 1923.

Scottish Golf (Ross, R. K.). *Swing-Minded.* Cornwall, England: privately printed, 1932.

Shapiro, A. *Golf's Mental Hazards.* New York: Fireside, 1996.

Shoemaker, C. J. *Juggling Golf.* Carmel, Calif.: C. Jonothan Shoemaker, 1994.

Shoemaker, F., with P. Shoemaker. *Extraordinary Golf.* New York: G. P. Putnam's Sons, 1996.

Simek, T. C., and R. M. O'Brien. *Total Golf.* Garden City, N.Y.: Doubleday, 1981.

Simmons, M. L. *Golf and the Subconscious Mind.* Belleville, Ill.: privately printed, 1984.

Thompson, K. R. *The Mental Side of Golf.* New York: Funk & Wagnalls, 1939.

Travers, J., and G. Rice. *The Winning Shot.* T. Werner Laurie, 1915.

Vardy, D. *The Mental Game of Golf.* Nottingham, England: Castle, 1996.

Voorhies, C. L. *The Mental Game of Golf.* La Mesa, Calif.: privately printed, 1950.

Watson, T. *Tom Watson's Strategic Golf.* New York: NYT Special Services and Pocket Books, 1993.

Weidemnkoph, R. *The Science of Controlled Relaxation in Golf . . . and How to Apply It to Your Game.* Chagrin Falls, Ohio: Privately printed, 1936.

Wiren, G. *The PGA Manual of Golf.* New York: Macmillan, 1991.

Wiren, G., and R. Coop. *The New Golf Mind.* New York: Simon & Schuster, 1978.

PERIODICALS

Golf Illustrated 6, no. 7 (1990). Special feature on concentration.

Graham, D. *Golf Psych Update.* Boerne, Tex.: SportsPsyche, Inc. Newsletter.

AUDIOCASSETTES AND VIDEOCASSETTES

There has been an explosion in the production of golf audiocassettes and videocassettes. Golf psychology has followed suit. Although most of the tapes listed are audio (A), an increasing amount of information is being presented in videotapes (V), compact discs (CD), CD–ROM, and even an LP record.

Allen, E. *Golf: A Mental Warm-Up!* (A). Yorktown Heights, N.Y.: Elliot Allen Productions, 1993.

Attitudes: The Mental Side of Golf (A). Newport Beach, Calif.: Mental Dynamics, 1989.

Beale, G. *Mind Games* (A). Reno, Nev.: Sierra Center for Peak Performance, 1990.

Biles and Kistler. *Golf Audio Package* (A). Canton, Ohio: Clinical Concepts, 1993.

Blanchard, K. *Mastering The Mental Game* (V). Escondido, Calif.: Golf University, 1992.

Chenoweth, J. *Mind over Golf* (A). Jim Chenoweth Enterprises, 1989.

Cohn, P. *Think to Win* (A). Naples, Fla.: Peak Performance Publications, 1995.

Cohn, P. J. *Make Your Most Confident Stroke* (V). Orlando, Fla.: Peak Performance Sports, 1996.

Cook, D. *The Psychology of Tournament Golf* (A). Lawrence, Kans.: Mental Advantage, 1990.

Drake, C. *Pro-Putter's Mind Trainer* (A). Columbus, Ohio: Social Psychological Services, 1993.

Garfield, C. *Peak Performance Training Audiotape Series* (A). Oakland, Calif.: G. A. Garfield, 1990.

Grant, E. *Subconscious Golf* (A, with workbook). Scottsdale, Ariz.: Subconscious Golf, 1981.

Harriet, S. *Golf before You Golf!* Fresno, Calif.: Agents, Inc., 1991.

Hebron, M. *Building and Improving Your Golf Mind, Golf Body, and Golf Swing* (V, with workbook). New York: Michael Hebron Productions, 1993.

Hogan, C. *Nice Shot!* (V and A). Sedona, Ariz.: Monitor Productions, 1988.

Hogan, C. *The Player's Course* (V, with handbooks). Sedona, Ariz.: Chuck Hogan, 1991.

Hogan, C. *Self-Hypnosis for Better Golf* (A). Sedona, Ariz.: Chuck Hogan, 1992.

In-Synch Golf (CD). Nellysford, Va.: In-Synch Sport International, 1994.

In-Synch Putting (CD). Nellysford, Va.: In-Synch Sport International, 1994.

IntelliPlay. *ESPN Interactive Golf: Lower Your Score with Tom Kite: The Full Swing and Putting (with Bob Rotella)* (CD–ROM). Atlanta, Ga.: Intellimedia Sports, 1993.

IntelliPlay. *ESPN Interactive Golf: Lower Your Score with Tom Kite: Shot Making (with Bob Rotella)* (CD–ROM). Atlanta, Ga.: Intellimedia Sports, 1992.

Jacobs, A. A. *Sports Psychology: The Winning Edge in Sports* (V and A). Kansas City, Mo.: The Winning Edge, 1987.

Jensen, P. *The Golfer's Inside Edge* (A). Rockwood, Ont.: Performance Coaching, 1993.

Kubistant, T. *Be the You You'd Like to Be* (A). Reno, Nev.: Performance & Productivity Specialists, 1989.

La Treill, D. *Mental Golf* (V). Van Nuys, Calif.: Westron Video, 1993.

Nicklaus, J. *Golf My Way. I: Playing the Game* (V). Jupiter, Fla.: Jack Nicklaus Productions, 1989.

Pate, S., with J. Petralia. *Steve Pate's Strategic Golf* (V, with booklet). Pasadena, Calif.: Green Management Productions, 1988.

Powers, M. *Golf Like a Pro* (33⅓-rpm record). Los Angeles: Wilshire
  Books, 1964.

Ram D. *Golf and the Spirit* (A). Carmel, Calif.: Shivas Irons Society, 1995.

Reynolds, M. *Golf in the Zone* (A, with booklet). Mt. Laurel, N.J.:
  Learn, Inc., 1997.

Rotella, B. *Putting Out of Your Mind* (A). Trumbull, Conn.: Golf Digest Books, 1986.

Rotella, B. *Playing to Win* (A). Duluth, Ga.: Golf Training Systems,
  1996.

Rotella, B., and R. Coop. *Golfing Out of Your Mind* (A, with workbook). Charlottesville, Va.: Creative Media Productions, 1985.

Small, K. G. *Golf: 80% of Your Game Is Mental* (A). Mechanicsburg,
  Pa.: Intrinsic Development, 1993.

Smith, L. W. *Concentration* (A). Part of the Mastery of Golf Tape
  Series. Livonia, Mich.: Golf Control, 1987.

Vicory, J. *The Mind Zone in Golf* (A). Aurora, Ill.: The Mind Zone in
  Sports, 1996.

Whitaker, J. *Brainwaves Golf* (V). Clearwater, Fla.: TeleVisual Communications, 1991.

INDEX

ABOUT THE AUTHORS

Dr. Syd Harriet has four advanced degrees, including a doctorate in speech communication and a doctorate in clinical psychology. He has been a college professor for more than twenty-eight years, a communications consultant for private and nonprofit organizations, a licensed psychotherapist in private practice, an author of numerous articles in psychology, and an avid golfer. Since 1992, his column, "Ask the Shrink," has appeared in *Golf Today*. He offers answers to hundreds of golfers' questions related to all aspects of the mental game of golf.

Dr. Sol Grazi is a board-certified family practitioner. He has taught and practiced medicine in Denver, Colorado, for 20 years. He has been a high school team physician and director of the Colorado Holistic Health Center, where he supervised the treatment of back and musculoskeletal injuries. Currently, he is on the staff of Denver General Hospital. During his career, Dr. Grazi has treated thousands of injuries related to sports and has taught holistic philosophy to patients in various primary care settings. He also has taught the concepts and practice of holistic medicine and the nature of psychosomatic illness to medical students and residents in his capacity as assistant clinical professor in the Department of Family Medicine at the University of Colorado Medical School.